10668919

BOURBON WHISKEY

Our Native Spirit

From Sour Mash to Sweet Adventures With a Whiskey Professor

Bernie Lubbers

Blue River Press
Indianapolis, IN

Bourbon Whiskey © 2011 Bernie Lubbers

All rights reserved under International and Pan-American Copyright Conventions

No part of this book may be reproduced, stored in a database or other retrieval system, or transmitted in any form, by any means, including mechanical, photocopy, recording or otherwise, without the prior written permission of the publisher.

Cover designed by Phil Velikan
Editorial assistance provided by Dorothy Chambers
Packaged by Wish Publishing

Printed in the United States of America
10 9 8 7 6 5 4 3 2 1

Published by Blue River Press
Distributed by Cardinal Publishers Group
Tom Doherty Company, Inc.
www.cardinalpub.comed by

To Virgil, David, Steve and the Whiskey Chicks (Sam and Paige—and yes, that means you all, too, Kathleen and Linda)

Whiskey professor Bernie Lubbers and U.S. Vice-President Joe Biden.

Table of Contents

FOREWORD
By Fred Noe 7

PROLOGUE
Whiskey Professors are Born Not Made 11

CHAPTER 1
How I Became a Whiskey Professor 15

CHAPTER 2
What Makes Bourbon, Bourbon? 35

CHAPTER 3
Distilling and Aging Bourbon 47

CHAPTER 4
How to Read a Label 69

CHAPTER 5
Bourbon's Place in American History 91

CHAPTER 6

Visiting Kentucky and the Distilleries, and You WILL 121

CHAPTER 7

How to Host a Bourbon Tasting at Your Home 159

CHAPTER 8

My Favorite Bourbon Recipes 167

CHAPTER 9

Bourbon: Our Native Spirit 181

APPENDIX:

Frequently Asked Questions 185

Foreword

Bernie asked me to write a foreword for his new book, so I figured I should tell ya'll just who the hell I am. I'm Fred Noe, seventh-generation distiller in the Beam family. My great-grandfather was Jim Beam. He's the one most people know of since his name is on the bottle, and he's the one who started our distillery again after Prohibition in 1934. Pretty amazing for a guy to restart a whole distillery at 70 years old. But it was his great-grandfather, Jacob Beam, who started our family legacy by distilling and selling his first barrel of whiskey back in 1795. To think our family has stuck in this business for over 200 years is really amazing. I'm glad they did, because I don't know what I'd be doing otherwise. It's literally and figuratively in my blood.

Fred Noe (courtesy of Beam Global Spirits & Wine)

My dad, Booker Noe (of Booker's Bourbon), taught me all about the business, and I think he was one of the very best. I remember traveling with him on trips where we would promote the small-batch bourbons that Pop created in the early 1990s, actually creating a new category. He taught me not only about distilling, but also how to be a guardian and an ambassador for the brands he created. You see, brands have lives and live on way longer than us human beings. When Dad passed away a few years back, it was just me serving as the ambassador for these brands, and the world was craving more bourbon, more stories, more everything.

I have a son, Freddie, but he needs to get out of college before he can even think about joining the family business. Bourbon is so popular now that we couldn't wait for him to graduate, so we brought in Bernie Lubbers to help promote Knob Creek and our other bourbons. Now Bernie's not from a distilling family, but he caught on pretty darn quick. I had heard Bernie's name and voice on the "Bob & Tom Show" radio program in the morning, so I knew he'd have a leg up, as a lot of this job is being able to talk to just about any type of person around and to communicate a fairly complicated topic like bourbon.

I guess he had a lot of passion for it since his dad and grandfather worked in a brewery in Louisville, so maybe something rubbed off on him, or poured off on him somewhere along the line. Bourbon is something you don't just learn overnight. It takes years—really it takes a life time—and even though there's a lot more for us all to learn, I'd say Bernie knows his shit pretty damn good.

Being bourbon ambassadors, we have people who come up to us and tell us that they could do our jobs since they love bourbon. But being an ambassador requires quite a few unique skills. Enjoying bourbon and having bourbon knowledge is a good start, but it's just the tip of the iceberg. You've got to enjoy traveling. And when I say traveling, I mean flying more than 100,000 miles a year, sometimes to several cities in a week. A typical ambassador is gone at least two to three weeks a month. We do staff trainings and educational tastings at bars and restaurants with our sales people during the day. Then we might have a bourbon dinner or other type of consumer event that night. Then there are the whiskey shows, where thousands of people attend to taste their favorite whiskies and try new ones. Drink bourbon all night, all day and night sometimes. The next morning you might have to wake up early and catch a plane to somewhere to do it all again, or maybe be on a morning radio/TV show and look and act fresh, and be the life of the party all over again wherever they take you afterward. But if you can, it's a true brotherhood of people, and it's a truly incredible ride.

I think Bernie's book brings some of that to life for you, and I think you'll also learn quite a bit about bourbon, even if you already know a lot about bourbon. Once you finish this book, you may want to come visit us here in Kentucky at our distillery. Come on down and come thirsty and come by and say hey to me and Bernie. If you keep drinking it, I'll keep making it.

Here's lookin' at ya.

Fred Noe

Prologue: Whiskey Professors Are Born Not Made

The first question that people ask after they find out I'm a whiskey professor is, "How did you get that job?" Well, the truth is that the job came to me. I didn't go after it. I performed stand-up comedy for 20 years, and "whiskey professor" wasn't on my radar screen. Hell, I didn't even know it existed. But it's a career where you use verbal skills and your personality to explain and promote a product, so in many ways, stand-up comedy was a perfect background.

It also may have helped that I grew up in a family in the beer business. My dad worked at a brewery for 45 years, and my grandfather was one of the founders of that brewery. In some ways you could say I grew up "under the influence."

For example, every summer we closed our house in Louisville and moved up to a "camp" my parents owned on the Ohio River in Utica, Indiana. Utica is like that little town in *To Kill a Mockingbird* but without a lawyer and with more Boo Radleys. Our "camp" was (and still is) a two-bedroom concrete block house on a slab that my dad built with his friend Evvers Johnson. Nothing luxurious, but it was awesome to us, and best of all we had our own little beach on the river. We would swim, hike, skip rocks, and fish every day. We had a ball. The Fourth of July was the climax of the summer, with fireworks going off all day, and parties, parties, parties.

We knew all of our neighbors along the river – we referred to ourselves as the "river rats." And river rats are the most friendly and gregarious folk around. Even though Dad went to work every day, it was like a summer vacation for our parents, too.

Beer was a big part of those summers. On weekends, my parents let us take sips of beer when we fetched them one from the house to the beach or patio overlooking the river. Because I had been exposed to beer and adult beverages as a youth, I never went to or threw crazy high school parties like other kids did when their parents went out of town. The idea of playing quarter bounce or anything like that was silly and ridiculous to my siblings and me. The first time we went to a high school party like that, my buddies and I turned around and went home and played pool and poker, and probably drank Mountain Dew or Coke. We never drank beer just to drink beer. It was a nice little treat, but not something you just drank. It just wasn't forbidden fruit at my house, so I really could have taken it or left it.

Do you remember your first official beer? I'll never forget mine. It was July 20, 1969. Something called the lunar module had just landed on the moon with Buzz Aldrin and Neil Armstrong tucked inside. The whole world was glued to their televisions. There are times in your life when you watch history in the making and don't know it. That July night we were watching history, and we knew it. There was no event bigger than this, and I was sharing it with my mom.

My mom's name was "Champie." She got that name by winning the freckle face contest at the Kentucky State Fair in 1939. She had a great sense of humor and everyone who met her, loved her. That July night was a night we would spend bonding along with the entire world.

Walter Cronkite was in great form. He was interviewing a never-ending string of scientists and astronauts. He had the coolest plastic models showing just how the lunar module worked; we were mesmerized. After a couple hours of delay after delay, though, my mom turned to me and said, "How long is this gonna take? Would you be a dear and go get me a beer?" And then she added, "It's not every day a man walks on the moon, so why don't you get one for yourself, too." Two historic occasions in one night! I was so excited.

I was 10 years old at the time.

After another hour of watching for Neil Armstrong's lunar debut she looked at me and said, "If he doesn't come out and climb down that ladder soon, we're going to be drunk!"

Neil and Buzz finally did come out somewhere near the end of my one beer. We watched as they skipped and hopped across the lunar surface. I will not forget that night for the rest of my life.

When I tell people that I travel the world teaching bourbon classes, running consumer events, and hosting bourbon tastings, they just can't believe there's a job like mine. The fact that there is a job called Whiskey Professor is probably why the terrorists hate us so much. I'm sure glad there is because I am having the time of my life. How many people in the world can say "My life is a paid vacation"?

I can. This is a story about living on a paid vacation, the people I've met along the way, and the host of that vacation: bourbon whiskey. So pour yourself a highball and come along for the ride.

My sister Katie, me (holding a silver mint julep cup), Mom, and my brother Lar.

1

How I Became a Whiskey Professor

"I never drink water; that is the stuff that rusts pipes."
—W.C. Fields

My name is Bernie Lubbers. I love bourbon, and that's a good thing since I am a whiskey professor. Now that is one sweet job title! And the answer is yes: I do have a business card that says whiskey professor right on it. It's a job your counselor doesn't tell you about when you're in college. And in many ways, it's not really a job, it's a lifestyle. You can't just stop being *The Whiskey Professor*. If you see me in an airport anytime soon, which is pretty likely since I travel 100,000+ miles every year promoting bourbon, odds are I was out late the night before sharing my passion and probably a couple drinks. Just this morning as I was coming through the airport security, a gentleman saw my Knob Creek bourbon shirt and asked me for a sample. I rolled up my sleeve and said, "You want a sample? Here you go, lick my arm."

People ask me just how I got this job and what it takes to be a whiskey professor. Well, besides a strong liver, the first requirement is a deep passion for our country's "native spirit." Second, a person must have an unquenchable thirst for studying the history and heritage of bourbon and the whiskey men and women who forged its legacy. And I guess it doesn't hurt to be born in Kentucky and be part of a distilling family, even though in my case that was brewing beer. But you will soon learn, you've got to make beer before you make bourbon!

My grandfather was one of the 13 saloon keepers in Louisville, Kentucky, who started the Falls City Brewing Company in 1905. They produced Falls City, Drummond Bros., and finally Billy Beer. For those of you under 30, that was named for President Jimmy Carter's famous beer-swilling brother. The brewery couldn't produce beer during Prohibition, so they manufactured soda pop and sold ice to stay viable. My grandfather was also forced to close down his saloon. So he decided to start selling hardware ... and bootleg whiskey. He sold hardware in the front and hard liquor in the back. The back room business was more brisk than the front.

After Prohibition my grandfather moved the bar from the back room to out front and reopened the saloon, and the brewery started brewing Falls City Beer again. When my father graduated from Xavier University in Cincinnati, he went to work at the brewery. He spent his entire career there, starting in the ice house and retiring as Vice President of Purchasing and Labor Relations 45 years later. He would have had 49 years of service at the brewery, but the U.S. Army drafted him in WWII at the age of 32! Because he took a couple law classes at Xavier, he was chosen by the company to be one of the first people in Kentucky and the country, for that matter, to strike deals with the Teamsters and other unions on behalf of the brewery. I'm sure there were some pretty good stories he never shared with us about those times.

Greasing the garbageman

I guess it was my dad who taught me that if you represent a brand or company, you do it in all aspects of your life. When I was six or seven years old, the garbage was picked up at our house every Saturday. My father gave me the job to go out and count how many guys were working on the truck and then bring them each a frosty cold bottle of Falls City Beer ... two each if it was going to be really hot. Can you imagine doing that today?

I thought this was an awesome responsibility – after all, I was a little boy, and little boys *love* garbage trucks. Here's a giant truck that grown men get to hang off the side of; I mean, how cool is that? And then the men get to take garbage cans and dump them in this big hopper, pull a lever till it smashes the garbage away to the back somewhere and clears the way to dump more in. Fabulous, right? The guys on the truck would ask me every week what I wanted to be when I grew up, and I would smile and shout, "I want to be a garbageman!"

So every Saturday morning about 8:00, I'd look out the living room windows eagerly awaiting the arrival of the magical truck. And every Saturday morning several thirsty garbagemen would look out their windshield eagerly awaiting the sight of this magical little boy who dispensed frosty cold bottles of beer.

Needless to say, our family was very popular with our garbagemen. Our neighbors, who didn't give them beer, never got the same degree of service we did. If they left out old broken swing sets or large appliances, the garbagemen wouldn't pick them up because they were not suppose to fill up their trucks with those kinds of bulky items, so the neighbors would have to borrow a truck and haul it off to the dump themselves. But at the Lubbers household, the garbagemen would take old jungle gyms, dishwashers ... hell, they probably would have hauled dead bodies away without comment! The old man was pretty smart in a couple of ways on that one. Not only did it save him from borrowing a truck and hauling things down to the city incinerator, I bet when those garbagemen bought beer on their own, they'd pick up a 12-pack of Falls City Beer. I didn't know it then, but Dad taught me a valuable lesson in walking the walk, and drinking the talk. Anyone you meet in life–from garbagemen to CEOs—is a potential customer, especially when you're in the beer/liquor business.

My mother was a homemaker and did what most moms did in the '60s. She raised kids, and she was busy with four of us. Back then you didn't have 25 versions of Benadryl or other over-the-counter wonders. When we were teething, she would rub bourbon on our gums. When we were sick, it was whiskey with honey and lemon. We either weren't sick anymore, or we didn't care. Either way, we slept soundly all through the night. Nowadays they'd probably call child services on her for doing that, but that was standard operating procedure for most moms of that generation. My guess is that it got me used to the taste of bourbon, because I never had to acquire a taste for it or beer.

Growing up in Kentucky, at least for my generation, bourbon was sacred. I'm glad to see it's becoming that way again, not only in Kentucky but all over the country and the world. For example, bourbon is extremely popular in Australia and New Zealand. To say they are nuts about it is an understatement. The largest-sized bottles of bourbon we can sell in the United States is a 1.75 liter (about a half gallon). In Australia and New Zealand, they sell 4.5-liter bottles of bourbon! It's so big, it comes on a cradle so you can rock and pour it since it's so big and heavy you can't lift it up easily. I mean, ya don't want to run out of your Jim Beam over the weekend, do ya, mate?

Other places that bourbon is finding an increase in popularity include Germany and some countries in Asia. Even whiskey drinkers in the U.K. are embracing our native spirit. And in the U.S., bars specializing in bourbon tasting are opening up everywhere from San Francisco to New York. A place called Rick House opened up just last year in San Francisco. This place is decorated like a bourbon rick house, and it's packed. It's the place to see and be seen, and bourbons flow every day there to a young crowd. Char No. 4 in Brooklyn, New York (196 Smith Street), is a very popular place to be, and it features 150 bourbons and American whiskies. Char 4 is the level of char we fire the barrels for the aging of bourbon. Big Star in Chicago (N. Damen Avenue between North Wicker Park and West Pierce Avenues) is a new place started by the same folks who own the famous cocktail bar, The Violet Hour, which is right across the street. While you're in Chicago, you gotta stop by Delilah's, where Fred Noe, Jimmy Russell, and all us ambassadors and distillers hang out after Whiskey Fest there. Michael Miller owns the joint, and you'll find bourbons there you can't find anywhere, and not even Michael can tell you where he got them. He either forgot or won't tell you in case you're a government agent! Bar Sable inside the new Kimpton Palomar property in downtown Chicago (505 N. State Street) is another great cocktail bar run by Mike Ryan, who came from the Violet Hour. Ask him what he thinks about Old Grand Dad, Old Fitz and other great bourbons. Are you getting the idea that bourbon is really in vogue? We are smack at the beginning of the Golden Age of Bourbon, so get your ass out there and start enjoying our country's native spirit. OK, off my soap box now, back to my story.

Age is more than just a number

My mom drank a four-year-old bourbon because she enjoyed highballs. My dad claimed he didn't "trust" a bourbon over six years old. He said that there were too many wood notes from the barrels over six. Pappy Van Winkle of Old Fitzgerald bourbon didn't sell his bourbon when it was under fifteen years old. It doesn't make any of them right or wrong, it's just their opinion and preference. That's part of what makes bourbons different. Age and proof. Like any rebellious son, I wanted to find my "own" bourbon to claim.

In college and before, I drank beer, and a little bourbon. Well, we were in the business, so my parents knew I was drinking some, and they kept more than a watchful eye on me. As my dad said, "We don't want the boy to be one of the poor saps to go away to college and never had a sip of liquor in his life, and on his first night on his own, die of alcohol poisoning like those poor Southern Baptist kids do!"

Like most beginning drinkers, I mixed my bourbon. I never had "the talk" from my father that some stricter bourbon parents had with their children about only mixing bourbon with a couple cubes of ice or a little water. I think my parents wanted me to find my own way. So I started out by mixing my bourbon with 7UP and a slice of lemon. Keep in mind, this was before the small-batch and single-barrel bourbon craze of the early '90s. This was late '70s and early '80s. Extra-aged and higher-proof bourbons were rare in the bars, and younger bourbons are fine for highballs.

Soon I was enjoying the flavor of the bourbon, and I was drinking it with either soda water, ginger ale, or a combination of the two. I loved to order the combination because my father told me that drink was called a Presbyterian. I later found out from my friend Chris, who was raised Presbyterian, that it was called that because it looked like a regular ginger ale. If you mix bourbon with ginger ale it becomes dark and looks like you're drinking bourbon. Adding soda water lightens it back to the color of ginger ale. So a Presbyterian could enjoy a drink without appearing to be drinking. Plus it's a deliciously refreshing cocktail.

I think I'll have one right now, since I brought it up. Be right back...

Ahhhhhh, yes indeed, it IS deliciously refreshing. How fun to go to a bar and order a drink named after a religion. Being raised Catholic, I was all over that, and a little jealous to boot! But, back to my story…Eventually, I went from drinking a Presbyterian to just bourbon and soda, and then to just bourbon with ice or water. I had found my way after all. Thanks for trusting me, Dad.

I attended the University of Louisville my freshman year. U. of L. is a commuter school, and it just felt like high school on steroids. So when I visited friends at the University of Kentucky, it seemed more like college life to me. I transferred as a sophomore. It was at UK that I discovered tailgating. "Handles" of Jim Beam and bottles of Old Crow and Old Forester were everywhere before, during and after football games. Now this was big time college! Because you couldn't major in tailgating, I chose to study marketing because there was little math. I still had statistics and some advanced math to negotiate, but after some summer classes, I graduated on time in four years with a whopping 2.6 cumulative. Actually it was a 2.66, so for résumé purposes, I round it up to a 2.7.

After graduating, I went to work at a local bank as a loan officer (now *that* will make you drink). It was a small family-owned bank that I called Nepotism Fidelity (that's a joke that

I earned). I learned that the best thing I could say about working at the bank was that you always knew the time and temperature from staring at the sign out the window, wondering if this was what the next 30 years of your professional life was going to be like.

After three open mic nights at a local comedy club, I quit my job and hit the burgeoning comedy circuit for the next 20 years. I had grown up watching Johnny Carson on TV when I should have been asleep, but I thought his monologues were the most unbelievable things to witness. I wanted to make people laugh and write my own routines, and so I did just that.

When you leave Kentucky, you find that some bourbons that are popular in your home state are not even available in other regions of the country...and vise versa. I took this as an opportunity to try different bourbons and local brews. You tend to drink what your parents drink at first. When those brands were hard to find in other places, I branched out.

I will never forget the day I found *my* favorite bourbon. It wasn't my dad's bourbon or my mom's bourbon, it was *my* bourbon. That bourbon was Old Grand Dad Bonded, and it's still one of the best bourbons out there, in my opinion. I found this bourbon in Drew Carey's stomping grounds in Parma, Ohio, a suburb of Cleveland. When I tasted it on the rocks, it just spoke to me. To this day, I enjoy 100-proof bourbons. It was also the start of what would put me on the bourbon map, teaching people to read whiskey and bourbon labels 20 years later.

This reminds me of a story that happened after I discovered Old Grand Dad bourbon

My longtime friends Paul Halloran and his wife, Amber (which is my favorite color–it's the color of bourbon), entertain frequently at their house. Often Paul's parents would be in attendance, and they were both about 75 years old at the time of this story. Both of Paul's parents, Ryan and Louise, are die-hard bourbon fans and big-time Old Fitzgerald Bonded 100-proof drinkers.

When I got back from working in Cleveland, Ohio, and I enthusiastically shared with Louise the news that I had found "my" bourbon, she calmly and diplomatically informed me that "Old Grand Dad is a fine bourbon, yes, but it's no Old Fitzgerald." Now remember, this is a very proper Southern lady who was well into her 70s. She continued as she sipped her Old Fitz, "Ryan and I prefer the bonded 100-proof, but now that we're older, we drink the 86-proof."

Overhearing her say this, her son, Paul, who had made her drink, informed her, "Hey Mom, that's the 100-proof you're drinking right there." She looked at her bourbon and then up at me and said, "Oh...well, I thought this tasted especially good."

Then as she swirled her bourbon with just two small cubes of ice and looked at it, she continued, "Ryan and I used to only drink our bourbon neat, but now that we've gotten a little older, we cut it with ice." (You just *have* to love her.)

Louise passed away in December of 2009 at the age of 90, and being the "Emily Post of Kentucky" she wore high heels to the end. We all miss Louise, so as you read this, raise an Old Fitzgerald 100-proof to her memory, and if you have to cut it, just two cubes now!

A few years after my Old Grand Dad discovery, the small-batch and single-barrel bourbons hit the market, and I was eager to try them. This was also a time that I learned a very neat trick when it comes to high-end spirits. This is a tip you can use today as it's still true, so pay attention. I found that the Jim Beams, Evan Williams and Wild Turkeys of the world always had a speed pourer on the bottles at the bar so they could be measured out on what bartenders call "a three count." You've seen a bartender pick up a bottle and just start pouring the spirit into a glass. They turn it upside down and count to three, and that's an ounce and a quarter every time, if they count right.

I noticed that the small-batch and single-barrel bourbons had a cork on them, not a speed pourer. So if I ordered a Knob Creek or similar high-end bourbon, the bartender pulled the cork out and just glug, glug, glugged it into the glass, and as a result I got a double (or more) for the price of a single. I took note, and even though I paid more for that one drink, it was really two really good ones. Buying this book just paid for itself, so use the information to your benefit!

When I traveled the comedy circuit, my big ending was my routine about my father, who was approaching 90 at the time and drank a quart of bourbon a day. That's not my guess, by the way, those were his words to his doctor when he was asked how much he drank. I'd always order a bourbon on stage and salute my dad with a toast.

Oh, all right – I know you want to know what it was

My comedy routine about my father

My dad is 90 years old and he's started having trouble with his vision. He's seeing double, and in his mind, it couldn't be the bourbon. Of course it wasn't the bourbon, but then again, he did drink a lot of it. You never know how much they drink, of course. My dad has the magic cup. He drinks from a 24-ounce Styrofoam cup because it doesn't sweat or leave a mark, and it never seems to empty. He has a bottle in the fridge in the garage, so he walks out there with an empty cup, and when he gets back to the dining room—bam!—his cup is full again. My dad is also very quick witted and funny. He told me once, "Son, always date someone that's homeless…that way the next morning, you can just drop them off anywhere."

My dad is an alcoholic. There it is, I said it. I can tell people that my dad is an alcoholic and it doesn't bother me for two reasons. Reason # 1, I like how things turned out. I'd be a different person if my dad was different, and I kind of like myself. So if Dad was a different guy raising us, we'd all be different. Reason # 2 that I am comfortable telling you that my dad is an alcoholic, is that *everybody* has someone in their family, someone they know, who's an alcoholic, and if you don't think you know someone or have someone in your family who's an alcoholic…it's you!!!

Back to my dad's vision problem. So my mom took him to the doctor. Actually it was a new doctor of his ... his fourth doctor, as a matter of fact. You see, he'd outlived the first three. I joked with Dad that we should call this new doctor to make sure he's still alive so we didn't waste a trip!

Now, we all know the questions a new doctor will ask when you get a checkup. How much do you smoke? How much do you drink? And the answers aren't lies you want to rush in to. You try them out on your friends. You'll ask them, "Does three drinks a day sound like a lot?" It doesn't sound like a lot to me, but then again, I'm a whiskey professor.

But for the first time in my dad's life, instead of lying to his doctor, this time he was going to be totally honest. I mean, he's 90, so what's the worse that can happen, he drops over dead? Plus my dad loves to read, so seeing was very important to him. He decided he wasn't going to lie, he was just going to give succinct truthful answers. So the doctor came in and said he was going to ask a few questions and get down to the root of this vision problem. My dad was seated and ready. My mom was there to hear this exchange, and as they say, you can't write stuff like this, it's much funnier when it's the real deal.

Doctor: "How old are you, Joe?" Boy, my dad had that one nailed.

Dad: "90," he said loudly and clearly.

Doctor: "Do you smoke?"

Dad: "No."

Doctor: "Do you drink?"

Dad: "Yes."

Doctor: "How much do you drink?"

Dad: "Quart."

Now that made the doctor stop and look up. And that's hard to do.

Doctor: "Did you say quart?"

Dad: "Quart," my dad was on a monosyllabic roll!

Doctor: "A quart of what? Beer?"

Dad: "Bourbon."

Doctor: "In what time frame do you drink a quart of bourbon? A month? A week?"

Dad: "A day."

My dad drank a quart of bourbon each and every day! That sure connected a lot of dots. Kind of explains why I went to a state college!

Me and Dad, taken around 2002.

I don't know what's funnier about that. The fact that my dad drank a quart of bourbon a day or the fact that he still thought we measured bourbon in quarts!

So the doctor left the room and probably went to the nurse's station and said, "Look at this. The man's 90, and he drinks a quart of bourbon a day. And he's breathing ... right there in exam room #2."

When he returned, my mom said he looked at my dad and scolded him like a little kid. He said they were going to give him a few tests and get down to the bottom of this vision problem, but as a man of his age, he really should consider *quitting* drinking altogether.

Now I ask you, what the hell kind of doctor could this man be? My dad couldn't, no...no, more like *shouldn't* stop drinking just like that. I mean, how long has he been drinking a quart of bourbon a day? 50? 60? 70 years??? You can't go from a quart to nothing. He'd drop over dead.

You see, my dad's organs are busy! They've been processing and filtering a quart every day for all these years. If my dad did stop drinking, his liver would look at his kidneys and say, "This is the chance we've been waiting for!" and then just shut down.

If my dad dies, and I think it's just an "if," because I don't' think cancer can exist in a bourbon-ridden environment. My dad's probably had cancer seven times and just shook it off.

"Burrrrrrrrr....."

"What's wrong there, Dad? You got a chill?"

Dad: "I think I just had cancer again. Cancer always gives me a headache; I need a drink."

If my dad dies, the second that embalming fluid hits his liver, he's going to sit up straight in the casket and say, "Now this is top-shelf shit right here, boys!"

I also wrote a song about my dad and performed it on the popular syndicated morning radio program, "The Bob & Tom Show." The song is titled "He's My Dad," and it goes a little something like this:

He's My Dad

He'll eat the fat off your steak, he don't like it too lean
He's outlived three doctors, thanks to ole' Jim Beam
He eats a pork chop sandwich most days for lunch.

Fries everything in butter or bacon grease
Passes constant gas through his BVDs
He swills Citrucel like its gourmet fruit punch.

He's my dad. He's my dad.
94 years old and still walkin' that ain't half bad.
Claims he's older than Santa Claus and that's a fact.

Graduated with Moses, how 'bout that?

Now that's old school, that's my dad.

He'll do the Sunday crossword without even tryin'

He says, "I can't see" but he's still drivin'

But if he hits you, you won't get hurt, he don't drive that fast.

Tracks the "Storm Team" all through the day

Then checks his rain gauge after every rain

He's going cross-eyed readin' all that crap scribbled on the bottom of CNN.

He's my dad. He's my dad.

His toe nails look like Fritos corn chips right out of the bag.

He's sittin' home right now with his glass of cheer

I bet he outlives half of us sitting here

He's pickled, he's not going no where, he's my dad.

So here's to my dad

Raise a toast to my dad....

I'm sure glad I got to know ya,

I love ya, Dad.

You can see a version of this sung and performed by me on YouTube. I recommend watching it with a drink in hand so you can join me in a toast at the end.

My dad passed away just shy of the age of 94. He lived a long life. He was born in 1911 and passed away in 2005. Can you imagine what he saw? When he was a kid, people were still riding horses to get places. He put us all through college all on his dime. When we graduated we just had to get a job and not worry about loans. He got to see me perform stand-up comedy and then work for Jim Beam. He was really proud of what I was accomplishing, although he didn't really understand how going around drinking bourbon and telling stories was a real corporate job with health benefits. But then again, he sure thought it was cool.

Truth be told, I didn't get to really know my dad until my mom passed away. We all figured Dad would pass away first, not only because of his age, but in addition to his drinking, he had a horrible diet. For breakfast he'd take a glazed donut and cut it in half, put a pat of real butter on each half, and put it in the toaster oven. Then he'd wash that down with half-and-half. For lunch, he'd eat a fried pork chop sandwich; for dinner, bean soup and a nice marbleized fatty steak. The only thing we could think of was that the fat in his diet clogged his arteries, and the bourbon cleaned them out!

So when my mom passed away at 79 after a brave battle with cancer, we all thought, "Well, what are we gonna do now?" I mean, we really didn't know our dad very well. As odd as that sounds, my mom was the one we all really spent time with. Dad was just kind of "there" through the years. He was cranky most times when he came home, and he was a big intimidating man, so we kinda stayed away from him, and he from us. I mean, he was a great provider, and don't get me wrong, I wouldn't change a thing. But now we were "stuck" with this guy we really didn't know and were a little intimidated by.

He lived alone after Mom passed away and was very self-sufficient. He read five books a week. (On stage I'd joke that with his age, they were the same five every week! He sure loved those mysteries!) He'd read two books at one time and on the side do *The New York Times* crossword puzzles.

He was also still driving, which was scary to think of until you noticed he didn't drive that fast. The impact couldn't have done more than spill your coffee. He would shop, then cook. He cooked food for all of our families and the neighbors. We all took turns having a different "Dad day" and mine was

Wednesday. He'd always have a steak he had bought at the store to prepare to my liking. He was always great at finding a good deal at the grocery, too, his favorite pastime. He'd always peruse the sale bin in the meat section, or what I called the "green meat bin."

He'd say, "Hey, look at this, I got this rib eye steak for $1.29."

I'd say, "Dad, there's mold on it."

And he'd retort, "Heat kills everything, son, it'll cook up just fine. Look at all that good fat on there."

He finally did give up driving on his own. I'd drive him to his weekly visit to the grocery store. He'd shop for a good hour and a half, and then when he checked out, I'd pick him up after going to his home to do the cleaning that he couldn't see to do anymore. One time the 18-year-old checkout clerk said to him, "For an old man, you sure do buy a lot of groceries." Without missing a beat Dad fired back, "I have a voracious appetite."

When I drove him to the store for the first time, I pulled up to the second entrance of the store, and he said to me, "You missed the damn exit, boy!"

I said, "Well, I have to drop you off, and so I have to take this entrance to drop you off the right way." He pouted for a couple moments and said back to me, "Well, you're not doin' it the way I'd do it, so you're doing it wrong!"

He was something else.

After a few months of eating lunch with him and spending time actually "talking" to him for the first time in my life, a funny thing happened. I realized my mom gave us all a beautiful gift when she died first: our father. And we all got to fall in love with the man my mom fell in love with. If he would have passed away first, we would have been robbed of that, so cheers to you, Mom. (Sip.)

I found out that I get my wit and humor from him. He was truly hilarious. He'd cut obituaries out of the paper and have me read them. I mean, have you read some of them? They might start out like, "Last night Jane Doe, 42, stepped through the door to Heaven breathing in the wonders and mysteries of being in the presence of God." One of his all-time favorites was, "John Doe, 54, died approximately November 15th, 2003."

Some were *very* long and cost several hundred dollars, especially if a picture accompanied it. He just couldn't believe all that money wasted on someone who was dead. He told me that when he died, we should just say he died and that was that.

When my dad passed away, I wrote the obituary. As he would be the biggest critic of it from "beyond the threshold" (which is where I know he is now reading this book and sipping bourbon), I wanted to have one befitting him. Sorry I wrote more than you wanted, Dad, but here's what it said in the *Courier Journal* that day:

> **OBITUARY**
>
> LUBBERS, H. Joe, 93, of Louisville, passed away Tuesday
>
> He was born May 5, 1911. At the age of 32, he was drafted in the U.S. Army to serve in WWII. He fell in love with and married Helen, his first wife, and they had a son, whom they named Lawrence "Lar." She unfortunately died too early. He then married Agnes "Champie" Kruse and they had three children: Katie, Bernie, and Gretchen.
>
> He started out working in the icehouse at Falls City Brewing Company and retired as vice president.
>
> He drank good Kentucky bourbon, so let's all raise a glass to Joe. He made it almost 94 years. He was Herman Joseph Theodore Christopher Lubbers–PROST!!!"

(Prost is a shortened version of the old German toast, Ein Prosit.)

So back to how I became the whiskey professor...

Fast forward through 20 years on the road performing comedy in 160 cities from Hawaii to Florida to the day when one of my best friends, Karen (one of the best liquor distributors in the business), introduced me to a guy named Rob who was just hired by Jim Beam in Kentucky. Rob saw that in my act I talked about bourbon and even ordered and drank his products on stage. He figured that I was a person he'd want to support, since I was on stage for an hour at a time in front of more than 1,000 people a week. So for two years, Rob invited me to tastings and events that Beam put on. One day Rob came to me and asked if I'd be interested in working full-time for Jim Beam hosting events and running promotions. It sounded like fun, and being a personality job, seemed a good fit. So I took the gig, and this is when I started to learn more about bourbon, but with a comedian's approach.

Most bourbon distillers' presentations that I saw focused on how they distilled their specific bourbons. But just about everyone distills bourbon the same way. So I realized it was my job to find a way to talk about bourbons in a new way. We also hired my cousin Bobby and a couple other recent college grads who wanted a career in the spirits industry, and we leveraged their passion and energy with the fact they were out and about a lot by making them ambassadors for Knob Creek. We kicked ass and drove the brand up 129%! The brand manager for Knob Creek took a shine to me and asked if I'd help start the Whiskey Professor Program with them. Too dumb to be afraid, I took on the job, and after two-and-a-half short years, my colleagues David Mays and Steve Cole and I collectively won Whiskey Ambassadors of the Year for 2009 by *Whiskey Magazine's Icons of Whiskey Awards* out of London, England. We won Best Ambassadors of the Year for the United States, and then for the entire world! We were blown away, to say the least. I never thought that stand-up comedy would be a good entrée for a corporate job, but there it is.

We were told by several of the judges that we won that year because we not only had the knowledge and passion for bourbon, but we did things in new and creative ways. I was particularly proud of that because we looked at it from the ground up. We even took a look at how we dressed. I didn't think that wearing slacks, tie and sport coat was ever the way to go. My friends know that if I have a suit on, there's probably a dead body in the room.

With 20 years of experience as a stand-up comic, I knew that we had to look, act, and present in a new and creative way. We decided that we would dress like they do down at the distillery—in blue jeans and a nice shirt. Fred Noe had some really cool cowboy boots made along with the band we sponsor, Montgomery Gentry. So I thought I'd have some custom boots made that had Knob Creek Bourbon on them. The only problem was that custom-made boots are like crazy expensive. So I stopped in to see Nick and Lynn over at Leatherhead down the street from my condo in Louisville. Nick is a true craftsman with leather. He's made custom collars for Oprah's dogs. Nick made the boots for Orlando Bloom in the *Pirates of the Caribbean* movies, and I couldn't think of anyone who could do it better. Plus he and Lynn have a farm next to the Booker Noe Distillery, so serendipity was in full force. Nick and Lynn came up with a solution to have the custom-made look without blowing our budgets. And they are awesome!

So now we have a different look than most bourbon ambassadors. And instead of just talking to people about how bourbon is distilled, we talk about the whole whiskey category and teach people how to read a whiskey label. Just like with wine, you can learn how to read a whiskey label and know quite a bit about it before you even taste it. (You will learn how to read a label later on in Chapter 4.) Then we bring to life the fun and riveting stories in the history of bourbon, just like Jimmy Russell, Fred Noe and the guys with the rich family legacies do. And lastly, we have *fun* with it. We don't just give bourbon presentations. We laugh and joke, drink and hang out with other people who love bourbon. Some of the best fun and best presentations I've ever given were just sitting at a bar and getting into a bourbon conversation with a total stranger, and by the time we part company we've shared a few bourbons, talked about history, and bonded. We really

Whiskey Professor Bernie Lubbers (photo by Dean Haynes)

have a lot of fun being whiskey professors. When you never feel like you're working, then you really start to take things to another level.

When you visit Kentucky and stay in Louisville, stop by the Blu Café at the Marriott Hotel for Bourbon & Bluegrass Night every Thursday (corner of Second and Jefferson–it's also one of the stops on the Urban Bourbon Trail) and have a Basil Hayden's with Claire at the bar, and listen to some of the best live music with Hickory, Jim and Chris. Be sure to ask them about it. Hell, they play at every bourbon festival and up at Jim Beam's house on Distiller's Row in Bardstown every year, as well as every time we have VIPs and folks in from all over the world. Make sure to buy a CD from 'em too. I did.

I'm not married and I don't have kids, so I tend to be out listening to live music and meeting friends and family for a cocktail most nights of the week. Being a comedian and a musician, I really enjoy being social and going out, and that really comes in handy as a whiskey professor. Some people ask me why I "gave up" comedy. I use my comedy talents and skills every single day. I travel as much or more now than I did working the comedy circuit. I just integrate it all into my sales and consumer presentation and make it damn entertaining as well as educational. This is not the job for someone that likes to stay home. But it's not for someone who just likes to go out and drink all the time, either. It's a real balancing act. Adding to that is the need to continue educating myself on the category of whiskey and bourbon. Like I said before, my life is a paid vacation, so it doesn't feel like a job to me. Whiskey professor happens to be my job title, but I feel that I'm not just called the whiskey professor, I *am* The Whiskey Professor.

2

What Makes Bourbon, Bourbon?

"I feel sorry for people who don't drink. When they wake up in the morning, that's as good as they're going to feel all day."

–Frank Sinatra

Well, now that you know what made me, me, you should ask what makes bourbon, bourbon. People had been making whiskey for hundreds of years. But it took Kentucky to make it bourbon. Make no mistake about it: Because of Kentucky and the Kentuckians who distilled it, their whiskey had a different recipe with the corn, giving it a fuller body and sweetness. They made bourbon in North Carolina, Tennessee, Indiana, Illinois and other states, but Kentucky bourbons were the ones left standing, for the most part.

What makes Kentucky bourbon so special? The big difference is the charred barrels. The interaction of the charred barrels with the aging whiskey enhances the flavor and makes the delicious liquor even more smooth and easy to drink. The specialty barrels also give the whiskey that beautiful amber color it never had before. Kentucky is also responsible for the name–Bourbon–as that was the port city that the liquor came from in the Bluegrass State.

Most–97%—of all bourbon is still produced in Kentucky. There are a few reasons for that. When settlers started moving west, Kentucky was about as far west as you could go. Many of those settlers were displaced after the Whisky Rebellion in western Pennsylvania and were whiskey men. The conditions in Kentucky have always been perfect for whiskey making. Fresh springs, creeks and lakes are abundant, and those aren't

Limestone filtered water (Photo courtesy of the Louisville Convention and Visitors Bureau)

just any water sources; they carry pure, limestone-filtered water. Kentucky has a great limestone shelf, and that limestone filters out all of the iron in the water.

The water in Kentucky also contains a good amount of calcium, which is one of the reasons the horse industry thrives here. When the horses eat the grass and drink the water, they get the calcium they need for strong ankles, which helps them run around the race track on the first Saturday in May and at the Bluegrass Stakes at Keeneland a few weeks before. (Unfortunately, the limestone that filters the water for the bourbon also filters out the extra calcium, so drinking bourbon does not guarantee that *you* will have stronger ankles. So don't go thinking you can outrun Usain Bolt just because you've been enjoying some of our native spirit.)

Then there's the handy location of Kentucky right in the center of the country. We get extreme cold in the winters and extreme heat in the summers. These temperature fluctuations allow the whiskey to work its way in and out of the barrels, imparting that beautiful color and flavor to the bourbon.

Kentucky was also ideally situated right there on the Ohio River, which runs into the Mississippi, so it was easy to get the bourbon to market. That, coupled with the Louisville/Nashville Railroad (L&N), made Kentucky bourbon easily distributed throughout the United States.

Kentucky is also where many of the distilleries were located. If you wanted to start a distillery after Prohibition, you could build a brand new one from the ground up or just buy an empty one. Colonel Beam bought the old Murphy Barber Distillery and started the Beam Distillery in 1934. Others followed suit.

From barley to rye to bourbon

From un-charred new barrels, to charred used barrels, to brand new charred barrels

Ben Parley Moore was down in Kentucky representing his employer in 1857 and wrote back to them about his experience: "Everywhere, sir, I am greeted by gentlemen with their hearts in their right hand, and their right hand in mine, and certainly in their left, a bottle of unequalled Old Bourbon Whiskey."

The whiskey of these early settlers in colonial and post-colonial times was a beautiful work in progress. Hard work, along with some lucky mistakes, transformed colorless rye and corn whiskey to the beautiful amber Kentucky Straight Bourbon Whiskey we enjoy today.

When the Scotch and Irish whiskey men landed in the Northeast, they brought with them barley. What grew prevalently in Maryland and Pennsylvania was rye and some corn. So the early whiskey was made with rye and a little corn until their barley plants started to grow. Even George Washington made rye whiskey. We know this from the records kept by his distiller, a Scotsman named James Anderson. The president's whiskey was 60% rye, 35% corn and 5% barley. The whiskey was stored in barrels, and those barrels were made right on site at Mount Vernon. George Washington was of course a very rich man, so he was able to have a cooperage on site. What distinguished a better grade of whiskey back then was how many times it was distilled, not by how long it was aged in the barrels – and no one had even thought of the benefits that charring the barrels would give the liquor within them.

The most expensive whiskey at that time was the highest proof and was distilled four times or more. Multiple distillations not only drove the proof up, but it also distilled out fusel oils and other congeners. Whiskey distilled twice was called "common whiskey" and fetched around 50 cents per gallon, and whiskey distilled up to four times could be as much as a dollar a gallon.

As distillers moved west to Kentucky, barley and rye were not common crops, but corn was plentiful. So corn became the predominant grain used in whiskey making. "Whiskey is made either with rye, barley, or Indian corn. One or all of these grains is used as they are more or less abundant in the county. I do not know how far they are mixed in (all of) Kentucky, but Indian corn is here in general basis of whiskey, and more often employed alone." (Kentucky Bourbon–Henry Crowgey)

Unlike Washington, these whiskey men were not rich and had no cooperage on site. They bought their barrels from dry good stores or from anyone who had barrels to sell. Barrels were handy to use because one person could roll one down the dock and onto the Kentucky boats (simple Tom Sawyer-style rafts, but much larger and able to transport up to 50 tons) or onto steamboats which also sit low in the river.

Frequently, the second-hand barrels had been used to ship pickles, meats, fish and other perishables, and many of the barrels had used salts, vinegars and pickling agents so the contents would not spoil. When the whiskey makers bought these barrels, they didn't just put their liquor in them right away. They would sterilize the barrels by scraping and then setting the inside of them on fire so that their whiskey would not be flavored with what was shipped in the barrels beforehand.

When you snap a branch off a tree, that tree sends sap to that area to heal itself. When the inside of the barrel is fired and charred, the natural sugars in the oak used to make the barrels rush to the damaged area, and a caramelized layer of natural sugars sets where the char ends and the wood begins. This is known as the "red line."

During the day, the sun would beat down on the barrels traveling down the Ohio and Mississippi Rivers. When a barrel heated up, the liquor expanded and went into the wood, passing through the red line to pick up some of that amber color and, more importantly, absorb flavors from the wood. At night when it got cooler, the whiskey would be forced out of the wood and back into the barrel, again passing through the red line, picking up flavor, and rounding out that rough spirit.

In the six months it took the whiskey to travel downstream, it was drastically changed in sight and taste. Remember, it had started differently than traditional whiskey and was sweeter because the predominant grain was corn instead of rye. But the interaction with the charred barrels made it something entirely new. As we like to say in the whiskey business, the barrels rounded off the rough edges and softened up that white dog. When people tasted it, they fell in love with it and asked what it was. The barrel heads were printed with the name of the port the liquor was shipped from, the county in Kentucky named after the French royal family—the Bourbons—just like Bourbon Street: OLD BOURBON KENTUCKY WHISKEY. And so the drink we all know and love came to be. Fans would say, "I sure like that bourbon whiskey from Kentucky."

Did the whiskey makers know what was going to happen to their liquor on that journey? Or was it just an accident that people liked?

My friends Larry and Rob down at Heaven Hill Distillery tell another story. According to them, Elijah Craig was the first distiller to char a barrel before storing whiskey in it, and I personally hope their version is true.

Elijah Craig was a Baptist preacher and a distiller (talk about an oxymoron) and had some empty barrels stored in his barn. There was a fire in the barn, and being a thrifty God-fearing Christian man who felt that wasting anything was sinful, he went ahead and used those barrels to store his whiskey. When he did this, the barrels did their work, and bourbon was discovered because someone was too cheap to replace his materials after a fire. It's a great story and like I said, I really want it to be true, and perhaps it is indeed how *his* barrels became charred.

By the way, Elijah Craig is a damn fine bourbon, and the 12-year expression is my favorite one to toast Brother Elijah with. There is also a single-barrel 18-year-old expression that is quite tasty. And for the price, you can't beat these whiskies, especially for their age.

Of course with these stories, you've got to keep in mind that in France they were storing cognac and brandy in toasted barrels, and barrels were being used to add some color/flavor to other liquor. The French tripped upon extra aging when they were at war with Spain, because Spain was their big export market for cognac. Most of the cognac sat in the toasted barrels for more than 12 years before peace made its export possible again. The VSOP, XO and extra-aged cognacs can trace their origins to this time. So maybe some of the folks in the New World had heard about the benefits of aging liquor in oak barrels. Was it this information that made the folks in Kentucky, North Carolina and other states char their barrels deeper to add more color and flavor? Was it a barn fire? Was it an accident? Perhaps we'll never know, but it sure is fun reading old books and records and seeing the evolution of bourbon aged in charred barrels. I know for sure that George Washington wasn't charring barrels, and David Beam and David M. Beam were charring barrels in Kentucky in the 1800s, so *something* happened somewhere in there.

Maker's Mark barrels being charred. (Maker's Mark is a registered trademark of Maker's Mark Distillery, Inc. and is used with permission.)

Regardless of how the barrels came to be charred, until the Bottled in Bond Act of 1897, most bourbons were shipped to a tavern in a barrel right from the distillery. Bourbon makers didn't supply bottles, or ship the liquors in bottles, with the exception of Old Forrester. Old Forrester was bottled in 1870, but that was distributed as a prescription from doctors at the time. So previous to that time, if you owned a tavern, you'd bring your own bottles from home—wine bottles, apothecary bottles—and use them to sell whiskey to your patrons. If you could put liquid in it, you could sell bourbon in it. As an aside, a lot of single-barrel or small-batch bourbon makers, such as Basil Hayden's Woodford Reserve, Knob Creek or Booker's, remember their history by packaging their bourbons in similar bottles today.

Because the bourbon was sent to the tavern in a barrel, some unscrupulous shopkeepers would water down the whiskey to make more money. If you suspected this, you might take a bullet out of your gun belt, take it apart and dump the gun powder on the bar in a little pile. You'd then wet the gun powder with the whiskey. Alcohol will burn at just over 50% alcohol content (57.06 to be exact), so if you lit a match and put it to the gun powder and it burned yellow and fizzled out, the whiskey had been watered down. But if it burned blue and made that gun powder flash, it was *proof* of how good the whiskey was. And that's where we get the term 100 proof or 86 proof. It's also one reason Bottled in Bond bourbon was 100 proof. It was considered the good stuff!

So how did bourbon go from being stored in used charred barrels to being stored in brand new charred-oak barrels each and every time? After Prohibition, the Standards of Identity were written and enforced. The coopers' union lobbied their congressmen and senators, who had a vested interest in the cooper industry in their districts, and to insure the coopers had work forever, these legislators made it a law that bourbon had to be stored in a brand new charred-oak container.

Would bourbon distillers still use a brand new charred barrel if they didn't have to? We'll never know. But when you reuse a barrel, it's like reusing a tea bag. You get less and less out of it with each use. You do get more wood notes and characteristics out of a brand new charred barrel than from a used one and in a shorter period of time. But as of now, if you do reuse a barrel even after following all the other laws of bourbon, all you are left with is whiskey, not bourbon whiskey. Examples of this are Michter's American Whiskey and Early Times Kentucky Whiskey. This doesn't mean they are not as good in quality; their wood notes just won't be as pronounced. Some of these can be as enjoyable as bourbon; they are just not bourbon by definition, is all.

A friend of mine who happens to be in his 70s told me a story that he heard from his friend who was one of the government agents who actually lived in a distillery. You see, up to the 1970s government agents actually lived on site at distilleries. There were millions of dollars in tax money involved here. They would inspect the "bonded warehouses" and make sure the appropriate taxes were being paid on the right amounts of bourbon. On each warehouse there would be two padlocks on every door. The master distiller would have one key, and the government agent would have the other key. Neither one could get in with out the other.

So anyway, a government agent told my friend that several years back, Jim Beam was experimenting with aging bourbon in caves, like wine. Two years later when they came back to taste the barrels that were locked away in the caves, they opened up the doors ... and all the whiskey was gone! So much for national–or alcohol–security.

Aging today

As you travel the bourbon trail in Kentucky and visit the different distilleries, you'll notice the rack houses where the bourbon is warehoused dotting the landscape. Most are tin-wrapped wooden structures facing north to south so that they get as much exposure to the sun as possible.

A traditional rack house has from five to nine stories, with three barrels on each floor. It takes a crew of five people to put barrels up in these houses. The newly barreled bourbon is placed in the house from top to bottom, and left to right. The barrels stay in the same place the whole time, and after aging is complete, they are pulled out in the same order. The alternative to this placement is to rotate barrels between storage facilities every two or three years. As you can imagine, rotating the barrels is very labor intensive. However, the distilleries who rotate believe that's the best way to make quality bourbon, and the distilleries that don't feel it's unnecessary. There really

Heaven Hill rickhouses (Photo courtesy Heaven Hill Distilleries, Inc.)

is no "better" way, but if you ask them, they will tell you their way is the better way every time! You gotta love distillers! Ha!

Another type of storage facility for bourbon is an escalator house. The escalator house uses a conveyor system to help get the barrels up, so it only takes three people to fill the building. Yet another type of rack house is the palletized warehouse, which is only a couple stories tall, so it only takes one person on a forklift to put the barrels in. They are stacked on top of each other on pallets.

Anyway, as you can see, all these barrels in these different houses age differently. It takes a distiller experience and know-how to get a consistent flavor profile for their best small-batch or single-barrel bourbons. Should they rotate the barrels over the years? Should they take a cross section from top to bottom, and left to right? There's no single answer for any of these questions. For example, Four Roses is the only distillery in Kentucky exclusively using single floor warehouses so that extreme temperatures never affect the bourbon. Other distilleries want those extreme temperatures and marry barrels

Of course, the fun stories you get told over a drink by a new friend are part of what makes bourbon so special. I wish you all could hear my buddy from Tennessee, Nick Lambert, tell this story. He is an exceptional storyteller. I'll give it my best, though.

One May I was doing a bourbon tasting in Memphis at the famous Bar-B-Q festival. Our team there is the wonderful "Peg Leg Porkers." Pit master Carey Bringle has an artificial leg, a great sense of humor and a great way with BBQ.

I gave my talk to the Peg Leg Porkers and their friends, and it went just great. We laughed, we tasted, we learned about our native spirit, and then we all took the bourbon pledge. One of the guests there was already half in the bag and was heckling me a little during my presentation. It seems my presentation broke into his beer drinking time since he was not a bourbon drinker or fan. So after the tasting, he staggered up to me—I was up close to the beer cooler—and said that he enjoyed my presentation, but he thought I went about 10 minutes too long.

My comedy background turned on like a switch, and I treated him like a heckler. "So just what would you have done in my place?" After toying with him a while and having as much fun as I could at his expense, I thanked him for his honest yet uninvited input. We all moved on to eating BBQ, drinking bourbon, and sharing stories the rest of the night.

When we walked back to the hotel, I noticed the same guy who had been critical of me staggering around with his wife, looking for their car. His wife was totally sober and not at all happy with her intoxicated, boisterous, butting-in husband. After a few minutes, the man started cussing because he realized they had parked in an illegal spot and their car had been towed. He came up to me in our team's car and said, "Can you believe the damn city towed my f@%&ing car?"

I replied, "Well buddy, I guess you parked there about 10 minutes too long."

from top to bottom. Maker's Mark rotates their barrels. Buffalo Trace has two different types of brick houses and two different types of block houses. A new distiller just has to work with the different methods, taste the results, and then make some choices. That's one of the reasons it is so hard to get into the bourbon business from scratch. There is a *big* learning curve here.

The bottom line is, if you want to get into the bourbon business, you'll find that the most expensive things you'll incur are wood, time and mistakes from lack of experience. A barrel costs around $125 a piece, and the average rack house holds 20,000 barrels. Experience is priceless. You'll have to cross your fingers and pray over all those years of aging, and hope you distilled and aged it right. What a blow that would be if after eight years in the barrel, the bourbon you made just didn't taste very good.

Even so, there have been hundreds of applications approved for micro distilling in the United States. It will be quite a journey for those new distillers, who will no doubt be calling up the old timers and bourbon experts and bending their ears for advice. Most will be happy to give it. The rising tide raises all ships, so these micro distillers will bring a lot of excitement and pride in regional distilling, just like micro breweries did with craft beers. But whether it's a giant industrial distillery like Jim Beam that makes 1,200 barrels a day, or one that can only turn out a couple of barrels a day, they all have to follow the same strict laws. That's one of the beautiful things about bourbon, there are no short cuts. The word "bourbon" is a quality stamp, like cognac, 100% pure agave or champagne.

3
Distilling and Aging Bourbon

"I have known several men who drank too much, and they were all extremely interesting." –Katharine Hepburn

Why the hell did folks distill grains in the first place? Was it just for catching a buzz? Back several hundred years ago, water was the liquid you least wanted to drink in most places. Unless you were located on a spring, the water in ponds or lakes was usually full of bacteria and other nasty things that would make people sick. Our forebearers found that if they fermented the water with fruits, grapes or grains and created mead, cider or beer, the water was then safe to drink and could keep longer.

By the same token, these grapes, fruits and grains could normally only be consumed when they were in season. But fermentation meant that they could be kept around and consumed over a longer period of time. So the earliest distillers were farmers. Whether they were growing fruits or grains, there were certain to be excess crops from time to time. Instead of just throwing that food out, they would preserve it by canning them or (even better) making beer from the grains, or wine from the grapes and fruits.

So how did this lead to distilling? Well, in Spain and France, for example, they had lots of grapes. They would take the excess grapes and make wine, which was great until they started exploring the world. They took wine with them for the voyages since it kept longer than water, but because the wines were made at low alcohol per volume, they would go bad and turn to vinegar. So they began distilling the wine. Those evolved into what we know today as brandies, cognacs and Armagnacs.

Scotland and Ireland grew a lot of barley for their breads and cereals. They often had excess grains after a growing season, so they made beer from it. When they distilled the beer, they got what they called *usquebaugh*, and thus were born Irish and Scotch whiskies. *Usquebaugh* (pronounced Ush-ka-bay-ha) means "water of life" in Gaelic.

Most nations had their own version of the "water of life"—water made drinkable by distillation: Aqua Vitae (Latin), Aquavit (Scandinavia), Eau-De-Vie (French), Zhizennia and Voda (Russian). Some were made from grapes, some from grains, but all were high in alcohol content.

So when the Scottish, Irish, Spanish and French immigrants came to the New World, they brought their knowledge of distilling. If you look at where these various nationalities settled, you get a clear idea of how North American drinking trends were shaped even before 1600.

The Spanish landed in Florida, and the French settled in Louisiana. As the French and Spanish were experienced in making brandy from grapes and fruits, they made brandies and apple jack from the fruit trees that are indigenous in the South. The Irish were more prevalent in the northeastern United States; the Scottish in Canada. Both nationalities were whisk[e]y drinkers, and in those areas of the new continent, rye was the most abundant grain. In Canada, the Scots followed in the tradition of Usher's and Johnny Walker so Canadian Whisky used a neutral grain spirit along with rye, malted rye and malted barley as flavoring grains. Because of their Scottish influence, they also did not spell their whisky with an "e". The Irish and other whiskey men who settled around Maryland and Pennsylvania used mostly rye, and some corn in their whiskey (and beer, for that matter). The Irish influence meant they spelled their whiskey with an "e."

In 1789, George Washington was elected as the first president of the United States. At that time, he had a big debt to repay to France and others for their help in the Revolutionary War. An estimated $54 million in debt was racked up since the 1776 declaration of war. So in 1791, the Secretary of the Treasury Alexander Hamilton suggested an excise tax on domestically distilled spirits. Because of the British embargo on rum and sugar cane, whiskey was the spirit that was being distilled domestically. The people affected most by this tax were the farmers in Western Pennsylvania near Pittsburgh. They had just fought a war based on taxation without representation, and this tax was levied from an Eastern-based national government. Western farmers owned small family stills and did not operate year-round, so they ended up paying a higher tax per gallon, making them less competitive. Farmers in Western Pennsylvania thought that Hamilton was deliberately trying to run them out of business and promote big businesses that could pay more taxes to the new government.

On September 11, 1791 a newly appointed tax collector by the name of Robert Johnson was tarred and feathered in protest in Washington County, Pennsylvania. Shortly after that, a man was sent to Washington County by government officials to serve warrants to those who attacked Robert Johnson, and that government man was whipped, tarred, and feathered as a result. In the frontier Kentucky territory of Virginia, no one would volunteer to take the job of collecting the tax, and all the other states in the Appalachian region followed suit. .

In August 1792 a convention was held in Pittsburgh to discuss resistance to the whiskey tax. A militant group known as the Mingo Creek Association took over the convention and issued radical demands. Washington and Hamilton were embarrassed by this insurrection, since the nation's capitol was located in Pennsylvania at that time. Washington signed a presidential proclamation drafted by Hamilton himself on September 15, 1792, and it was published in every newspaper and plastered in every town. Resistance continued until 1794, when a militia was called up from New Jersey, Maryland, Virginia and eastern Pennsylvania. A force of 12,950 men was gathered, which was larger than the forces involved in the Revolutionary War. The sheer size of the militia helped to squash the insurrection, and there were few casualties. Later Washington pardoned many of the rebels, since he had made his point. He had successfully shown that the new national government had the willingness and ability to suppress violent opposition to its policies. Interestingly, the Washington administration's actions met widespread approval among most citizens. Ironically, George Washington became the nation's largest distiller of rye whiskey in 1797 and 1798 until his death in 1799.

After the Whiskey Rebellion was over, farmers like Jacob Beam and others from Pennsylvania and Maryland moved as far west as they could to get away from the government control. They moved to Kentucky, which had just become a state (actually a commonwealth) in 1792. At the time, new settlers were given a free parcel of land if they built a cabin on it and grew the native crop, corn. This was part of the Corn Patch and Cabin Rights established in 1776 by the Virginia Assembly to encourage western development.

The settlers brought their rye and barley with them to Kentucky and planted that in addition to their corn. As everyone was growing corn to get their free land, there was a lot of surplus lying around in corn cribs at the time. So settlers started distilling it into their whiskey as well. After all, you could more easily transport a bushel of grain in liquid form than in its natural form. The settlers found that they could make more money from a gallon of corn liquor than from an equal amount of grain.

It was soon true that corn became the main grain in whiskey recipes, and they found that it "softened up" the whiskey. Keep in mind, this was clear, like moonshine, and not the "red whiskey" that we associate with whiskies today. But still, it was sweeter than the rye and barley whiskies they were making before in the East and in Europe. This sweeter corn was the foundation that separated what would become bourbon from the barley-based Scottish and Irish whiskies and from the rye whiskies from the northeastern United States. The corn-based whiskey was so popular that some farms used all of their crop to make whiskey – you've probably heard the songs about how people drank their corn from a jar.

Distillation

Pot stills at Laphroaig Distillery "The Magnificent 7" (Laphroaig is a registered trademark of Beam Global UK Limited and is used with permission.)

Let's take a look at just what distillation is. I'm not going to cover every holding tank, pipe and temperature...I'm basically going to distill down the distillation process. I am not going to mention how many gallons a cooker or fermenter holds, or what temperatures are set, etc. This can get a little confusing, plus it's slightly different from distillery to distillery. I'm just going to talk about distilling overall. I don't want to get too technical, and trust me, folks, I can't, since I was publically educated in Kentucky!

The word *distill* literally means "to strip away." So the higher proof you bring the whiskey off the still, the more congeners, flavors and character you strip away. The more times you distill something, the more you strip away. The highest you can bring anything off the still is around 190 proof.

With single-malt scotch, distillers must use copper pot stills by law. A copper pot still is kind of like an old-fashioned tea kettle. Each time a distiller makes a new batch of whiskey, he puts the fermented beer in, gets the temperatures up, and the whole time the proofs are going up and down erratically. That's

A column still (Photo courtesy of Heaven Hill Distilleries, Inc.)

where they split off the heads and tails and just keep the heart. They make their distillates in batches. Then when they finish distilling that batch, they clean out the still and start a new batch.

Most bourbon distilleries, however, use a column still. All but one of the 10 distillers in Kentucky use column stills. With a column still, once the steam under the column still gets to the correct temperature, you can pump in the fermented distiller's beer 24 hours a day at a constant level proof. Temperatures and proofs are more constant in a column still, so it's very efficient and does extremely well. It doesn't mean scotch or pot stilling is inferior, it just means there are different ways to do it.

So here's how the process works: Let's say you're making vodka (God forbid). With vodka, your goal is an odorless, colorless, and tasteless spirit. (Damn, I can't wait to taste that vodka.) You might not just double distill, but triple distill, quintuple, or continuously distill. Each distillation strips away most of the character, and you end up with a very clean, crisp, tasteless spirit. (I know I'm selling vodka pretty aggressively here, but that really is the definition of vodka.) Distilling to that high proof over and over again has stripped away most of all the characteristics of whatever you fermented.

The lower proof we bring a distillate off the still, the more characteristics we leave in the distillate. With bourbon, we want the flavors from the grains we have fermented. So we only use two distillations to achieve more flavors from these grains. The laws of bourbon state that it must be distilled under 160 proof. In practice, most bourbons are brought off the still at under 140 proof.

Grains before milling (photo courtesy of the Louisville Convention and Visitors Bureau)

The whole process begins with the grains. The grains are sent to a grinding mill. Mill grinds are set to get maximum breakdown of the starches so they convert better. Each grain is milled separately, weighed according to the percentage of the recipe of that mash bill, and added to a cooker. In that cooker the grain is mixed with pure limestone-filtered water and a thin slop, known as the *sour mash process*. All are cooked until proper pH conversion and flavor consistency are achieved. *Sour mash* is the liquid that is left over from the previous distillation minus the alcohol. When the mash is first put into the fermenter it is sweet since all the starches and sugars are present. After fermentation, the yeast eats all the sugars, and at the end it actually tastes sour. The corn and the rye are where we will be getting body and flavor, and the enzymes in the malt turn the starches into sugars. Are you with me so far? To summarize, we've just added the ground-up grains to water and thin slop.

Cooker at Jim Beam (Jim Beam is a registered trademark of Jim Beam Brands Co., and is used with permission)

So now that we have grains and liquid in a large vessel, we heat it up and cook

Jug yeast and fermenter at Maker's Mark (Maker's Mark is a registered trademark of Maker's Mark Distillery, Inc. and is used with permission)

it. This helps to release the grain starches into fermentable sugars. After cooking, we take all this liquid and grain and put it into a fermenting tank where the liquid jug yeast is added along with more thin slop for the sour mash process for consistency of flavor. Each distillery has its own proprietary yeast strain. Yeast is very important congener-wise. You can take the same grain bill, but if you add two different yeast strains in two different fermenters, you would end up with two totally different-tasting bourbons at the end of it all. Yeast is a living enzyme that feeds on the sugars. As the yeast feeds, they produce three things:

(1) carbon dioxide

(2) alcohol

(3) heat/temperature

We're not so interested in the carbon dioxide and heat, but we are interested in that low-proof alcohol. The fermenters produce a 17.5-proof beer or 8.75% alcohol (this differs from distillery to distillery) which actually does taste like a stale beer. Well, that's probably because—minus the hops—it *is* beer! We call it distiller's beer.

Now we take this distiller's beer, and we pump it continuously into our column still. This will be the first distillation. We pump the beer and grains into the still about 2/3 of the way up. Imagine a tall cylindrical column with steam heat underneath it. In this column are a series of plates/trays with tiny holes and weirs (troughs) in the bottom of each plate, kind of like a thick pizza tray with smaller holes.

As the liquids and solids fall down from plate to plate from top to bottom, the heat from the steam works its way from bottom to top. Water turns to vapor at 212 degrees. Alcohol turns to vapor at a lower temperature. So the alcohol vapors rise through the perforated trays to the top of the still, and the beer stair-steps down from tray to tray to the bottom of the still.

The leftover solids (grains) are taken and spun in a centrifuge and further dried by heat and steam and sold as high- quality feed grain for livestock. The liquid is used for the sour mash process; that is the thin slop that is added to the next cook and fermenters so the flavor of the next batch is consistent with the previous batch (kind of like a starter loaf in a friendship bread).

The vapors that escape from the top are then surrounded by tubes of cold water, and this condenses that vapor back into a liquid. This is called *low wine*, and the proof of the alcohol has been raised from 17.5% to 125 proof. This differs from distillery to distillery. I'm using the example of Jim Beam. This low wine is clear like water or vodka. We've taken out most of

Fred Noe asked his dad, Booker, the legendary distiller and grandson of Jim Beam, why the new bourbon whiskey was called white dog. Booker said, "Well, Dumbass..."

Fred claims he thought that his real name was Dumbass until he was 20.

"Well, dumbass, it's called white dog because it's clear (white), and if you drink enough of it, it'll bite you in the ass like a dog!"

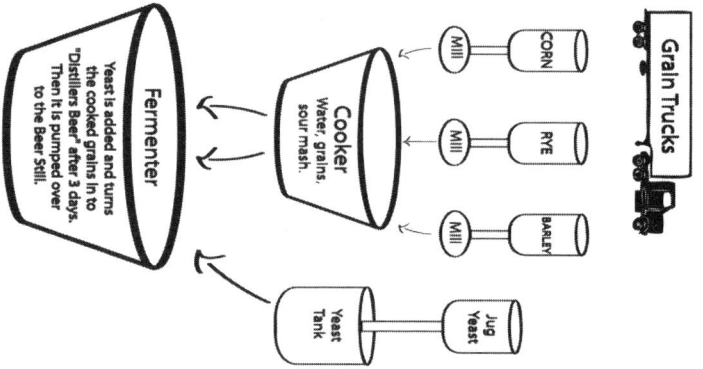
Grain Trucks
CORN
RYE
BARLEY
Mill
Mill
Mill
Jug Yeast
Yeast Tank
Cooker
Water, grains, sour mash.
Fermenter
Yeast is added and turns the cooked grains in to "Distillers Beer" after 3 days. Then it is pumped over to the Beer Still.

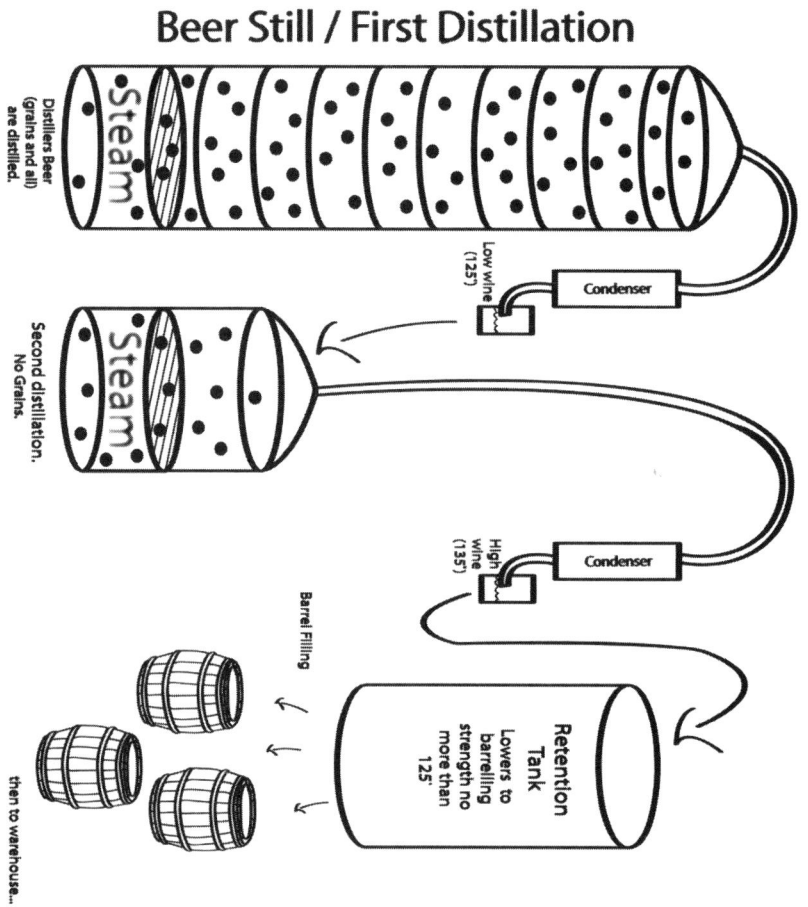
Beer Still / First Distillation
Steam
Distillers Beer (grains and all) are distilled.
Condenser
Low wine (125°)
Steam
Second distillation. No Grains.
Condenser
High wine (135°)
Retention Tank
Lowers to barrelling strength no more than 125°
Barrel Filling
then to warehouse...

the congeners and fusel oils (the stuff that gives you a headache) in this first distillation. But we need to distill it one more time to get the proof up slightly and to eliminate the rest of the undesired fusel oils and congeners.

We send this low wine down to what we call the *doubler*. The doubler is not a column still; it is a hybrid between a column still and a pot still. We don't have any grains in this liquid, so we just pump the low wine in over steam coils underneath, and that alcohol is turned to a vapor and escapes out the top. Once again the pipe for the vapor is surrounded with tubes of cool water, and it condenses it back in to a liquid. Viola! We have *high wine*, or what is called *new bourbon whiskey*. It is at 135 proof now. It tastes cleaner and not as oily as the first distillation, because we have taken out more of those fusel oils. Out of around 44,000 gallons of fermented distiller's beer, we only yield around 6,000 gallons of new bourbon whiskey. New bourbon whiskey is also called *white dog*.

Now we need to put that new bourbon whiskey into a brand new charred-oak barrel and put it up in the rack houses to let it age. But according to law, we cannot store that distillate at more than 125 proof. So we add enough de-mineralized water to get that new bourbon whiskey down to just under 125 proof, and then we put it into the barrel for aging.

The laws of making bourbon are very strict. So if we put that white dog directly into the barrel at 135 proof, even if we put it in a new charred-oak barrel, the resulting product could not be labeled bourbon. It could only be labeled as whiskey. So we have to add more of the limestone-filtered water to get that down to 125 proof before it enters the barrel. Also, if you distill to 150 or 160 proof, you'll have to add even more water to get it down to the 125 in the barrel, resulting in a lighter end product.

The reason for barreling at 125 proof or less is because, as the whiskey ages, we lose approximately 4% a year to evaporation, also known as the angels' share. It's what the angels drink. The old boys say that if the angels don't take their share, it's not worth drinkin'. The barrels that age on the higher floors where it is very hot and dry will rise from 125

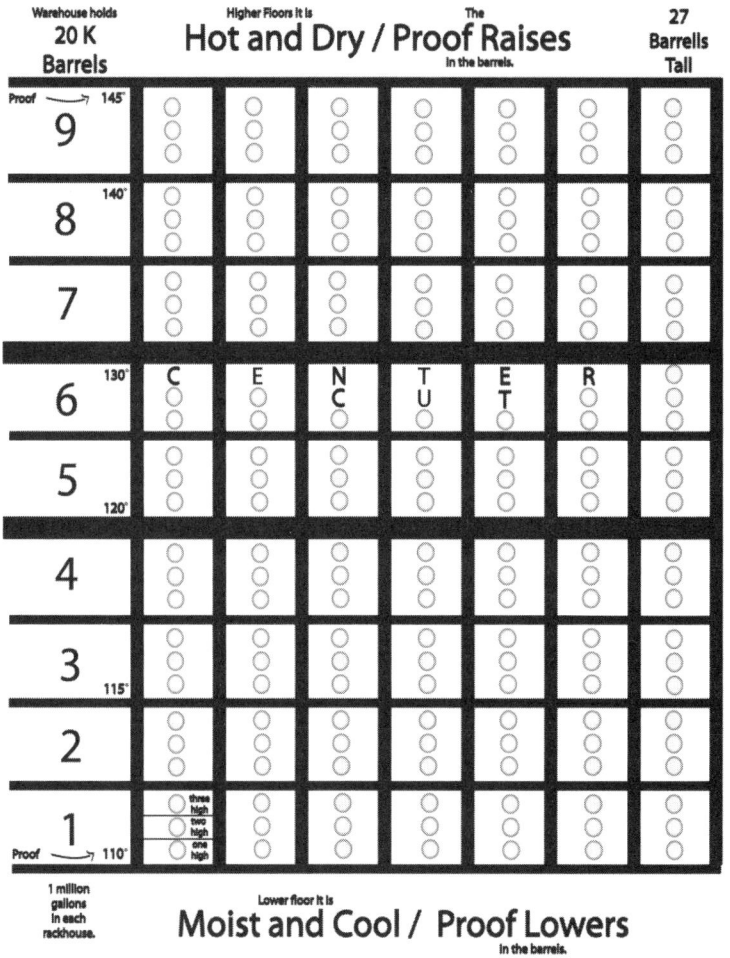

How barrels age inside a traditional rackhouse.

proof to 145 proof after evaporation. If we put the 160-proof whiskey in the barrel, it could rise all the way up to 180 proof or so. And if you add water after aging to get that bourbon down to 80 or 100 proof in the bottle, you've just watered down everything you worked so hard for, and you don't get the flavors you need at the end. So bourbon can't enter the barrel at anything more than 125 proof.

Buffalo Trace Barrels in rackhouse (Photo courtesy of Buffalo Trace Distillery)

For small-batch bourbons or single-barrel bourbons, the proofs of the low wine and high wine are typically lower, leaving in more flavors and characteristics from the grains. The process of making all bourbon is the same, so if you do want to make a more flavorful, or "premium" product, you can really only change the grain bill, yeast strains, or bring it off the still at different/lower proofs or bottle it at higher proofs. Are you getting the hang of just how regulated bourbon is?

Bourbon and Moonshine

You'll find that some bourbons now have flavorings added to them as a shout-out to the tradition of adding a flavor to moonshine. Wild Turkey and Evan Williams make a honey and cherry flavor, and Jim Beam's Red Stag is black cherry flavored. There are some folks that scoff at this or say distillers shouldn't add flavors, but I'd argue moonshiners have been doing it longer than we've been aging in barrels.

After distilling, we go into the aging process. Aging is just as important to the final flavor of the bourbon as the distillation. You can take the same recipe, put it in two barrels at the same proof, and then bottle one after four years and the other after six years, and you will get two very different bourbons. This is where it really starts to become interesting.

How the Aging Process Works

If you've ever had moonshine (and you should once in your life), you'll remember it being served in a mason jar with something else in it. There's often fruit in it, like strawberries, cherries or a peach. The fruit softens up the taste of the harsh moonshine and adds some sugar and flavor to it. The barrel serves a similar purpose. It just takes a lot longer to do it.

Aging sounds pretty simple. You take your whiskey off the still, put it in a "brand new charred-oak container" as the law specifies, and then store it until you decide to bottle it, right? Sounds simple. But there is way more to it than that. How long do you store it? Where do you store it? Do you move the barrels around or just let them rest? From where do you pull the barrels after aging?

First of all, let's put to rest the myth that bourbon has to be aged for two years in the barrel. This is not true. The Standards of Identity only say that bourbon should be "stored" in a brand new charred-oak container. As Jimmy Russell from Wild Turkey says, with bourbon you can use the "Fifteen/Fifteen" rule: As long as you put the new under-125-proof bourbon whiskey in the new charred-oak bucket for 15 seconds or carry if for 15 feet, you've got bourbon. It wouldn't be very tasty, but by law it would be bourbon. The designation of "straight" bourbon means that

Barrels charring at Independent Stave Cooperage (Jim Beam is a registered trademark of Jim Beam Brands Co., and it used with permission.)

you have followed all the laws of bourbon and have stored (aged) the whiskey for a minimum of two years.

Let's talk about the barrels. We all use white oak, since that variety allows the bourbon to penetrate the wood but also can hold the liquid for the years needed without losing integrity. Before being made into barrels, the wood is cut and set outside in the open air for several seasons to allow it to age in the elements. This helps get all the green out of the wood and tempers the wood against some tannins and other elements that are undesirable during the aging process.

As I explained in the last chapter, charring makes the natural sugars come to the surface of the interior of the barrel so that the bourbon can imbibe the qualities, flavor and character of the wood, which is what gives bourbon its beautiful color and seductive taste. Most distilleries use the deepest, or level four, char. In contrast, wine is typically aged in lightly toasted barrels with no char. Bourbon distillers are

Buffalo Trace Warehouse C (Photo courtesy of the Louisville Convention and Visitors Bureau)

allowed to select their char level, but barrels must be charred, not just toasted or seared. The way the coopers char the barrels is to assemble the barrel staves, and before they put the heads on the ends, they introduce a flame through the inside of the barrels. If you've ever seen a hot air balloon and its burners, it's similar to that.

Storage while aging has developed differently at each distillery, and each master distiller or warehouse manager has his/her own opinion about it. Some use brick rack houses and others use wood-and-tin construction. Some use four-story rack houses that are 12 barrels tall and others prefer nine-story rack houses standing 27 barrels tall. Maker's Mark rotates its barrels the old-fashioned way. Four Roses only uses one-story warehousing. Buffalo Trace and Woodford Reserve use brick rack houses. There are as many ways to age the liquor as there are ways to make it, and one way is not necessarily more correct or better than the other; they are all just different. Although if you ask one of the distillers, he might say his way is better ... I just love the pride in this industry.

The atmospheric pressure in the rack house and location of the barrels make barrels age differently from top, to middle, to the bottom of the rack house. It's very hot and dry at the top of the rack house—think of it as being just like your attic. So the barrels on the top floor start out at 125 proof and will rise all the way up to 145 proof (or more) due to evaporation during the aging process. Barrels on the bottom floor, however, where it is moist and cool, will have the alcohol and water molecules interact. Those barrels start out at 125 proof and will go down in proof to 115 or so. The middle of the rack house is where the temperature is the most consistent, so the barrels will stay around the 124 to 128 range. Confusing? Well keep in mind that the bourbons on the outer parts of the rack houses will get more heat than those on the inside.

Where do you pull the barrels from after aging? From one floor in the rack house? From all floors? How much from each floor? Do you rotate the barrels? Do you just use a single-story rack house? Are you discovering that generations of

Barrels resting at Heaven Hill Distillery (Photo courtesy of Heaven Hill Distilleries, Inc.)

experience passed down from distiller to distiller really comes in handy here? That's why distilleries talk about their family lineage and experience all the time.

Distilleries used to rotate barrels as standard operating procedure. Maker's Mark still rotates its barrels, but as the number of barrels has increased for everyone, the practice of rotating has been replaced by letting the barrels rest, and then taking a cross section of barrels from the top to the bottom, and left to right diagonals.

Distillers also found out that by rotating the barrels, the barrel bung would dry out at the top of the barrel after a couple years, and by rotating it and rewetting the bung, they lost another 1% or 2% angels' share. That translates into thousands of gallons of bourbon we could all be sipping here instead of passing it on to the angels through evaporation.

Each distiller has a different opinion on the optimal age for their bourbons. Baker Beam (Baker's Bourbon) says that after seven years you've gotten everything out of the barrel you can, and it's the perfect time to dump the bourbon. Fred

Noe says that number is nine years for his Knob Creek, and you've really hit the wall at 12 years. Bill Samuels says between five and six years. He ages by taste, not years. Julian and Preston Van Winkle age their bourbons from 15 to 23 years. Parker and Craig Beam age the Elijah Craig bourbon 12 to 18 years. Remember, my dad thought that six years was the perfect time. Jimmy and Eddie Russell like between four and five years, but they like to distill and barrel at very low proofs, the old-fashioned way. If all bourbon tasted the same, it would be a boring category of whiskey indeed. But thank God they all *do* have a different opinion.

Another way to age whiskey that's a lot quicker is the Lincoln County Process that Tennessee whiskies employ. Many people think that Jack Daniels is not a bourbon because it's made in Tennessee. This is not true. Bourbon can be made anywhere in the United States. But Jack Daniel never wanted to make bourbon. Back in the 1860s was a dangerous time to live, and people didn't want to wait six years for a bourbon to age when they didn't know whether they'd be alive in six days. So they found a way to speed up the aging process.

They burned the maple trees that grew around their distillery and then took the charcoal that was left after burning and piled the ashes and char in a 10-foot column. Then they took the white dog and put it in this column and let it slowly drip, drip, drip through all that charcoal. After a good six or seven days of dripping through all this charcoal, they'd put it into a new charred barrel. This process is called charcoal mellowing, not filtering. This adds flavor to the whiskey. That's why Jack Daniels has the smoky quality that Tennessee whiskey drinkers like. If you spent a week in a vat of charcoal, you'd taste a little smoky, too.

Small-batch and single-barrel bourbons are typically aged longer than main line Wild Turkey, Jim Beam and Evan Williams. Some people think that scotch is higher quality than bourbon because it is aged 10 years or more, but that's not true. Keep in mind that every year a barrel of whiskey is aged in Kentucky is equivalent to about four years in Scotland. The average temperature in Scotland is 55 degrees, so they aren't getting the variety of temperatures we're getting, and they are not using a brand new, charred-oak barrel on top of that. They are using one of our once-used bourbon barrels, so they have to age it longer. I'm not saying our bourbon is better than scotch or vise versa; I'm just explaining the differences. Each distiller in Scotland or Kentucky uses their experience and geography for what's best for their whisk[e]y. That's also why scotch tastes so good. Every drop of scotch has some of our bourbon in it!

They did a test a few years ago. Jim Beam sent a barrel of bourbon to Scotland to age, and the Laphroaig Distillery sent a barrel of scotch to Kentucky to age. It turned out that the switch just didn't work. Both tasted below par, proving that bourbon and scotch need to be aged in the environment and landscape of where they are distilled.

I had the great opportunity to visit Scotland, and it was a magical experience. I visited the Dalmore Distillery in Inverness, Laphroaig on the Island of Islay, and then the Ardmore Distillery, home of Teacher's Blended and Ardmore Single Barrel, in Aberdeenshire. The highlands of Scotland really resemble Kentucky. Both places are basically the same size geographically and population-wise (around 4.5 million). Both are known for excellent water and whisk[e]y making, and both are full of excellent whisk[e]y men and women who are extremely passionate about their craft.

Although I don't get to see them as often as I'd like to, I'm lucky to call John Campbell at Laphroaig and Alistair Longwell at Teacher's my colleagues and friends. But I do get to work with, debate, and drink good whisky with Simon Brooking, their global ambassador. If you ever get the chance to see any of these whisky men, by all means do!

A Word About Recipes or Grain Bills

By far the most frequently asked question that I get is "What is the recipe for your bourbon?" Some people seem to want to know the exact percentage of barley, rye and corn that we use. It's a question that every distiller and ambassador has been asked. A couple distillers will just tell ya straight out. Maker's Mark is 70% corn, 16% red winter wheat and 14%

barley malt. It's right up on the wall at the distillery on a chalkboard. That's pretty damn cool. Maker's Mark just makes one recipe. Other distilleries have two or more different recipes for their bourbons. Jim Beam and Buffalo Trace don't reveal their different grain recipes. It's a family secret, if you will, and that's pretty damn cool, too. I mean, do you think you could discern that one bourbon could possibly be "better" than another simply because it had 1.5% more rye or corn than another? And would that make a big difference over four to 12 years of aging in a barrel?

No one ever asks what the grain bill is for a single malt scotch, do they? That's because there is only one recipe, and that's 100% barley. And there are over 90 distilleries in Scotland producing the same recipe in the same whisky. It depends on where that distillery is and how that location affects the whisky in production and during aging. The size and shape of the still has an effect on the final product as well. But everyone wants to know the exact percentage of grains in bourbon and then pretend that this combination defines what is, in their own head, a "good bourbon." I think that's ludicrous. I personally think that some people just don't know what to ask, so that seems to be a good question, especially in front of a group of people.

Now that being said (and I'm glad I got that off my chest), a considerable change in the percentage of grains can have an effect on a bourbon. In studying bourbon and being around all the distillers, I have concluded (and I'm not the first one to conclude this, but it's an "aha" moment when you get to this point) that there are only three (that's right, three) recipes in *all* of bourbon. From this I've put together the following "chart." This chart is based on information from articles and books I've read and distillers I've talked to. It shows what you can learn when you read *Whisky Magazine, Malt Advocate, The Bourbon Review*, Liquor.com, straightbourbon.com and books on the subject.

Corn is what gives bourbon its signature flavor and is considered the "engine" that provides the highest yield of alcohol per bushel of all the grains. The flavor of corn is very prevalent fresh off the still in the white dog. But over years of aging, corn becomes neutral and lends mostly in the overall sweetness to the finished product.

Bourbon flowing from the barrel in the dump floor. (Jim Beam is a registered trademark of Jim Beam Brands Co. and is used with permission.)

Barley is prized mainly for its enzymes that convert starches to sugar for the fermentation process so the yeast can feed on the sugars. Where corn is the "engine," malted barley is considered the "work horse" that delivers these enzymes. Barley provides some of the underlying malty and chocolate notes, along with some dryness. Usually around only 5-12% of any grain bill, barley is mainly used for those enzymes, and not so much for flavor, but it does gives the bourbon that biscuity texture.

Rye and Wheat contribute most significantly to the flavor of mature bourbon. They are referred to as the "flavoring grains." Any grains can be used, like oats or rice, but these two are the only ones used, with rye being the dominant flavoring grain with distillers.

Rye brings a range of spice notes including pepper, nutmeg, clove and cinnamon, which are all intensified during the aging process. Think of eating a piece of rye bread. Rye gives bourbon that wonderful flavorful "bite" that it is known for.

Wheat results in a sweeter-tasting bourbon, but not because the grain is sweeter. Wheat is not as rich as rye, so it allows more of the sweetness of the corn and vanilla to show through, compared to rye, which can overshadow some of those sweet flavors.

The three recipes or mash bills in bourbon

- Traditional Bourbon Recipe—70-80% corn, balanced with rye and some barley. Think of a sweet-and-spicy, back- of-the-tongue experience. *This is my term for this, not the industry's, but I think it describes it well since the next two are accepted terms in the industry.

- High Rye Bourbon Recipe—20-35% rye–dials back on the corn and keeps the same amount of barley as a traditional bourbon.
- Wheat Bourbon Recipe (or simply referred to as "Wheated")—70-80% corn--similar to traditional, but replaces the rye with wheat. Wheat allows the sweetness of the corn and the sugars from the barrel to be more pronounced. Think "soft and sweet," with a front-of-the-tongue experience.

Barrels and aging

The recipe is the soul of the bourbon, and the barrel and aging provide varying flavors depending on the length of the aging process, the type of warehouse, and the location of the barrels inside a rack house. Barrel aging is responsible for between 50% and 75% of the final flavor of a bourbon.

There are six different types of vanillas you get from a barrel. And it takes a good six years to get bold vanillas out of a barrel. So younger bourbons will not have pronounced vanillas, and bourbons six years or older will have more pronounced vanillas.

4
How to Read a Label

"Always carry a small flagon of whiskey in case of snakebite and furthermore always carry a small snake." –W.C. Fields

Growing up in Kentucky I would hear from many people that "All bourbon is whiskey, but not all whiskey is bourbon." But when I got into the bourbon business I also learned that "All scotch is whiskey, but not all whiskey is scotch," and "All Irish whiskey is whiskey, but not all whiskey is Irish." So after my head started hurting, I asked, "What makes bourbon different from all whiskey?" It had to do with aging it in barrels, but then I found out that all whiskies are aged in barrels. I threw my hands up in disgust and decided not to even think about it anymore.

It wasn't until working with distillers Fred Noe, Jerry Dalton and Tommy Crume at the Clermont Distillery that it all became clear to me. What really did it was when Jerry Dalton gave me a copy of the Standards of Identity from the Bureau of Alcohol, Tobacco, and Firearms, which defined whiskey and bourbon.

The Standards of Identity came out shortly after bourbon was named the native spirit of the United States in 1964. But it wasn't the first paperwork on bourbon; the Standards of Identity were preceded by a couple other acts. The Bottled in Bond Act of 1897 was a bill championed by one of my heroes in the bourbon world, Colonel Edmund Taylor. Bottled in Bond is still in effect today. If a whiskey is labeled "bonded," then it was aged in new, charred oak for a minimum of four years and is exactly 100 proof. It comes from one distillery and from whiskies distilled from one season (January to December). So if you see "bonded" or "bottled in bond" on your bourbon label, you are guaranteed that it is an honest 100 proof, at least four years old, and distilled in one place in a specified period of time. In short, the good stuff. Up until the 1970s federal marshals used to actually live at the distilleries and inspect the bonded warehouses on a daily basis. It doesn't take long to inspect a warehouse with added barrels, or barrels being removed, so I've heard that those federal agents were really good golfers.

However, the first act that affected the bourbon business was 1906's Pure Food and Drug Act. The act defined three different types of whiskey:

1. Straight Whiskey–aged for two years
2. Bonded Whiskey–aged for four years, 100 proof, and from one distillery and one season
3. Imitation Whiskey–product of rectifiers and compounders

Imitation whiskey? Let me explain a little: Rectifiers do not distill. They buy whiskey stocks from one or more distilleries and then process and bottle them under another name. They can buy barrels from one or several distilleries and marry them. They can age them longer and come up with their own flavor profile, or bottle it at varying proofs.

Some use a variety of aged whiskies to create a different flavor profile. If you know the meaning of the words on a label, and you know whether some words are missing, you can tell a great deal about the liquor. You can find some bourbons that are diamonds in the rough, that are really great whiskies at low retail prices. Others you can see are still a great quality, but perhaps a little overpriced for what the label is telling you. When I see these, I'll just wait for someone to buy me one instead of me putting my own money down for them.

Compound whiskies are those that contain grain neutral spirits for filler. These are better known as "blended whiskies." Brands like Seagrams 7 and Eight Star come to mind. These are still quality products, but they have a very different flavor profile than straight bourbon whiskey and are produced much more cheaply.

The 1906 Pure Food and Drug Act was further refined in December of 1909 by the Taft Decision. This created the formal definition of whiskey that is still present today. Taft said that for a whiskey to be called "straight," water was the only thing that could be added. If anything other than water was added to the whiskey, it had to be called "blended" whiskey.

But of course, you can't really know what bourbon is until you know just what whiskey is. So let's look at the definition of what I call the four foundation words: Kentucky - Straight - Bourbon -Whiskey. We'll look at them one at a time and learn how each word is defined by the Standards of Identity for Distilled Spirits. (Please note that the Standards spell whisky and bourbon whisky without an "e" in all definitions.)

Whisky

Whisky is "an alcoholic distillate from a fermented mash of grain produced at less than 190 proof in such a manner that the distillate possesses the taste, aroma, and characteristics generally attributed to whisky, stored in oak containers and bottled at not less than 80 proof, and also includes mixtures of such distillates for which no specific standards of identity are prescribed."

So the general category of whiskey requires that whiskey should be made from grains (similar to vodka) distilled under 190 proof (similar to vodka) and aged in oak (a distinction from vodka).

You can add neutral grain spirits (pure grain alcohol which is basically vodka). And you can add colors and flavors to get it to meet the requirement that it looks, smells, and tastes like whiskey (not vodka).

Bourbon Whisky

(Rye Whisky, Wheat Whisky, Malt Whisky and Rye Malt Whisky)

"Bourbon whisky, rye whisky, wheat whisky, malt whisky, or rye malt whisky is whisky produced at not exceeding 160 proof from a fermented mash of not less than 51 percent corn (rye, wheat, malted barley, or malted rye grain respectively), and stored at not more than 125 proof in charred new oak containers, and also includes mixtures of such whiskies of the same type."

So unlike just plain whiskey, bourbon can't be made from just any grains. The majority has to be corn. Whiskey can be distilled up to 190 proof, but bourbon must be distilled at under 160 proof. Whiskey can be stored in any type of barrel at any proof, but bourbon must be stored in a brand new, charred-oak container, and at less than 125 proof. (Remember: The reason they put an upper limit of 125 proof on bourbon in the barrel is that barrels at the top of the rack house will rise in proof.) Whiskey can have colors and flavors added, but bourbon can only have water added to achieve barreling and bottling strengths. Ah, now I get it! All bourbon is whiskey, but not all whiskey is bourbon.

As they all share a definition, this means that rye whiskey has to be at least 51% rye and follow the same standards. As do wheat, malt and rye malt whiskies.

Straight

"Whiskies conforming to the standards prescribed in the definitions of Bourbon whisky, rye whisky, wheat whisky, malt whisky, rye malt whisky [and corn whisky] which have been stored in the type of oak containers prescribed [charred new oak] for a period of two years or more shall be further designated as 'straight.'"

So basically "straight" means that all grains were distilled at lower proofs and contain no grain neutral spirits. Only water has been added, and the whiskey has been stored for a minimum of two years in new charred oak.

I was told that when the railroad was being laid across the country, two railroad ties were called a "straight." I don't know if the term comes from aging whiskey two years, but until you can prove me wrong, I'm running with this one here.

Kentucky

"State of distillation of domestic types of whisky and straight whisky, except for light whisky and blends…"

Bourbon can be distilled anywhere in the United States, but if you list a state on the label, it must be the state of distillation. Kentucky makes 98% of all bourbon because of the reasons we've already discussed: It has iron-free water and a suitable climate, and, perhaps most significantly, it was where many of the distilleries were already located when Prohibition ended. It is much easier–and cheaper–to retool an old distillery than to build one from the ground up.

There is a bourbon called Virginia Gentleman (General McArthur's favorite bourbon), and it says "Virginia Bourbon" on the label. There are over 200 applications for the development of microdistilleries to make bourbon, whiskey and other distillates. So you'll see many regional whiskies popping up all over the United States, from New York to Montana. This will be great for the industry. It is hoped that people will embrace them, just as they did microbreweries, and I think it will increase awareness and sales in bourbon and rye in general.

Kentucky state law requires that in order to put the word "Kentucky" on a bourbon label, the bourbon should be aged at least a year and a day in Kentucky. This is for Kentucky state tax purposes, since $2 per barrel property taxes are levied per year. Doesn't sound like a lot, but when you figure distillers have anywhere from 100,000 to 1.5 million barrels on hand, that starts to add up. More than half the price you pay for a bottle of bourbon is taxes!

What to look for in a label

So if you see the words "Kentucky Straight Bourbon Whiskey," that's a quality stamp. I call these words the four foundation words. If you see these words, you know where/how it's made. Just like if I see a bottle of brandy, that's one thing, but if I see the words Courvoisier Cognac XO, that's another story altogether. That word "cognac" is a quality stamp, and the designation XO is a statement of age.

Look for the words "distilled and bottled by" when you are selecting a bourbon. If it says "distilled and bottled by" then you know by law that bourbon was distilled at that distillery. If it just says "distilled in Kentucky, bottled by..." then all you know is that bourbon was made in Kentucky, but not by any specific distillery. Pappy Van Winkle of Old Fitzgerald Bourbon used to say you should look for "distilled and bottled by" because "any fool with a funnel can bottle whiskey."

Labeling laws

There are labeling laws for bourbon whiskey. These laws require:

Information about the aging process

- If the bourbon is under four years old, an age statement is required.
- If the bourbon is over four years, an age statement is optional.
- If an age is stated, it has to reflect the age of the youngest whiskey in the bottle.

Proof/alcohol by volume must be printed on the label. The higher the proof, typically the less water has been added after aging to get it to the bottling proof.

Are you starting to clearly see the differences between whiskey and bourbon? If so, that's a huge step in the right direction. So pour yourself a nice 100-proof bourbon, grab some bourbon/whiskey bottles, and let's sip and read some labels together.

(Old Grand Dad is a registered trademark of the Old Grand Dad Distillery Company and is used with permission.)

BOURBON LABELS

Old Crow

Kentucky Straight Bourbon Whiskey

"Distilled and bottled by"

Aged for 3 years

80 proof

I know where it was distilled (Kentucky), I know it was distilled by the company that bottled it, so they had control from grain to glass. I know that it was more than 51% corn, stored in new charred oak at no more than 125 proof, and that nothing was added to it other than water to get it to barreling or bottling strength. We also know that it was aged for a full three years in new charred oak and bottled at 80 proof.

Since it is under four years old, an age must be stated. It follows all the laws and is a true bourbon. As you can see, the word "bourbon" is the largest word on the label of the four foundation words. It will be a lighter bourbon since it aged for only three years, but it is a bourbon nonetheless. Bourbon = quality.

Let's compare and contrast:

Early Times

Kentucky Whiskey

"Distilled and bottled by"

Aged for 36 months in reused cooperage

80 proof

Michter's, Small-Batch, Unblended American Whiskey

"Decanted and bottled by"

no age statement

91.4 proof

On the Early Times, two of the four foundation words are missing: "straight" and "bourbon." It is 36 months old, so you can figure out why it cannot be called "straight." If you look at the back label, it states that it is aged a full 36 months in "reused cooperage," which means that they are storing the whiskey in used barrels. So this is a whiskey instead of a bourbon.

But it's over two years old, so why isn't it "straight" whiskey? Remember, straight whiskey has to be aged in *new* charred barrels. I can tell by this piece of information that this will also be a lighter whiskey, even lighter than Old Crow because they are reusing the barrels. This is still a purer product than a blended whiskey, but it is not a true bourbon. Early Times is a well-made, perfectly fine whiskey, but it just won't be as full-bodied and flavorful as a bourbon.

It's also not expensive, and the label confirms that it is a good quality product that should not necessarily cost a lot. I've heard that they are talking about reintroducing a bourbon version of Early Times soon. I would look forward to tasting that.

With Michter's, "unblended" means they are trying to alert you to the fact that there are no grain neutral spirits, and by the statement "unblended," and "American Whiskey" means that is it is not a bourbon. This probably means that it, too, has been aged in used barrels. There is no age statement, so it must have aged for at least four years. This is a $30 bottle of whiskey, so I have a few questions about this product. "Decanted and bottled by" means the producers are rectifiers that purchase whiskey on the open market and then age and process it to their standards, but they have no distillery. The proof is a nice high proof that would be worth a few more dollars, but I would like some more information on the age for it being a whiskey and not a bourbon.

Seagram's 7, Kessler

"American whiskey–a blend of distinctive character"

"Bottled by"

80, 80 proof

75% and 72.5% grain spirits

A "blended whiskey" or "whiskey–a blend" is a mixture which contains straight whiskies or a blend of straight whiskies that are not less than 20% on a proof-gallon basis, excluding alcohol derived from added harmless coloring, flavoring, or blending materials, and separately, or in combination, whiskey or neutral spirits. Also, the percentage of neutral grain spirits must be printed on the label for U.S. whiskies.

Sure enough, if you look on the back label of Seagram's 7 it states "75% grain spirits." A neutral grain spirit comes from a grain (usually corn, as there is a bigger alcohol yield from corn than from small grains like rye, wheat or barley) that is distilled up to 190 proof. What's an example of a grain spirit? I'll bring back a high school or college memory–Ever Clear Pure Grain Alcohol. Ever Clear is made from corn and distilled to 190 proof. As a side note, I also get a kick out of the other words on the Ever Clear label:

DO NOT APPLY TO OPEN FLAME

CONTENTS MAY IGNITE OR EXPLODE

CAUTION!! EXTREMELY FLAMMABLE

HANDLE WITH CARE

NOT INTENDED FOR CONSUMPTION UNLESS MIXED WITH NON-ALCOHOLIC BEVERAGES

Have you ever been to a party where grain alcohol is being served by your classy host? How do they usually serve it? With a mixture of fruit juices. That hootch is equivalent to putting colors and flavors and sugars into it–much like the peach or strawberries in our moonshine example earlier. You have to soften it up and make it palatable, so you make a blend of juices to do so.

Back to Seagram's 7. So 75% of this is pure grain alcohol, and 25% is whiskey (which can also be produced up to 190 proof), so you've basically got Ever Clear that has been watered down to 80 proof. It must "look, smell, and taste" like whiskey to be a whiskey, so they add caramel coloring, sugars and flavors to get it to look, smell, and taste like whiskey. This is done instantly. And there you have "whiskey–a blend."

To show you what sugar and coloring can do, in my youth I would make Kool Aid in the summertime. My mom always bought the concentrated pouches that had no sugar added. I always liked the sour sensation the Kool Aid would give me without the sugar, but I could only drink a spoonful. But as soon as I added a cup and a half of sugar to it, I could drink the whole pitcher! Same thing with blended whiskey. It starts out kind of harsh because it's basically pure grain alcohol watered down to 80 proof. But as soon as you add caramel color and sugar to it, it becomes really smooth. And how do people drink Seagram's 7? In a seven-and-seven: They mix it with 7UP, which has more sugar and flavor. No wonder it's so smooth, and no wonder you wake up with a giant headache the next morning from all that sugar!

There is absolutely nothing wrong with drinking blended whiskey. Some people prefer it over other whiskey. But know what it is. Blended whiskey is cheap whiskey by definition. They do not cost much, and they shouldn't, but there are still some bourbons like Old Crow which cost several dollars less than blended whiskey. I'll buy Old Crow or Old Charter over blended whiskies when the occasion calls for it. Knowing how to read a label could be saving you money, too!

Jim Beam, Evan Williams, Old Forester, Old Fitzgerald, Wild Turkey

Kentucky Straight Bourbon Whiskey

"Distilled by"

4 years old stated

Some state no age

80 proof.

I don't have to wonder how these bourbons are made. I know this is a quality stamp since the words Kentucky Straight Bourbon Whiskey appear on it.

Jim Beam states four years of age, the others state no age. I look at the back to see whether they are four years old. If the bourbon is four years old, the age statement is optional. Jim Beam makes four-, five-, seven-, and eight-year-old bourbons. They put age statements on their white labels to distinguish the differences between the bourbons.

Evan Williams, Old Forester, Old Fitzgerald and Wild Turkey do not state an age on their labels. What I assume here is that these are four years old. That's what the label is telling me, anyway. Some have varying proofs, but the ages are the same according to the labels.

Remember, it takes at least six years to get pronounced vanilla notes. So if you like big vanilla, caramel, maple and ginger flavors, look for something that is at least six years old.

Jack Daniels, George Dickel, Prichard's

Tennessee Whiskey

Old No. 7, Old No. 8

"Distilled and bottled by"

80 proof

Tennessee Whiskey is not a designation in the Standards of Identity, so Jack must follow all the rules of whiskey but not of bourbon. Jack uses the same basic rules of bourbon regarding grain bills and distillation. They distill to 140 proof, so that's well under 160. They use new charred-oak barrels. The big difference is what is called the "Lincoln County Process" of aging and leaching the whiskey off the still through a 10-foot column of maple charcoal. Gravity propels the whiskey to drip down through the charcoal into the barrel. It takes a whole week to get this done.

Jack Daniels uses new barrels to get as much flavor out of the wood as possible in the time that they age. If they used a previously used barrel, they would have to age the whiskey longer than the four to five years they do. The "No. 7" on the label is not an age statement. Even folks at their distillery aren't sure what it really means. I know this because I was watching the History Channel one night and on came a show about whiskey. They were at the Jack Daniel's Distillery, which was fascinating, but the representative for the distillery said that no one at the distillery had any idea what Old No. 7 stood for. The first thing that came to my mind was, "Sude, you're on the History Channel! Make some shit up at least!"

Old No. 8 for Dickel Tennessee Whiskey is a fine tradition, and they produce good whiskey. But it is not bourbon by their design and tradition in Tennessee. I don't see anything on the website about what Old No. 8 Stands for, but my guess is that it is a play on Old No. 7 from Jack, which would be really hilarious since Old No. 7 means nothing.

Apart from Jack Daniels, George Dickel and Prichard's are the only other Tennessee Whiskies. They do it slightly differently, but still in that same style. Mr. Prichard is also using white corn to mirror the style of the Tennessee whiskies made in the 1800s in the Volunteer State.

Old Grand Dad, Heaven Hill, Old Fitzgerald, Old Bourbon Hollow—Bottled in Bond

Kentucky Straight Bourbon Whiskey

"Bonded – Bottled in Bond"

"Distilled by"

All are 100 proof

No age statement

We know by definition that these are at least four years old and exactly 100 proof, from one distillery and from one season.

The 1,000,000th barrel produced after prohibition by the Sunny Brook Distillery in front of one of the bonded warehouses. (Photo courtesy of the Louisville Convention and Visitors Bureau)

A NOTE ON SMALL BATCH

"Small batch" is a term that was first coined by legendary distiller Booker Noe in 1987 with the introduction of Booker's Bourbon. The bourbon is not made in small batches, although it can be, as in the case of Parker Beam's Elijah Craig 12-Year. This bourbon was launched around the same time as Heaven Hill, which is produced in batches of 70 barrels or less. But then again, Booker and Parker are cousins and learned the old ways from the Beam family. It's probably a lock that Booker, Parker and Elmer T. Lee all were picking each other's brains on their projects. Elmer T. Lee came out with Blanton's Single Barrel in 1984, and Elijah Craig and Booker's came out a few years later, and "small batch" became a designation that was supposed to mean it was not a single-barrel bourbon.

The definition of small batch can differ from distiller to distiller. Booker Noe coined the term when he created Booker's Bourbon in 1987. He used the term "small batch" to differentiate his bourbon from his friend Elmer T. Lee's new bourbon called Blanton's, which was a "single-barrel bourbon." A single-barrel bourbon is bourbon from only one barrel. That barrel and its location in the rack house are noted on each bottle. Small-batch bourbons are taking more than one barrel from certain places in the rack house and then mingling those barrels for a consistent flavor profile. A single-barrel bourbon can taste different from barrel to barrel, and that's the magic of single-barrel bourbon. We don't make batches of bourbon since we use continuous column stills, so the batch is at the end where you take selected barrels from the distiller's "sweet spots" of the rack house.

Now Parker Beam at Heaven Hill introduced Elijah Craig around the same time as Booker's, and he defined his Small Batch Bourbon as a batch of 70 barrels or less. Because Booker and Parker are cousins, and both buddies with Elmer T. Lee, it's probably a logical assumption that they were picking each other's brains without really telling each other completely what they were working on. Elmer T. Lee released Blanton's Bourbon in 1984, and Booker's and Elijah Craig came out around 3 years later. So even though Small Batch Bourbons are not distilled in small batches, it still defines the category. So small batch is kind of like an oxymoron, like peace keeper missile. Oxymorons that I came up with on my own include vodka tasting, vacation Bible school and Fox News.

Knob Creek 9-Year, Elijah Craig 12-Year, Pappy Van Winkle 23-Year, Russell's Reserve 10-Year

Kentucky Straight Bourbon Whiskey

"Distilled and bottled by"

Small-batch

Aged 9 to 23 years

100, 94, 95.6 and 90 proof

These all have the four foundation words, so there's the quality stamp. Every drop in that bottle is at least as old as the age that is stated on the label.

"Distilled and bottled by" shows that they are each controlled by their own standards. Some state "small batch," which has no definition, but was coined to differentiate it from a single-barrel bourbon. It's a mingle of barrels.

I'm left with few questions, if any, about these bourbons. I know how they are made, where they are made, and how long they have been aged. But there is a risk in putting an age statement on a bourbon label. If the demand for that bourbon outpaces the supply of barrels that are in a warehouse, you might see a shortage or outage of a product until the next lot of barrels reaches maturity.

Woodford Reserve, Bulliet, Maker's Mark, Buffalo Trace, Four Roses

Kentucky Straight Bourbon Whiskey

"Distilled by"

Small batch

No age statement

90.4, 90, 90, 90, 90 proof

You don't have to worry about quality with the four foundation words. We know the bourbon in the bottle is at least four years old since there is no age statement. But with many small-batch or other handmade bourbons, their stocks are limited so they often mingle ages. If you mingle bourbons from four to eight+ years old, you get a unique flavor profile. Some call this "bottled to taste." They are not trying to mislead you about the age of the bourbon, but they are most likely trying to keep themselves from running out of older whiskey and not being able to supply the demand. If there is an age on the bottle, that number must reflect the age of the youngest bourbon in the mix. If you don't state an age, the youngest bourbon has to be at least four years old. So the distiller can use younger bourbons with the same flavor profile to continue the run if they run out of the older stock, as long as the youngest is at least four years old.

Bourbon with ages on the bottle aren't "better" than those without ages, but remember, if you like big vanilla or other barrel notes in your bourbon, age statements might be more important for you.

Corner Creek, Rowan's Creek, Jefferson's Reserve, Pogue Master's Select

Kentucky Straight Bourbon Whiskey

Small batch

"Distilled in Kentucky, bottled by"

No age statement

88, 100.1, 82.3, 91 proof

These are quality products with the four foundation words. But the language "distilled in Kentucky" means that it was not distilled *by* them. This tells you that they are rectifiers. This means that they are buying the bourbon from one of the distillers that sells on the open market. What are they doing to make it "their" bourbon? Look for age and proof. Master's Select has no definition, but the name would suggest the master distiller is selecting barrels.

There is no age statement, so we can assume that the bourbon in the bottle is at least four years old. It could also be a mingle of ages, but we are going by the label here. Then note the proof. For additional information, you can check the "necker labels" that often dangle from the bottles or check the companies' websites. In many cases this can give more information than the label. But remember, there are not the same strict laws on neckers or the web that there are for the label itself.

Make no mistake, I would *love* to be a rectifier and have my own bourbon. It's a way for passionate people (some who are descendants of famous whiskey distillers) to continue or start a bourbon legacy. Distilleries cost millions of dollars to build and maintain, so rectifying is a great way to get into the business. I just like as much information on the label as I can get.

Blanton's, Four Roses, Hancock's, single-barrel bourbons, no age statement

Kentucky Straight Bourbon Whiskey

"Distilled and bottle by"

Single barrel

No age statement

93, 100, 88.9 proof

Elijah Craig 18, Eagle Rare 10, single barrel with age statements

Kentucky Straight Bourbon Whiskey

"Distilled and bottled by"

Single barrel

Proof

18 years old, 10 years old

Single barrel means that all the bourbon from one barrel is bottled at one time. Because every barrel in a rack house can have a slightly different taste, distillers usually list on the label or necker the location of each barrel from which they pulled the bourbon. If you find that you consistently like high-storage or low-storage barrels, you can go for that single barrel over another. Or you might enjoy the varying flavor from barrel to barrel. That's the magic of single-barrel bourbon. And that explains the difference between "small batch" and "single barrel."

If no age is listed, all you can assume is that it has been aged for at least four years. With small-batch and single-barrel bourbons that have no age listed, I look for "distilled and bottled by." I'd like to know that I'm dealing with a distiller and then I can assume they are bottling to a flavor profile. An example of this is Buffalo Trace with their Blanton's and Hancock's brands—it is important to know which warehouse the bourbon was pulled from since they age different labels in different warehouses to get a certain flavor profile. You also want to check the proof and see how much water has been added after the aging process. When the age is stated, I get a very clear idea of what to expect from the taste.

Now let's check out some straight rye whiskey labels. Rye whiskey has to be at least 51% rye, and all the other rules are exactly the same. Check out wheat whiskey. There's only one, Bernheim Wheat Whiskey. It has to be 51% wheat and follow all the same laws.

STRAIGHT RYE WHISKEY

Rye brings a range of spice notes, including pepper, nutmeg, clove and cinnamon, which are all intensified during the aging process. Think of eating a piece of rye bread.

Jim Beam Rye, Old Overholt Rye, Sazerac Rye, (ri)1 Rye

Look for state of distillation, if any

Straight Rye Whiskey

"Distilled and bottled by"

Age

80, 80, 90, 92 proof

Rittenhouse Rye Bottled in Bond

Straight Rye Whiskey

Bottled in Bond means at least 4 years old, from one distillery, exactly 100 proof, and all from barrels from one season (January-December of one year)

"Bottled by"

100 proof

Rye whiskey has to follow the same laws as bourbon. Rye indicates that the whiskey must be made from a fermented mash of at least 51% rye instead of corn. That's the difference between it and bourbon. Less corn and more rye means that the spirit will be less sweet and have more spice to it. Some of the companies (and this is just my opinion) leave off "Kentucky," even if they are distilled there, to tie their product to the history of the classic Pennsylvania or "Monongahela" rye whiskies.

It's also a distinctively American spirit, and the category is on fire right now. Rye is enjoying its second "Golden Age."

STRAIGHT WHEAT WHISKEY

Bernheim Original

Kentucky Straight Wheat Whiskey

Small-batch

90 proof

What is this telling you? Well, we know it's 51% wheat. Wheat results in a sweeter-tasting whiskey, but not because the grain is sweeter. Wheat is not as rich as rye so it allows more of the sweetness of the corn and vanilla to show through, compared to rye, which can overshadow some of those sweet flavors.

Hey, you're catching on. I wonder how long it will take for someone to produce a straight malted rye whiskey?

So now you know how to read a label. Head out to the liquor store and spend some time looking at the labels. You will find that instead of just looking at the price of a bourbon and assuming it's really good, you'll be able to read the label and know something about it before you even taste it. When you do that, you'll find some real diamonds in the rough. Old Grand Dad, Ancient Age, Elijah Craig and Old Forester are just a few.

Some do cost more and are more than worth it. I'm always surprised when someone asks me why a bourbon can cost anywhere from $25 to $50+. Remember, distillers have to use a brand new barrel every time and then age the liquor for at least four years. I'm surprised we sell it as cheaply as we do. These are the same people that go to dinner and think nothing of spending $50 on a bottle of wine, and it's gone when dinner's over. That $50 bottle of bourbon will be around a little longer than that, and you get more than four glasses out of it! So quit bitching and buy the bourbon…jeez!

5
Bourbon's Place in American History

"Tell me what brand of whiskey that Grant drinks. I would like to send a barrel of it to my other generals." –Abraham Lincoln on Grant's drinking. Grant drank Old Crow.

When I sell liquor, it's called bootlegging; when my patrons serve it on Lake Shore Drive, it's called hospitality." – Al Capone

"Prohibition is better than no liquor at all." – Will Rogers

Here's where I earn my "Professor" title. For those of you who don't have the attention span for an actual history chapter, please turn to page 101. I've put together a handy-dandy timeline that will give you an overview of my favorite drink's history. You can always come back for details later.

The history of bourbon is the history of America. As I mentioned in an earlier chapter, George Washington himself was a distiller and in 1798 was the country's largest distiller, producing 11,000 gallons of whiskey that year at Mount Vernon. George Washington wasn't the only founding father to distill or enjoy whiskey. Thomas Jefferson also grew rye and distilled it into rye whiskey, and James Madison was known to drink a pint of whiskey a day.

Early farmers didn't have a store down the street if they needed something, either. They had to barter with their neighbors. If you had something your neighbor needed, he'd trade you something for it—a pig or a chicken, for example. If you had whiskey and your neighbor liked it, you could trade it for something else. So many farmers were trading whiskey and other things for goods. Sometimes money was hard to come by out in remote areas of the new country.

Not only farmers used whiskey as money, but the military has a long history with the frontier spirit. As a young nation we learned from the British. The British Navy paid their sailors a weekly ration of rum along with their money. After the Revolutionary War, the British put a blockade on rum coming into the United States, so our government couldn't pay our soldiers with rum. Instead they got a weekly ration of whiskey. According to records, the calvary soldiers in 1782 received a daily ration of four ounces of whiskey. George Washington said that ... "the benefits arising from moderate use of strong liquor have been experienced in all Armies, and are not to be disputed." This practice continued as our country expanded into some pretty dangerous territory in the 1800s.

An 1800 advertisement for employment in the army reads: "an abundant supply of whiskey, food and clothing of the best quality – $12 bounty, and $10 per month with comfortable quarters and a 'life of ease.'" A federal act in 1819 increased the deal by 15 cents and an extra "gill" of whiskey or spirits a day for cutting roads and fortifications. Sounds like a pretty good deal to me.

The tradition of paying the soldiers a ration of alcohol continued through the Civil War, although the weekly ration was not enough to keep soldiers from pillaging the occasional distillery and stealing its whiskey. So distillers were forced to take precautions against both Union and Confederate soldiers (Kentucky was a border state, so both forces were there quite a bit). The distillery kept both Union and Confederate flags on hand and then raised the flag of whatever side happened to approach their distillery. They'd share some whiskey with the troops and cuss the opposing side...no matter what side it happened to be.

The Civil War dealt a blow to bourbon distilleries in a couple of ways. Kentucky was a neutral state, but it relied heavily on trading with the South; therefore, many distilleries sided with the South. Basil Hayden was one who sided with the South.

There are a lot of stories about Civil War general Ulysses S. Grant and his drinking. We know Grant drank off duty, as did most of his fellow officers, but there was never an eyewitness account of him being a drunkard or drunk on duty. Lincoln reportedly fired back to one of his critics to find out what brand Grant drank, and he sent a barrel to all his generals. What was the bourbon that was supposedly U.S. Grant's favorite? None other than Dr. James Crow's Old Crow Kentucky Straight Bourbon Whiskey.

The truth of the matter is that the stories of U.S. Grant's drinking were quite exaggerated. Many of the drinking stories come from jealous Northern generals who could find no other way to discredit this brilliant man who was delivering battlefield victories to the president. An easy way to do it would be to spread malicious rumors about Grant being drunk on the job. There were stories, there were innuendoes, there were suppositions. But, in truth, there are no reliable eyewitness accounts of any drunkenness on the part of General Grant during the Civil War.

Perhaps Lincoln, being a shrewd leader, made the comment of sending a "barrel to all his generals" so they'd stop smearing Grant's reputation and start smearing the Confederates.

He claimed that if the South lost the war, he would not venture off his property for the rest of his life. Well, he lived to be over 100 years old (he started his distillery in 1796!), and after the South lost, he kept his word and never ventured off his property. Good thing for him, his distillery was located on his property, so there was quite a bit of venturing he could do right there!

After the Civil War, though, bourbon didn't regain the ground it had lost during the war, and it steadily decreased in popularity into the early 1900s. Rye whiskies fared better, as they did not have the same issues with their northern markets, and trade flourished during and after the war.

Temperance Movement–a direct war on liquor!

"Total abstinence is so excellent a thing that it cannot be carried to too great an extent. In my passion for it I even carry it so far as to totally abstain from total abstinence itself."

–Mark Twain, 1881

The Reverend Howard Hyde Russell, an Oberlin College graduate, returned to northern Ohio and founded the Anti-Saloon League (ASL). From the pulpit of the First Congressional Church in 1893, Russell outlined his plan to end alcohol's death grip on the country. The group was focused and did not align with Democrats or Republicans, but it joined with anyone who would lend a hand to help extinguish the making, selling or consumption of alcohol. To them, if you did away with alcohol, that would take care of gambling, rape, murder, horse racing, theft and arson. They cared only about doing away with alcohol and freeing the nation's citizens from its hold.

The leadership and staff of the ASL were almost exclusively members of Baptist and Methodist churches. Because 75% of the board of directors were clergy men, they had a captive audience every Sunday and reached hundreds of thousands of voters. An ASL spokesman talked about the power of this. He said that he could dictate 20 letters to 20 men in 20 parts of the country and ignite 50,000 men to action against alcohol. At this time in history, an organization based on a network of churches could call up 100 churches mobilizing 20,000 men in Bible classes alone.

Russell's ASL inspired a man by the name of Wayne B. Wheeler to join his cause. Wheeler was small and slight in stature, but not in his effectiveness. Upon his death it was written in papers that without him, the country would never have had the Eighteenth Amendment. The *Milwaukee Journal* wrote that Wheeler's conquest was the most notable thing of their time. Wheeler was a short, slender man who looked totally harmless, but he was a relentless crusader for Prohibition. While attending law school and clerking in a law office, he bicycled from town to town speaking to churches and groups and recruiting those for the common cause. In 1898 he earned his law degree and took over the Anti-Saloon League's Ohio legal office. The more he put on his plate, the more he accomplished. Delivering speeches, initiating legal cases on the ASL's behalf, launching telegram campaigns, organizing demonstrations—Howard Russell commented that there just were not enough Wayne Wheelers to go around. From their Ohio base of 31 full-time staff they were able to influence the Ohio legislature and later the U.S. House and Senate.

Wheeler took the Temperance Movement to a new level when he got the Women's Christian Temperance Union (WCTU) involved to help further each group's interests of Prohibition and women's suffrage. Wheeler actually coined the phrase "pressure group" at this time.

Native Kentuckian Carry Nation joined the WCTU in 1899 in Kansas. In 1901, Carry wrote herself into the history books by getting arrested for smashing up a saloon with a hatchet in Kansas City, Missouri (a town known for its opposition to temperance). She would be arrested a total of 30 times for similar crimes between 1901 and 1910. Ms. Nation actually had a traveling vaudeville act where she talked about her agenda called "Hatchetations." After the show, she'd sell mini hatchets to the public. Sort of reminds you of buying light-up magic wands at Disney World, doesn't it? Perhaps that's where they got the idea.

Nation also published a biweekly newsletter called "The Smashers Mail," which appeared in a biweekly newspaper titled *The Hatchet*. In one of her articles, she wrote that she applauded the assassination of President McKinley in 1901. She had heard that he drank, and she felt that drinkers always got what they deserved. She died after collapsing at a lecture in 1911. As an aside, Carry Nation died the same year my father was born, in 1911. She only lived to be 65, and my dad lived to be almost 94. I think it's ironic that she died the same year my father was born. Way to show her, Dad!

Right before Prohibition started, WWI broke out. The war to end all wars meant all hands on deck, and many distilleries were making industrial alcohol for the war effort. This alcohol was used in the production of rubber for tires, antifreeze, ether and rayon, which was used in the production of parachutes. When the war was over, the liquor companies were not rewarded for their efforts in helping to defeat the Kaiser; they were put out of business because there was no legal market for their products. This seems like a real kick in the face, doesn't it?

I am not going to cover all the causes of Prohibition in this chapter. If you want to read a great book on the subject, I suggest *Last Call* by Daniel Okrent. But as we all know, Prohibition was the death of bourbon whiskey. The states that made it–Indiana, Kentucky, Virginia and Tennessee—are all right in the middle of the United States and in plain sight of federal agents, so they had to stop producing. Prohibition lasted 13 years, 10 months, 18 days, 7 hours and 27 minutes, until January 1, 1934.

People opposed to Prohibition pointed out all the tax dollars that would be lost if such a bill was passed. But when Congress decided to put in an income tax, it became feasible. Russell, Wheeler and Nation organized essentially the first-ever lobbyists and put the pressure on legislators until state after state began putting prohibitions of their own into effect. They became so powerful and were responsible for so many anti-Prohibition politicians being voted out of office, the government gave in to the pressure and Prohibition passed.

Prohibition took effect on January 17, 1920. As devastating as Prohibition was for bourbon, it was a boon for Canadian whiskey, Scotch, Rum, Tequila and, most notably, moonshiners and bootleggers in the states. Just ask the Kennedy family how profitable it was for their father, Joe, to bootleg Scotch and Irish whisk[e]y from Canada to the Northeast. The Caribbean produced a lot of rum, so rum runners supplied Florida and the Gulf with rum that was produced legally in Cuba, Puerto

Rico, St. Croix and elsewhere. Tequila producers in Mexico cranked up production, and tequila and mezcal flowed north to Texas, California and other border states.

The immense Canadian border allowed Canadian Club and other Canadian whiskies to make their way into the United States. Deals with Al Capone, the Purple Gang and other mobsters were struck because Detroit was just a stone's throw away across the Detroit River. The stance that Canadian Club took was that they were making legal deals with individuals, and then what they did with the liquor was none of Canadian Club's business.

My friends Dan Tullio and Tish Harcus at the Canadian Club Heritage Center are the company's ambassadors and serve as the "godfather" and "godmother" of Canadian Club. If you've not been to their headquarters in Windsor, Ontario, do yourself a favor and go. It just drips with history, as well as good whiskey. Try the CC Sherry Cask, we bourbon drinkers really go for it.

Dan and Tish tell me that all sorts of boats queued up on the Detroit River to get Canadian Club Whiskey. Bill McCoy and his son supervised the dock operations at Hiram Walker where Canadian Club was distilled. As you can imagine, there were a lot of imitators who would say they had Canadian Club Whiskey and would sell it to folks who didn't care or couldn't wait to deal with Bill and his son. But most people wanted the real thing because of its quality and reputation as a world-class Canadian blended whisky. So it became commonly known that if you dealt with Bill McCoy and his son directly, you had the genuine Canadian Club, or "the Real McCoy."

WINTER IN WALKERVILLE

I was visiting Canadian Club in Walkerville, Ontario, Canada, just across the river from downtown Detroit. I met fellow whiskey professors Steve Cole and David Mays and Laphroaig Scotch ambassador Simon Brooking there to learn more about Canadian Whiskey production. Our Canadian Club hosts were the passionate and fun duo of Dan Tullio and Tish Harcus. Walkerville is only a six- hour drive from Kentucky, so do yourself a favor and go up to visit Dan and Tish at the CC Heritage Center. You talk about history. Have you seen Boardwalk Empire *on HBO? They tell the story of how Canadian whiskey flowed over the border and was a key player in the story of Prohibition in the United States. The Heritage Center alone at CC is something to see. It was built by Hiram Walker, and it's just an amazing place. There is a speakeasy in the basement of the Heritage Center where deals were made with Al Capone, the Purple Gang and other infamous characters.*

We were up having "drinkypoos," which is what Dan and Tish call cocktails there. And not just *cocktails; we were enjoying 30-year-old Canadian Club Whiskey courtesy of Tish. But the hilarious thing was, she had it in a 1.75-liter plastic bottle, since it wasn't out yet and not in bottles yet for sale. So there we were, drinking 30-year-old whiskey out of a plastic jug—what a scream. Then Steve said, "Hey, we've all been drinking this great whiskey a while and are a little buzzed, so shouldn't we switch from the 30 year to Classic 12 year?" In unison we all promptly looked at him and said, "Hell no!" Later that night, Steve was out making snow angels on the lawn while we smoked cigars. It was an unforgettable moment that we ambassadors get to experience.*

What's fascinating to me is that these spirits are still popular in those regions of the country where they were bootlegged during Prohibition. Tequila is still popular in Texas and the Southwest. Rum is still big in Florida and New Orleans. Scotch is popular in New York and the Northeast, and in Michigan and all along the North, Canadian Whiskey is still strong. This is known as the "Prohibition effect."

So the abolitionists really had it blow up in their faces. The only thing Prohibition seemed to do was bankrupt the U.S. government (half of the government's tax revenues came from the taxes levied on alcohol) and make criminals out of otherwise honest citizens who bootlegged these spirits. Not only that, but Prohibition was the best thing that ever happened to moonshiners. On January 1st, 1920, the first day of the "Noble Experiment," the price of moonshine quadrupled overnight.

A few distilleries were granted a license to continue to sell bourbon as medicine available by prescription from a doctor. Old Forester, Old Grand Dad and Old Prentice were some of those brands. Now they still could not *make* bourbon during Prohibition; they could only sell what they had on hand. It had to be bottled in pint-sized bottles and labeled as "medicinal whiskey." Most often those bottles came in a box which touted cures for many ailments. They were also "bottled in bond" under government supervision, so they were at least four years old, 100 proof, from one distillery and from one season (January through December).

Booker Noe and Jimmy Russell tell stories of shiny black sedans with Illinois license plates that would come down at night from Chicago to Bardstown. The "medicinal" bourbon sat in barrels in the rack houses. The local sheriff and the federal marshal would both end up with a few extra dollars in their pockets, and those shiny black sedans would leave a few hundred pounds heavier on the drive back up to Chicago. Afterward, they would fill those barrels with water just in case anyone checked them later.

During many of these trips, Al Capone himself would come down, and he frequented the legendary Seelbach Hotel in Louisville, where he and his buddies would play poker in a private room. There was (and still is) a large mirror that tilts slightly down so Al could get a read on not only his opponents' poker faces but their cards. In case federal agents showed up to nab him, two panels slid out of place to secret passages.

One led down a hidden corridor and out the kitchen's back door, and the other back out to a side exit of the hotel where Al Capone always had cars waiting and running in case he had to make a speedy exit. The room is called the Al Capone Room for that piece of history. It's the same place described in F. Scott Fitzgerald's *The Great Gatsby* as the place of Daisy Buchanan's wedding. When you come to Louisville, go visit the Seelbach and ask them to show you that room off the Oak Room. Then enjoy the great jazz at the Old Seelbach bar off the lobby and have their signature cocktail.

My Medicinal Bourbon

If you got a bottle of medicinal bourbon in 1922, it might read on the tax stamp "Old Grand Dad Whiskey, barreled Jan. 1917 and bottled spring 1932." I was given a bottle just like that by my friend Gary Gish, who owns the bar Joe's Older Than Dirt in Louisville, Kentucky. Joe's is a fabulous bar that you should visit the next time you are in Louisville. Gary and his wife, Janet, are not only my customers, but great friends. You find this happens a lot in the whiskey business.

On my 50th birthday, I had the pleasure of celebrating with that bottle of Old Grand Dad. That's 15 years in the barrel. Remember, they couldn't distill new bourbon, so all that bourbon was what they had in their rack houses. Some of the bourbon near the end of Prohibition had lots of age on it, up to 15 years. It sounds marvelous, but some of the bourbon got too much wood from that extra aging. So drinking Prohibition bourbon whiskey can be a crap shoot. But I must tell you, I got lucky with that bottle of Old Grand Dad on my 50th. Just one little cube of ice opened that bourbon up, and it was a memorable experience. Just ask my friends Paul (Louise Halloran's son), Mike, Eric and Eric. They will confirm that! Not everyone gets to drink 92 years of history on their birthday. I highly recommend it! Thanks, Gary!

IF THERE WAS NO BOURBON, THERE'D BE NO NASCAR

Even after Prohibition the effects lingered. In the religious South, Prohibition is still felt in the "dry counties" where Brothers Carl, Bob and Fonty Flock, better known as the Flock boys, ran moonshine on the legendary Thunder Road from Dawsonville to Atlanta, Georgia. There weas also a number of other "thunder roads" in North Carolina and all through the South. A good moonshine driver could make $100 a night runnin' shine...damn good money, especially in the 1940s, and not too bad today!

In 1947 Bill France, Sr. seized an opportunity by organizing these moonshine drivers for competition, creating the National Association of Stock Car Auto Racing (NASCAR). This convinced the Flock boys, the Pettys, Junior Johnson and others to go legit, or to add to their moonshining income. At first the money Junior Johnson made running shine was a lot more than he made on the track. But later that changed, and Johnson became the best driver of his time and was on the cover of Sports Illustrated *when he retired. In a 2002 History Channel interview Johnson said, "I do believe the fastest car I ever drove was a bootleggin' car."*

Little brother Tim Flock joined the Flock boys and started racing, and he had a co-pilot...a spider monkey who was outfitted with a helmet and racing gear. The family became known as the fabulous Flocks. Moonshine drivers became some of the best drivers on the NASCAR circuit. No surprise. If you could race at night being chased by the cops on Thunder Road, then going around in a circle in daylight making continuous left-hand turns was a piece of cake.

Many people think that Prohibition is a thing of the past. But let's not forget it is still alive and well. Thirteen million people live in Prohibition today in dry counties all over the South and other states. In Kentucky we have 120 counties, and 79 of them are dry! The joke in Kentucky is that Bourbon County is dry, but Christian county is wet. I believe Bourbon County is "moist" now. You can order beer, wine or a drink but only at a restaurant.

Prohibitionists like Russell, Wheeler and Nation thought the country would be a better, more moral, and safer place to live. But nothing could have been further from the truth. It not only kept hundreds of millions of dollars out of the federal coffers, contributing to the Great Depression, but it allowed a level of corruption, violence and mafia rule that almost destroyed the country. Franklin Roosevelt realized that this act needed to be overturned to get the country back on the right path, and more importantly to create jobs in distilleries, liquor stores and saloons, and thus start more tax money flowing back in to Washington.

When Prohibition was repealed, it was a joyous day indeed – but it would be awhile before there would be good product for the devoted bourbon drinkers. Before Prohibition there were 75 distilleries; afterward, only 51 applied for licenses. And, of course, for a bourbon to be a bourbon, it has to be aged for four years or more, so the distilleries didn't have a marketable product until the late 1930s.

As soon as he could, Colonel Jim Beam applied for a license to open a distillery in 1934. He almost had to, because he was going broke. Like other distillers, he simply got into other lines of work when Prohibition started. Colonel Beam got into citrus farming in Florida and the rock quarry business as well. Back in the 1920s it was hard to travel to Florida to oversee the operation, so he continued to live in Kentucky and lost quite a bit of money in that venture. He did OK in the rock quarry business, but not well enough. It seemed that bad luck followed him around during Prohibition. It was said that if Colonel Beam started a funeral home, people would suddenly just stop dying.

Other distillers filed for "medicinal licenses" and sold the bourbon they had in stock through druggists by prescription only. Brown-Forman did that and sold Old Forester. As a matter of fact, Old Forester is the only bourbon that was sold before, during, and after Prohibition by the same company. Old Grand Dad was also sold by the Wathen Distillery, and Stizel and Weller with Pappy Van Winkle sold medicinal whiskey. But this was a very limited market, and the bourbon could only be sold medicinally, and only with stocks on hand before Prohibition.

A few years later, WWII broke out and distilleries were mandated in 1942 by F.D.R to make ethanol for gun powder, vehicle fuel and rubber for tires. By the end of the war in 1945, bourbon inventories were all but gone—yet another devastating blow to the bourbon industry. Distilleries did more than their part for the war effort by putting aside the future of their own businesses for the good of their country.

So it really wasn't until after WWII that bourbon producers were able to get back to work and actually start aging their products again. It was almost 1950 before bourbon returned to shelves in abundance. By that time, Canadian and Scotch whiskey had a strong hold on the whiskey market, and tequila, rum and vodka were gaining on gin, which was the most popular spirit in the United States at the time. Bourbon was in trouble. Only "old timers" were drinking bourbon, and it was out of fashion with veterans and the new generation of drinkers.

It was also at this time that bourbon was being bastardized and made cheaper to save money. Labels and distilleries were being bought by bigger companies, and they cut corners where they could. Because bourbon is regulated so strictly, there's not too much a distillery can do to save money except add more water to the bourbon and lower the proof. Many distilleries did just that and lowered their bourbons' proofs from the bonded 100 proof to 86 proof, thereby creating a weak watery drink that did nothing to improve its popularity. You've heard the expression "86 it" when someone wants something to die or go away? Well, now you know where that came from.

By the late '60s, gin was replaced with the more neutral vodka as the most popular spirit. This was probably helped along by a certain movie character who enjoyed his martinis "shaken, not stirred." Bourbon starting gaining in popularity at this time, too, thanks to the military serving in Korea and Vietnam. Troops still received rations of whiskey as part of their pay package and could get Jim Beam, Wild Turkey and a couple other brands at the Post Exchange duty-free and pretty darn cheap. Some savvy traders would trade vouchers with their buddies who didn't drink, then buy up Jim Beam and resell it to nearby off-base taverns all over the world. This is how several labels got worldwide distribution. Not because of the distilleries' crack sales teams, but because of the Radar O'Rileys and Max Klingers of the world. Jim Beam and other distilleries owe a debt of gratitude not only for the soldiers' service to their country but for their service to bourbon!

Today bourbon is enjoying a great resurgence. Make no mistake about it, we are in the Golden Age of Bourbon. I'd say the first golden age was back in the 1850s when Ben Parley Moore was visiting Kentucky, and we are now squarely in the second. Since the early 1990s there have been about 50 single-barrel and small-batch labels added to the bourbon and rye categories alone. But make no mistake, it's still just a handful of labels that sells in the millions, and the whiskey category outsells the bourbon category. However, bourbon is coming on strong, with Jim Beam, Wild Turkey, Evan Williams and Maker's Mark as the category leaders. The bourbon business is up, even in these difficult economic times, so that should tell you something about the popularity of bourbon. There are eight distilleries offering tours in Kentucky and the number of people visiting is increasing exponentially each year. On average, around 90,000 people visit a single distillery each year, with a total of 250,000 people visiting distilleries overall. By 2012 those numbers are projected to reach 250,000 visiting each distiller, with a total of two million visiting the Bourbon Trail overall.

My Bourbon Time Line

"Too much of anything is bad, but too much of good whiskey is barely enough."—Mark Twain

1619 Virginia General Assembly passed laws against public drunkenness, with the first offense dealt with privately by the minister, and second offense dealt with "publiquely" (that being most probably stocks in the town square).

1600s-1700s Along with establishing grains of rye, barley and corn, fruit trees were planted in abundance. Farmers realized the trees matured in only six or seven years so they could bring in an orchard of abundance. They put up stores of cider and distilled brandy (also referred to as "mobby").

1716 According to Robert Beverley in *The History of Virginia, in Four Parts* (1722). "Their strong drink is Madera wine, Cyder, Mobby Punch (hard cider or brandy), made either of Rum from the Caribbee Islands, or brand distll'd from their apples and peaches; besides Brandy, Wine and strong Beer, which they have constantly from England."

1776 U.S. declares independence on July 4th, 1776.

Virginia Assembly established the Corn Patch and Cabin Rights, where people could claim 400 acres of land in Western Virginia and grow the native crop, corn, as long as they built a cabin on the property. This could be done until January 1, 1778.

1786-1788 On May 1, 1786, tavern rates were set in Kentucky Territory of Virginia. These were not taxes but were the *most* a tavern or a tippling house could charge for brandy, whiskey and other spirits.

1783 On September 3, 1783, the Treaty of Paris was signed, ending the Revolutionary War.

1789 In April 1789, George Washington was elected the first president being inaugurated in January 1790.

1792 June 1, 1792, Kentucky became the 15th state and becomes a commonwealth like Pennsylvania and Massachusetts. The U.S. made a flag with 15 stars and 15 stripes....later it changed back to 13 stripes and started adding stars for states so the flag wouldn't look like Joseph's amazing coat of many colors. Tavern rates were also set for tippling houses at this time.

1794 The Whiskey Rebellion took place in Washington County Pennsylvania, just outside Pittsburgh. Alexander Hamilton created the U.S. Marshal Service and sent agents to Pennsylvania and Kentucky and all states to collect taxes. In Washington County, agents were tarred and feathered and run out of town on a rail (a practice that I still encourage to this day... just kidding, Homeland Security).

1798-1799 After his presidency (and perhaps after seeing first hand that it could be lucrative), George Washington distilled 11,000 gallons of whiskey at Mt. Vernon to become the nation's largest distiller. A Scotsman named James Anderson made the whiskey and used the grains that were grown on Mount Vernon. Rye was still the more prevalent grain at this time and in this region, but corn was becoming more common. According to plantation records, James Anderson's recipe was comprised of 60% rye, 35% corn and 5% barley malt (*American Spirit Magazine* May/June 2008). Anderson also distilled fruit-flavored brandies and cider vinegar.

1802 President Thomas Jefferson repealed the excise tax of George Washington that caused the Whiskey Rebellion just a few years before.

1798-1810+ As at Mount Vernon, the most expensive whiskey was the highest proof. This was attained by distilling the whiskey up to four times or more. This not only was a way to drive up the proof, but also to distill out fusel oils and other congeners. Whiskey distilled twice was called "common whiskey" and fetched 50-60 cents per gallon; whiskey distilled up to four times could fetch $1.00 a gallon. At this time, barrels were merely used to transport the whiskey. Mount Vernon and other distilleries used brand new barrels, but they had no need to char them.

1810

Distilled spirits by state (in gallons)

Pennsylvania	6,552,284
Virginia	2,367,589
Kentucky	2,200,773
North Carolina	1,386,691
Ohio	1,212,266
Tennessee	801,245

(*Kentucky Bourbon* – Henry Crowgey)

A Lexington, Kentucky published account stated, "Whiskey is made either with rye, barley or Indian Corn. One or all of these grains is used as they are more or less abundant in the country. I do not know how far they are mixed in Kentucky, but Indian Corn is here in general basis of whiskey, and more often employed alone." (*Kentucky Bourbon* – Henry Crowgey)

1810 AND ON

The U.S. government, specifically the calvary, became one of the biggest consumers of bourbon whiskey by giving a weekly ration of whiskey to its soldiers as part of their pay. They received food, clothing, shelter and a weekly ration of whiskey. If the soldier helped build outbuildings or cut roads, they received an additional ration of whiskey.

1816

Hope Distilling Company opens in Louisville, Kentucky, with huge financial backing from the Northeast. They installed two giant stills and went *big*. Too big, too soon, as it turns out, and they closed a few years later when their capital ran out.

1820s Around this time, give or take 10 years, barrels were being used to ship the whiskey to the calvary and other customers. These smaller operations of whiskey distillers weren't like Mount Vernon, and they rarely had cooperages attached, so they would find, or more likely buy, barrels that had been used to ship meats and fish. These barrels had pickling agents used in them. The distillers didn't want to put their fine whiskey in these pickled barrels, so they would scrape the insides of them until there was no evidence of the pickling agents, and then to further sterilize them, they would light the insides on fire and char them before pouring in their whiskey. Their intent was only to sterilize the barrels, but charring happened to be very beneficial by causing the natural sugars in the wood to rush to the charred area to heal itself. As the sun shone down on the barrels, it forced the whiskey into the wood through this caramelized layer of sugar, and the cool evenings on the Ohio and Mississippi Rivers forced the whiskey back out through the wood. The movement in and out through the "red line" of sugars imparted an amber color, smoothed out that rough spirit, and gave some vanilla, caramel, maple, ginger, and other flavors to the whiskey, giving bourbon a distinctive look, taste and flavor.

1826 The American Temperance Society was founded in Boston, Massachusetts.

1831 Irishman Aenaes Coffey got his continuous still patented in Britain.

1836 J.W. Dant opened his distillery in Kentucky.

Bourbon Time Line

1838 Oscar Pepper opened the Old Oscar Pepper Distillery.

1840 George T. Stagg opened his distillery.

1844 T.W. Samuels opened his distillery.

1849 W.L. Weller, the original wheated bourbon, opened.

1850 David M. Beam moved his family's Old Tub Distillery to be closer to the railroad.

1855 Henry McKenna opened.

1857 Ben Parley Moore wrote his employer a letter during his visit to Kentucky. He was so struck by the folks here that he wrote, "Everywhere, sir, I am greeted by gentlemen with their hearts in their right hand, and their right hand in mine, and certainly in their left, a bottle of unequalled Old Bourbon Whiskey."

1860 David Beam's brother John started up the Early Times Distillery.

1861-1865 Civil War–Bourbon sales declined because of the war between the states. Kentucky remained neutral, but the bourbon industry depended on the South for a major chunk of their business. When the war ended, there were fewer distilleries than before. Between the end of the war and the turn of the century, bourbon didn't rebound to pre-war popularity, and gin started to overtake bourbon in popularity because it could be made easily in people's bath tubs.

1865 Benjamin Blanton opened up his distillery. (Elmer T. Lee created the bourbon Blanton's in 1984—the first single barrel bourbon.)

1867 The Chapeze Brothers started up Old Charter Distillery.

1870 John Fitzgerald opened up his distillery. He soon made Old Fitzgerald wheated bourbon.

1869-1870 Colonel Edmund Taylor (orphaned at a young age and raised partly by his uncle Zachary Taylor of Kentucky) opened up and named his magnificent state-of-the-art distillery O.F.C., which stood for Old Fire Copper, meaning that the whiskey only touched copper, making it cleaner and higher quality. Even today, everyone uses copper in distilling.

1870 Instead of shipping in barrels, the first bourbon was bottled and labeled. Before this, only bulk whiskey was available. Distilleries would ship barrels to a tavern, or people would come to the distillery with their quart jugs to be filled. In 1870, a pharmaceutical salesman by the name of George Garvin Brown bought whiskey stocks and rectified his brand and put the name of the most respected physician in Louisville on the label. Dr. William Forrester was that doctor, and Old Forrester was born. Others followed this and bottled and labeled their own whiskey. Later Brown-Foreman dropped an "r" after Doctor Forrester passed away, and it became Old Forester. Old Forester is the only bourbon around today that was produced before, during and after Prohibition, and owned by the same company!

1882 R.B. Hayden started up his distillery and used his grandfather's recipe from 1796. Hayden puts a picture of him on the label and called it Old Grand Dad!

1887 Edmund Taylor started up the Old Taylor Distillery and, at great cost, made it resemble a castle with elaborate sunken gardens. He was one of the first to realize that giving tours there and holding receptions and other events would help build his brands.

1888 Four Roses distillery opened.

1893 Wayne B. Wheeler teamed up with Rev. Howard Hyde Russell in Russell's recently formed Anti-Saloon League (ASL). Wheeler coined the term "pressure group" to turn up the heat on championing Prohibition.

1897 Bottled in Bond Act, the very first consumer protection in the history of the United States. Bonded whiskey had to be aged for four years and bottled at exactly 100 proof. It had to come from one distillery and be barreled in one season (January to December). Colonel Edmund Taylor was a galvanizing voice behind this bill.

1899 Carry Nation (born in Garrard County, Kentucky, ironically) joined the Temperance Movement in Kansas. She was arrested 30 times between 1900 and 1910 for smashing up saloons and their liquor with hammers (you gotta hand it to the old broad for style points, though), garnishing national attention for their cause. She died in 1911, which ironically was when my father, H. Joe Lubbers, was born!

1906
(June 30)

The Pure Food and Drug Act of 1906 was enacted establishing three separate classes of whiskey:

1. Straight whiskey
2. Bonded whiskey
3. Imitation whiskey – product of rectifiers and compounders

The Pure Food and Drug Act mandated that specified drugs, which included alcohol, be accurately labeled with contents and dosage. (Also labeled were cocaine, opium, heroin, morphine and cannabis indicta.) The Pure Food and Drug Act eventually led to the start of the Food and Drug Administration (FDA) as we know it now.

1909
(December)

The Taft Decision formally defined the types of whiskey still present today. Taft said that for a whiskey to be called "straight," water was the only thing that could be added. If anything other than water was added to the whiskey, it must be called a "blended" whiskey.

1914
(December 22)

A version of a Prohibition amendment came up for a vote in the House of Representatives. The vote went 197 for Prohibition and 190 against. Not a two-thirds majority, but a sign of the changing winds.

1914-1918 Distillation nearly ceased in order to focus on the war effort to produce neutral grain spirits to make fuels to run war machinery and to manufacture gun powder. Distilleries made some whiskey, but the bulk of what they made went to government contracts which were not as lucrative as selling whiskey on the open market. So Kentucky distillers had much to do with aiding the war effort and defeating the Axis powers.

1919 Volstead Act passed creating Prohibition ... the "Great Experiment." Only a few distilleries were licensed to keep bottling and selling (but not producing) bourbon whiskey for medicinal purposes, which required a prescription. Distilleries could not distill during Prohibition, so they had to use the aging stocks on hand that had already been distilled and barreled before Prohibition.

1920 (JANUARY 17) Distilleries, breweries, saloons and liquor stores were closed. A dark sad day indeed, and if anybody ever needed a drink, it was on that day...unless you had a prescription. To fill those prescriptions, 13 million gallons of bourbon were aging in Kentucky. They would run completely out of that supply by the end of Prohibition.

1920-1933 It was noted that from time to time many a resident of the Bourbon Capital of the World, Bardstown, Kentucky, would spot shiny black cars with Illinois license plates, seemingly heavily loaded down in the rear, making their way back north. Could these cars be tracked to Al Capone and other mobsters? Surely not!

1929 (December 7)

Stitzel -Weller and a handful of distilleries were granted permission under special licenses to run batches of whiskey for medicinal purposes from depleted stocks from the last nine years. This gave a select few the jump start they would need to have some stocks ready if and when Prohibition ever ended.

1933 (December 5)

Prohibition was repealed under F.D.R. Bottoms Up!

1934 (March 14)

Colonel Beam wrote up an invoice and purchase order for his first mash after teaming up with Chicago partners and purchasing and tooling up the old Murphy Barber Distillery in Clermont, Kentucky. Fifty other distilleries would reopen for a total of 51 distilleries in Kentucky. Colonel Beam spent $1,190.48 for grains, barrels, labor, taxes and a bond permit.

1938

Churchill Downs announced the official drink of the Kentucky Derby: the mint julep, and it continues to be the official drink today. During the Kentucky Oaks on Friday and The Kentucky Derby on Saturday, 80,000 mint juleps are consumed. It all started on that First Saturday in May of 1938. The winner that year was Lawrin, with Eddie Arcaro aboard.

1939

National Distillers commissioned a bust to be carved of Basil Hayden for the label of Old Grand Dad. This was to note that Old Grand Dad was the "head of the bourbon family." Before, it was a cartoon-like drawing that adorned the label.

1942

WWII–Just after returning to business after Prohibition, distilleries were again "drafted" to make ethanol for the manufacture of gun powder and other fuels for the war effort. This dealt another blow to Kentucky and other bourbon distillers who were just getting back on their feet from Prohibition. In part, if it wasn't for Kentucky bourbon, we just might all be *sprechen sie Deutschen* and working at Japanese car plants today. (Well, one of those has come to pass since then.)

1940s, '50s, '60s AND EVEN TODAY

Moonshiners hired runners to drive their whiskey (usually at night under the shine of the moon) to customers. The Flock boys, Junior Johnson, the Pettys and others soup up their Fords, Dodges and Chevys to outrun the cops. Bill France Senior figured out how to organize these good ole' boys to see who was the fastest, and in 1947 NASCAR was born. Junior Johnson won the second Daytona 500 shortly after serving nine months for moonshining.

1950s

Bourbon distillers began to lower the alcohol content of some labels from Bottled in Bond 100 proof to 86 proof (one of the ways we have come to know to kill or "86" something). This was done to match the more popular vodka and gin markets and to cut costs to keep bourbon viable in the market. At this time, brands were bought and sold to keep money coming in. Lots of distilleries were sold off or closed, and many labels went from being Kentucky Straight Bourbon Whiskies to cheaper blends and other whiskies.

Bourbon Time Line

1964

Congress declared bourbon the native spirit of the United States. Lyndon B. Johnson signed it into law. To be called bourbon, it must be produced in the United States.

1950s-1960s

Soldiers in the military stationed overseas were able to purchase Jim Beam, Wild Turkey and Jack Daniels very cheaply at the PX. Some industrious among the ranks would purchase or get vouchers from their Southern Baptist and other nondrinking buddies. They would then sell the vouchers to pub owners in European villages next to the base for those soldiers on R&R wanting a taste from back home. This was how Jim Beam and other products were "distributed" throughout Europe and Asia, and how those locals also got a taste of bourbon and whiskey from the United States.

1966

I made my first mint julep at seven years of age. My Aunt Bernadine allowed me to make the family Derby Julep to be passed around during the race. The winner of the Run for the Roses that year was Kauai King with Don Brumfield up!

Late 1960s

Vodka overtook gin as the # 1 spirit sold in the United States. A movie in which the lead character enjoyed his vodka martini "shaken, not stirred" boosted sales.

1970s

Bourbon companies sold off labels and just tried to survive with the few brands that were moving. However, blended scotches and Canadian Club and Seagram's and American blends were booming.

1984 Elmer T. Lee produced Blanton's Single-Barrel Kentucky Straight Bourbon Whiskey. It was 93 proof, about $45 a bottle, and only available in Kentucky. With Blanton's, Elmer T. Lee and Ancient Age Distillery created a new category. Keep in mind, bourbon sales were stagnant. Blanton's was well received, but by no means did the $45 bottle of single-barrel bourbon fly off the shelves.

1986-87 Jim Beam's grandson, Booker Noe, produced what he called "small-batch bourbon" to distinguish his Booker's from his friend Elmer T. Lee's "single barrel." At around the same time, Booker's cousin, Parker Beam at Heaven Hill, came out with Elijah Craig, which is made from a run of 70 barrels or less. Small batch could mean something different from distillers Parker and Craig Beam, Fred Noe, to Eddie Russell. But each would still be small batch since they were not from a single barrel.

1991 (MARCH) *Malt Advocate* magazine launched its first issue. *Malt Advocate* covers whiskies from all over the world, and its journalists are some of the most respected in the industry.

1992 The first Bourbon Fest was held in Bardstown, and hundreds of people attended. Today 55,000 people from 43 states and 13 countries attend Bourbon Fest on the third weekend in September.

1998 *Malt Advocate* magazine held its first "WhiskyFest," which sold out. They have since expanded to Chicago and San Francisco, and every event is always sold out in advance.

1999

Whisky Magazine was first published as a response to the rising interest and sales of single-malt scotches, small- batch/single-barrel bourbons, Irish, and Japanese whiskies. Based in London, the magazine is closer in proximity to scotch and Irish distilleries, but they make annual trips to Kentucky, and their journalists travel all over the world and are highly regarded as some of the best in the business.

2000

I believe this was the start of the second Golden Age of Bourbon. Not since Ben Parley Moore talked about that "unequalled old bourbon" in 1857 has bourbon been so recognized and enjoyed.

2007

The U.S. Senate unanimously passed a resolution declaring September "National Bourbon Heritage Month." With Bourbon Fest being held each September in the bourbon capital of the world, Bardstown, Kentucky, the Senate acknowledged the rich history and heritage that bourbon has contributed to the United States.

2008 (June)

Bourbon Review magazine hit the stand with its first publication. Based in Lexington, in the heart of Kentucky, this marked the first magazine to cover bourbon and no other whisk[e]y. Now that's making a stand!

2009 (February)

My fellow whiskey professors David Mays and Steve Cole and I received the Icons of Whisky Award, Global Whiskey Ambassador of the Year from *Whisky Magazine*'s distinguished panel. It is an honor that David, Steve and I cherish and strive to live up to every time we stand up and talk about bourbon!

6

Visiting Kentucky and the Distilleries, and You WILL

"I only drink two fingers of bourbon each day. Of course I use my index and pinky fingers." – Jimmy Russell, Master Distiller Emeritus, Wild Turkey

"May there be no hell..." –Booker Noe
"...and if there is, I'll see you there." –Fred Noe

So you're a member of the bourbon family now and inspired to come visit us down on the Bourbon Trail. Of course you are! I'm telling you, once you visit, you'll be back. They *all* come back. The biggest celebrities and political figures come back year after year to Kentucky for the Derby and just to visit. It's a great place, a fun place, and, as a nice bonus, it's not that expensive to visit. Since we are in the heart of the country, a large percentage of the population can just drive here.

We are in the second Golden Age of Bourbon. Why wouldn't you want to feel, smell, hold, and taste history? Not since Ben Parley Moore wrote his employer about that "unequalled old bourbon" has there been such unbridled enthusiasm about bourbons.

Napa Valley has hundreds of thousands of visitors a year. I've been myself, and it's wonderful. San Francisco is where most people stay and then drive up to the wine country. Then they come back and enjoy the food and nightlife of one of the most stunning cities in the world. The Bourbon Trail is very similar and much more accessible to most of the country than San Francisco. I would argue it is also just as stunning (just a different kind of stunning).

On the Bourbon Trail are the distilleries in Kentucky that welcome more than 250,000 visitors each year. Come on by anytime, but I'd avoid mid-July through August, since most distilleries do not distill during the hottest months. If you'd like a recommendation about the best times, I'd first suggest coming the third weekend in September for the Bourbon Festival. Also, Keeneland race track is open every April and October in Lexington, and Churchill Downs is running every May and November. I'd just avoid the last week of April and the first Saturday in May which is Derby, unless you have a bucket of money to get a hotel. Thunder Over Louisville in April is the largest fireworks display in the world and is one of the coolest days/nights ever. It's the opening ceremonies of the Kentucky Derby Festival, and throughout the day there is an air show while 600,000 people head downtown to assemble for the world's largest fireworks display over the Ohio River at night. Military cannons roar as fireworks light up downtown for miles. Don't believe me? Find it on YouTube, then go to www.thunderoverlouisville.org and you'll see. Hotels downtown can get pricey, but you can still find some deals, and it's quite something, especially if you have children.

Don't bite off more than you can chew in visiting the distilleries. You can only visit two on a given day. Don't try to do three, you just won't make it. Trust me.

WESTERN SHELF DISTILLERIES AND ATTRACTIONS

Split them in to 2 days to visit distilleries and the cooperage:

Day 1

Maker's Mark Distillery

3350 Burk Spring Road, Loretto, KY 40037

Phone:270.865.2881

www.makersmark.com

Master distiller is Greg Davis; president and family member ambassador is Bill Samuels, Jr.

Maker's Mark distillery house (Maker's Mark is a registered trademark of Maker's Mark Distillery, Inc. and is used with permission.)

The Maker's Mark visitor's experience gives you a look at how Bill Samuels, Sr. and his wife Marjorie (who is responsible for the bottle, name, font and wax) started up the family business again in 1959. A re-creation of their kitchen is here and you get an inside look at how this family created and built this now-iconic brand. Take your camera, there are photo ops a plenty. You top off your tour by being able to purchase a bottle of Maker's Mark and dip it in that famous red wax your own damn self.

Directions from Louisville: Take I-65 South from Louisville to Exit #112, (Clermont/Bardstown). At the ramp turn left onto Hwy. 245 South to Bardstown.

Take Hwy. 245 to the intersection of Hwy. 62, turn right and continue on Hwy. 62 east for approximately two miles. Hwy. 62 runs into Hwy. 150, where you will turn left and continue approximately two miles and past My Old Kentucky Home State Park. At the intersection of Hwys. 150 and 49, turn right onto Hwy. 49 South and follow the brown historical landmark signs to Holy Cross, which will direct you to go straight on Hwy. 527 South. Follow Hwy. 527 to St. Francis (5 miles), where you will turn left onto Hwy. 52 East into Loretto. Continue on through Loretto for approximately three miles,

1) Maker's Mark Distillery, 3350 Burk Spring Road, Loretto, KY 40037

2) Independent Stave Cooperage, 712 E. Main Street, Lebanon, KY 40033

3) Heaven Hill Distlleries Bourbon Heritage Center, 1311 Gilky Run Road, Bardstown, KY 40004

4) Jim Beam American Outpost, 526 Happy Hollow Road, Clermont, KY 40110

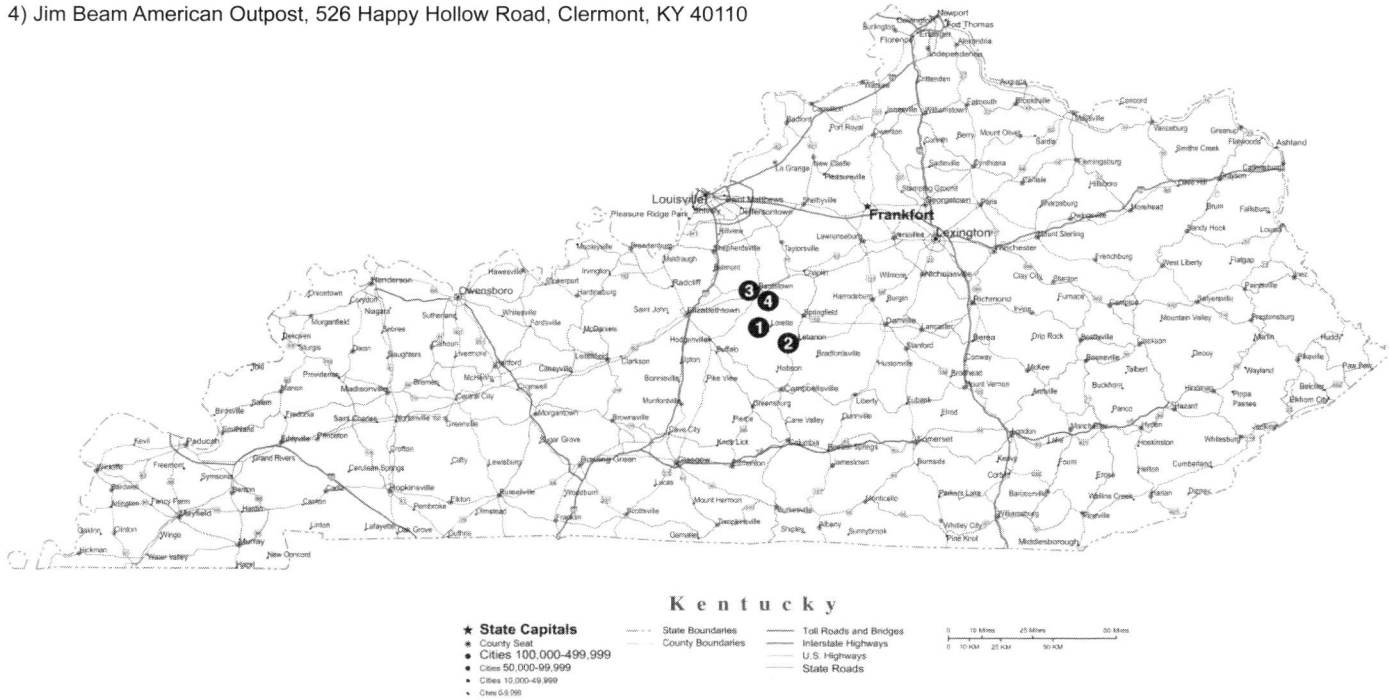

and at the end of Burks Spring Road you will see the sign, "You have just found the home of Maker's Mark." Approximately one-and-a-half hours driving time.

Directions from Lexington: Take U.S. 60 West six miles to Martha Layne Collins Blue Grass Parkway. Merge onto the parkway toward Elizabethtown and drive 30 miles to Exit 42 (Springfield/Lebanon). Take the exit and turn left toward Springfield/Lebanon on KY 555 S. After 14.8 miles, KY 555 S becomes KY 55 but continue straight for 8.9 miles to the traffic signal (Gen. Thomas Statue). Turn right onto KY 55 Bypass and drive to the next light (Circle K). Turn right onto KY 49/52 and continue 6.3 miles. Turn right onto KY 52 continuation and continue 2.2 miles. Turn right onto Burk's Spring Road and historic Maker's Mark Distillery is straight ahead. Approximately one hour, 15 minutes driving time.

Independent Stave Cooperage (Barrel makers)

712 E. Main Street, Lebanon, KY, 40033

Phone: 270.692.4674

www.independantstavecompany.com

This is something you've really got to see. The way they make barrels is just amazing! No nails, screws or glue here. Bending wood and using metal hoops along with hundreds of years of experience is what you'll see here at this facility. By law, bourbon must be aged in brand new charred-oak containers, so almost all the barrels you see being made are for the bourbon industry. The coolest thing is that this is a family-owned business run by the Boswells.

Directions from Louisville: Take I65 South toward Nashville for approximately 20 miles to Exit 112 (Clermont/Bardstown). Turn left onto Hwy. 245 toward Bardstown and drive 19 miles. Turn left onto Hwy. 150 E and drive 15 miles. Turn right onto KY 55 (Hardee's on the corner). Centre Square in Lebanon is nine miles straight ahead. From Centre Square drive one block south on KY 55/Spalding Ave. to the light at

Main Street. Turn left onto U.S. 68/Main St. and continue for about one mile. Independent Stave Cooperage is on the right. Driving time is about one hour, 15 minutes (63 miles).

Directions from Lexington: Take U.S. 60 West six miles to Martha Layne Collins Blue Grass Parkway. Merge onto the parkway toward Elizabethtown and drive 30 miles to the Springfield exit (Exit 42). Take the exit and turn left toward Springfield/Lebanon on KY 555 S. After 14.8 miles, 555 S becomes 55 but continue straight for 9 miles to Centre Square. From Centre Square drive one block south on KY 55/Spalding Avenue to the light at Main Street. Turn left onto U.S. 68/ Main St. and continue for about one mile. Independent Stave Cooperage is on the right. Driving time is around one hour, 10 minutes (59.8 miles).

Bourbon Heritage Center (Photo courtesy of the Louisville Convention and Visitors Bureau)

Day 2

Heaven Hill Distilleries Bourbon Heritage Center

1311 Gilky Run Road, Bardstown, KY 40004

Phone: 502.337.1000

www.bourbonheritagecenter.com.

Master distillers are Parker Beam and his son Craig Beam, and ambassador is my buddy Rob Hutchins.

Heaven Hill's Heritage Center really raised the bar for everyone else when they built their multimillion-dollar facility. They received *Whisky Magazine*'s Global Icons of Whisky

Award for Visitor Attraction of the Year in 2009. A fire destroyed a total of six rack houses and their distillery in 1996, so the distillery is no longer here at this facility. But they more than make up for this; trust me, you will be treated to one of the best experiences on the Kentucky Bourbon Trail.

Directions from Louisville: Take I-65 south to Exit 112 (Clermont/Bardstown). Turn left onto Hwy. 245 South. Take Hwy. 245 South to the end, then make a right onto 150 West. Turn left at the first light onto 49 South (by the McDonald's®). Follow 49 South one mile to Heaven Hill Distilleries Bourbon Heritage Center. It'll take you about 50 minutes to get there from Louisville.

Directions from Lexington: Take Bluegrass Parkway west to exit 25 (U.S. 150), turn right onto U.S. 150 West. Turn left at the first light (by the McDonald's) onto 49 South for one mile to the Bourbon Heritage Center. It will take you about an hour to get here from Lexington.

Booker Noe statue on Beam Hill (Jim Beam is a registered trademark of Jim Beam Brands Co. and is used with permission.)

Jim Beam American Outpost

526 Happy Hollow Road
Clermont, KY 40110
Phone: 502.543.9877
www.jimbeam.com.

Master distiller/family member and bourbon ambassador is Fred Noe, and ambassador and whiskey professor is Bernie Lubbers (yours truly).

I'm personally really proud of what is going on here at Beam's Visitors Experience. Jim Beam is the #1 selling bourbon in the world, so although the grounds are breathtaking, the distillery is large and industrial. But don't think that we're cutting any corners, goodness, no! Beam takes as much care as any of the smaller, quainter distilleries, just more of it.

Colonel Beam built big after Prohibition, and that's one of the reasons we're still around. He just had no idea any of you all would be coming around and visiting, so the distillery was set up to make *a lot* of whiskey. But they've done a great job renovating and showing off the distillery and everything that goes on at the world's largest bourbon distillery, and giving you an inside look at the process.

Directions from Louisville: Take I-65 South toward Nashville to exit 112 (Clermont/Bardstown). Go left off the exit, and 2.5 miles on the left is the Beam Distillery. You'll see signs for the Jim Beam American Outpost off Happy Hollow Road. Driving time is around 25 minutes.

Directions from Lexington: Take Bluegrass Parkway west to exit 25 (U.S. 150). Drive toward Bardstown and turn right onto KY 245. Drive 13.5 miles, then turn right onto Happy Hollow Road.

EASTERN SHELF DISTILLERIES AND ATTRACTIONS

For your visit to the Eastern Shelf I'd do it this way:

Day 1

Buffalo Trace Distillery

113 Great Buffalo Trace

Frankfort, KY 40601

Phone: 502.696.5926

www.buffalotrace.com

Filling bottles at Buffalo Trace (Photo courtesy of the Louisville Convention and Visitors Bureau)

Master distiller is Harlen Wheatley and distiller emeritus is Elmer T. Lee.

I love the grounds here at this distillery. I love the O.F.C. above some of the brick rack houses here. (Remember the Old Fire Copper from Colonel Edmund Taylor) They have different types of brick, block and traditional rack houses. The log buildings on the property are really cool too, and you can even rent the lodge for gatherings and meetings.

Directions from Louisville: Take I-64 East to exit 53B (U.S. 127 North). Continue straight about five miles, cross the Kentucky River and you'll see the Holiday Inn. Turn left continuing on 127 North which is also Wilkinson Blvd. The distillery is one mile down on the left.

Directions from Lexington: Take I-64 West to exit 58. Go North on U.S. 60 until it becomes 127/421. Go straight and follow signs to Civic Center/Downtown about 5.5 miles. Do not make any turns until you see the distillery on your right.

1) Buffalo Trace Distillery, 113 Great Buffalo Trace, Frankfort, KY 40601
2) Woodford Reserve Distillery, 7855 McCracken Pike, Versailles, KY 40303
3) Wild Turkey Distillery, 1525 Tyrone Road, Lawrenceburg, KY 40342
4) Four Roses Distillery, 1224 Bonds Bill Road, Lawrenceburg, KY 40342

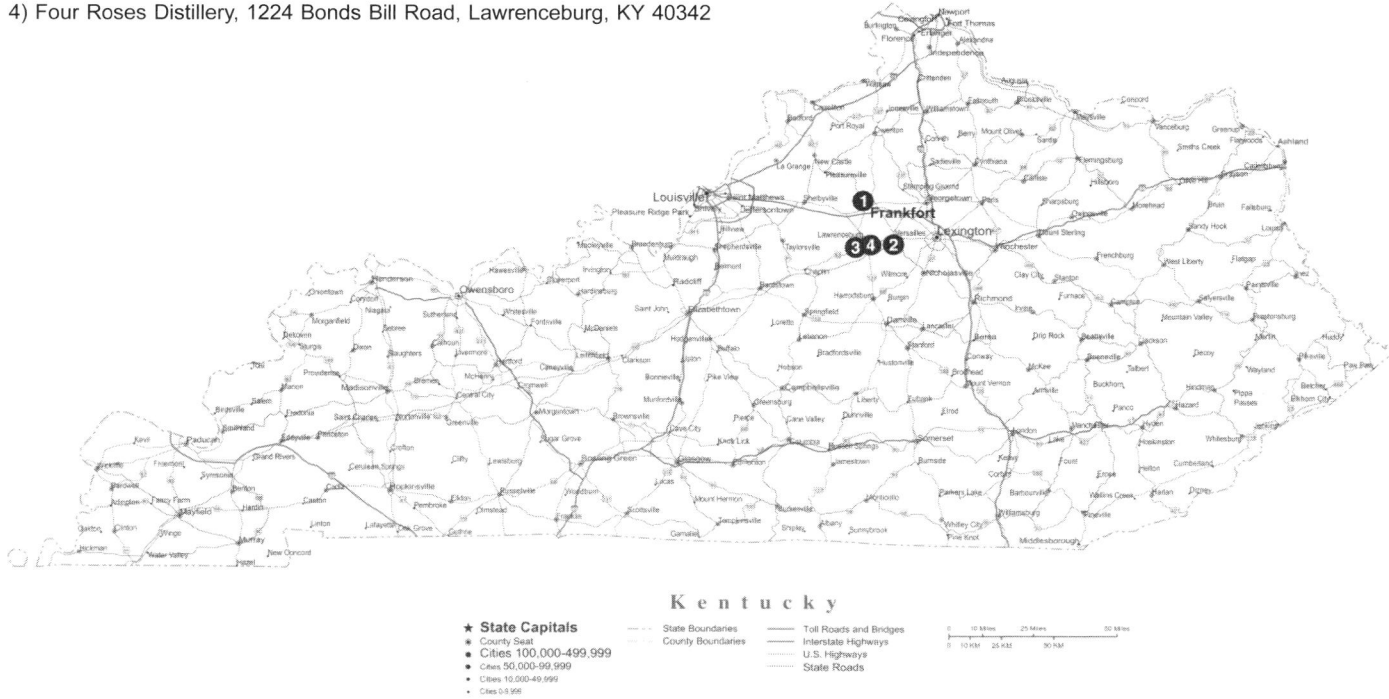

Woodford Reserve Distillery

7855 McCracken Pike

Versailles, KY 40303

phone: 859.879.1812

www.woodfordreserve.com

Woodford Reserve Barrel Head (Photo courtesy of the Louisville Convention and Visitors Bureau)

Master distiller is Chris Morris. Woodford is the gorgeously renovated former Labrot & Graham Distillery. Brown-Foreman spent millions of dollars rebuilding this distillery, and it shows. The brick rack houses are really cool, and the triple pot stills are something to see. since this company is the only one in the bourbon business to use them. They have many events at this distillery, including some really nice bourbon dinners, so call ahead and see what they'll have going on for when you visit.

Directions from Louisville: I-64 East to the U.S. 60 exit (Frankfort Versailles). Turn right toward Versailles. Go 2.5 miles and turn right on Route 3360 (Grassy Springs Road) until it ends. Turn right on McCracken Pike to the distillery.

Directions from Lexington: Take U.S. 60 (Versailles Road) out of Lexington toward Frankfort. Just after you pass State Road 1685, turn left onto Route 3360 (Grassy Springs Road) til it ends. Turn right on McCracken Pike to the distillery.

Day 2

Wild Turkey Distillery

1525 Tyrone Road

Lawrenceburg, KY 40342

phone: 502.839.4544

www.wildturkeybourbon.com

Wild Turkey Distillery (Photo courtesy of the Louisville Convention and Visitors Bureau)

Master distiller is Eddie Russell, and distiller emeritus is his dad, Jimmy Russell. This distillery sits way up overlooking the Kentucky River, and that alone is one of the coolest sights you'll see there. They've just renovated the distillery, so go take a look and enjoy it all. If you're lucky enough, maybe Jimmy Russell will be there to have a chat and take a picture or two with.

Directions from Louisville: Take I-64 East to 151 South. Take U.S. 62 East to the distillery. Driving time is around 50 minutes.

Directions from Lexington: Take U.S. 60 West to Versailles. Then take U.S. 62 West to the distillery. Driving time is around 30 minutes.

Four Roses Distillery
1224 Bonds Mill Road
Lawrenceburg, KY40342
phone: 502.839.3436
www.fourroses.us.

Four Roses Distillery (Photo courtesy of the Louisville Convention and Visitors Bureau)

Master distiller is Jimmy Rutledge. This distillery is built in the Spanish Mission style, and it's really picturesque. The rack houses you see across the way don'tbelong to Four Roses; those are the property of Wild Turkey, whose distillery is a few miles away. Four Roses is a small distillery, but Jimmy Rutledge does some of the coolest distilling there with their two recipes and five strains of yeast which can give them many options for a final product.

Directions from Louisville: Take I-64 East to exit 53 (U.S. 127 South). Go 14 miles to Highway 513 West (There's no sign there for the distillery, so pay attention). Go right on Highway 513. It's just one mile to the distillery on the right.

Directions from Lexington: Take U.S. 60 East to Bluegrass Parkway West. Take exit 59B off Bluegrass Parkway down a tenth of a mile to Highway 513 West (there's no sign to the distillery, so pay attention here). The distillery is just down a mile on the right.

WELCOME TO KENTUCKY

Since I'm the whiskey professor, I'll help guide you on your first visit here. Our airport in Louisville is a great little airport–one terminal. We have Southwest, U.S. Air, United, Continental, American, Delta, Frontier and a few others that fly here. We're only a five-hour drive from St. Louis and Chicago and seven hours from Atlanta. You can fly in to Bluegrass Airport (LEX) in Lexington, but I would venture to guess that Standiford Field (SDF) in Louisville is going to have more and cheaper options. Louisville is right in the middle of bourbon country and is a 25-minute drive from Jim Beam, and 45 minutes from Bardstown. On the other side, Lexington is only 72 miles from Louisville. It's not going to cost you much to get here, but you will need to rent a car or hire transportation to take you around to the distilleries if you'd like to do it that way, or come with a group. Mint Julep Tours (mintjuleptours.com) is a great company to tour with if you don't want to get a car or if you have a group of people you want to bring along with you. There are many hotels right downtown that start around $100 a night, and some on the outskirts of town (in Brooks or Shepherdsville) that are half that.

Taking tours is fun and interesting. Every distillery gives a different tour, and each has its own unique history and qualities. At some you'll see the distillation firsthand. At others you'll go into a rack house and see the barrels aging and smell the evaporation of the "angels' share" (what the angels drink ... the bourbon evaporating from the barrels). Louisville and Lexington are the cities you'd stay in as your home base, and then you'd journey out from there to the distilleries. You could also stay in Bardstown if you wanted to get that real small-town feel, being right there in the heart of the Bourbon Capital of the World. But there isn't as much nightlife or restaurants there compared to Louisville or Lexington. Once you've driven out through the rolling fields of horse country, met the passionate and friendly folks at the distilleries, and enjoyed the restaurants and nightlife here, you'll be back. Lexington is a fun college town, home to the University of Kentucky Wildcats and Transylvania University, with great restaurants and night life. And unlike most of the country, the bars in Louisville are open until 4:00 a.m. every night of the week, so bring your "A" game.

Louisville

The Louisville Visitors and Convention Bureau has done a really cool thing by creating the Urban Bourbon Trail (justaddbourbon.com). These are bars and restaurants where you can enjoy a large selection of bourbons after visiting the distilleries. Many of these are in the downtown hotels, so I'd suggest staying at one of those so you can sample the bourbons from the distilleries you visit. There are nine accounts on the Urban Bourbon Trail, and each of these accounts offers a minimum of 50 bourbons to be part of the Urban Bourbon Trail.

The following hotels are part of the Urban Bourbon Trail:

- **The Seelbach Hotel**–Fourth and Muhammad Ali Blvd–the Old Seelbach bar
- **The Brown Hotel**–Fourth and Broadway–lobby bar at the Brown
- **Marriott Hotel**–Second and Jefferson–Blu Lobby bar
- **21c**–Seventh and Main–named one of the top 100 hotels in the world by *Conde Nast Traveller*–Proof is the restaurant in the hotel
- **Galt House Hotel**–Fourth and Main–Jockey's Silk's Bourbon Bar and A.J.'s bar

The following restaurants are located on the Urban Bourbon Trail:

- **Z's Fusion**–Fourth and Market
- **Maker's Mark Bourbon House and Lounge**–Fourth Street Live!

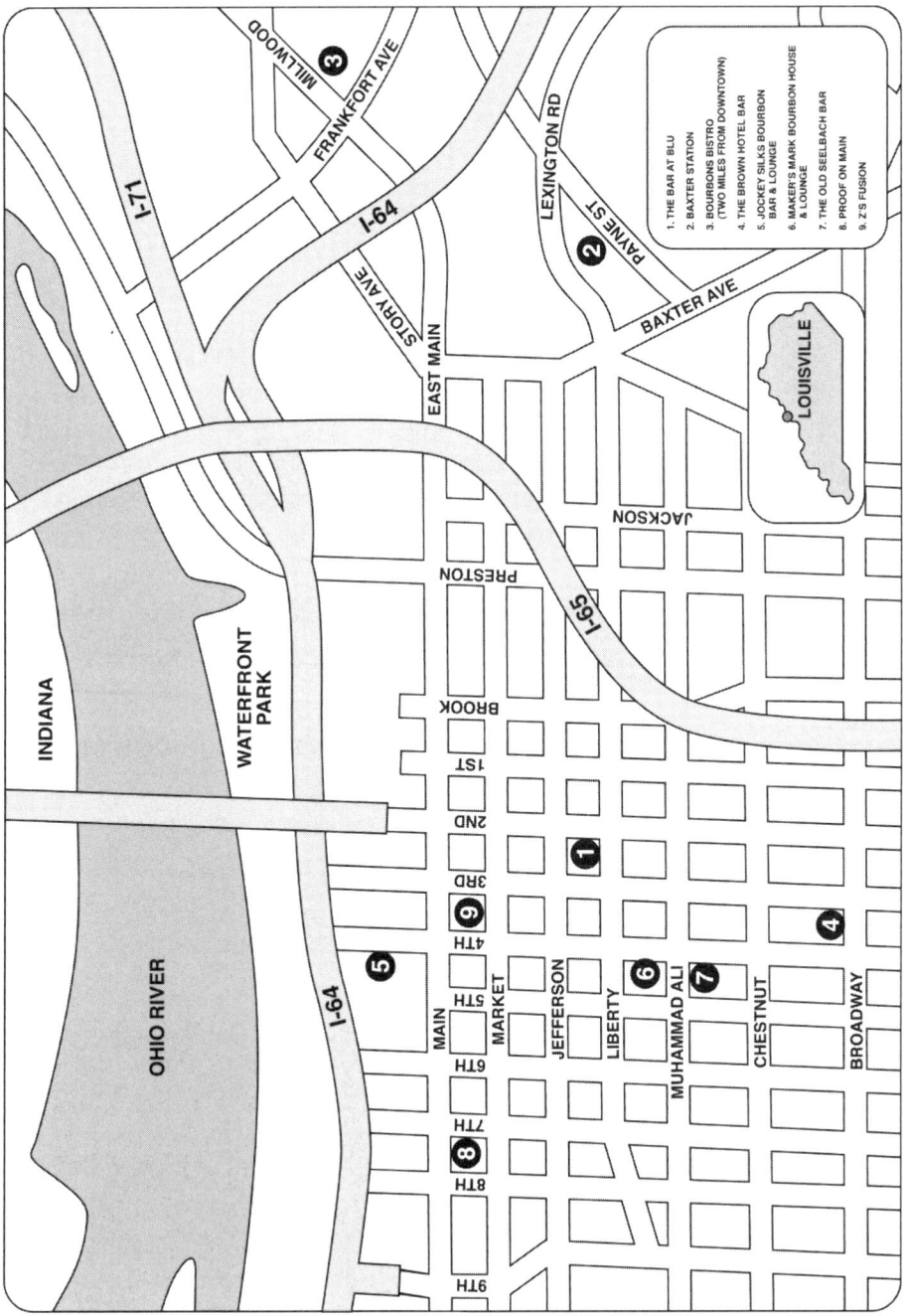
1. THE BAR AT BLU
2. BAXTER STATION
3. BOURBONS BISTRO (TWO MILES FROM DOWNTOWN)
4. THE BROWN HOTEL BAR
5. JOCKEY SILKS BOURBON BAR & LOUNGE
6. MAKER'S MARK BOURBON HOUSE & LOUNGE
7. THE OLD SEELBACH BAR
8. PROOF ON MAIN
9. Z'S FUSION
LOUISVILLE
INDIANA
OHIO RIVER
WATERFRONT PARK
I-71
I-64
I-65
MILLWOOD
FRANKFORT AVE
STORY AVE
LEXINGTON RD
PAYNE ST
BAXTER AVE
EAST MAIN
JACKSON
PRESTON
BROOK
1ST
2ND
3RD
4TH
5TH
6TH
7TH
8TH
9TH
MAIN
MARKET
JEFFERSON
LIBERTY
MUHAMMAD ALI
CHESTNUT
BROADWAY

- **Bourbon's Bistro**–2255 Frankfort Ave. (just two miles from downtown)
- **Baxter Station**–Payne Street and Cooper

All these accounts have at least 50 bourbons on the back bar to choose from. It's a nice array of accounts, too. From the historic Brown and Seelbach Hotels to the new and stunning 21c, all of these are within two to three miles of each other, and those that are downtown are just a few blocks from each other.

The Seelbach Hotel

500 S. Fourth Street

Louisville, KY 40202

phone: 502.585.3200

www.seelbachhilton.com

The Seelbach is a historic property built in 1905 which recently went through a $12 million renovation. F. Scott Fitzgerald and Al Capone were just a couple of the visitors to this hotel. The Al Capone Poker Room is off the famous Oak Room Restaurant, complete with slanted mirrors (to peek at his opponents' hands) and secret panels and passages to escape the Feds during Prohibition. F. Scott Fitzgerald was so inspired from his stay that he used the Seelbach as the backdrop for Tom and Daisy Buchanan's wedding in *The Great Gatsby*. The Old Seelbach bar oozes history and is famous in cocktail books for the Seelbach Cocktail made with bourbon, champagne, bitters and triple sec.

Old Seelbach Bar (Photo courtesy of the Louisville Convention and Visitors Bureau)

The Brown Hotel
335 W. Broadway
Louisville, KY 40202
phone: 502.583.1234
www.brownhotel.com

The Brown Hotel (Photo courtesy of the Louisville Convention and Visitors Bureau)

The Brown was built for $4 million back in 1923 and has been a magnet for celebrities and prominent guests for the Derby or visitors to the Bourbon Trail ever since. Extensive renovations in the 1980s restored it to its full elegance in English Renaissance design, and it remains one of the most treasured landmarks in the South. In the lobby bar, you'll be able to sip and enjoy a wide variety of bourbons and classic cocktails. The English Grill is a great restaurant, and I suggest you treat yourself and request the chef's table. There is a minimum number of people required for this table, but if you tell them the bourbons you want to pair and taste with dinner, they will accommodate. It's one of the most awesome dinner experiences I've ever had. Just across the street on Broadway is Freddie's Bar, and you'll swear you've walked back in time to the 1950s. It is one of the coolest, oldest bars in the city. Not a huge bourbon selection, but a place you've almost gotta experience.

The Marriott Hotel
280 W. Jefferson Street
Louisville, KY 40202
phone: 502.627.5045
www.marriott.com/hotels/travel/sdflm-louisville-marriott-downtown

Hickory, Chris, Claire and Jim at the Blu Bar (Photo by Bernie Lubbers)

The Marriott is right in the heart of downtown Louisville with 616 rooms. Built just a few years ago, this hotel is contemporary and comfortable. The Blu Lobby bar is cozy but open to the gorgeous lobby. Blu is where all the bourbons are showcased on the back bar, and it is also where my buddies Hickory, Jim and Chris play bluegrass every Thursday night from 9:00 until midnight. Hickory loves Basil Hayden's bourbon, Jim likes Baker's, and Chris likes Knob Creek, so your song request might just move to the top of the list if you buy them a bourbon. One of my favorite bartenders, Claire (also a Basil Hayden's girl), joins the band and sings a couple songs with the boys, too. It's a fun night and a great place to stay while visiting Louisville. If I'm in town on Thursday nights, you'll find me there, and most times Hickory invites me up to sing and play with them, too. It's a great fun night for all, so by all means, come on by.

If You Stay at the Marriott

Since Hickory and Claire are both Basil Hayden's fans, I'll tell ya this story that I share during my bourbontations around the country.

Bahsil or Basil? *I always refer to Basil Hayden's bourbon as "Baaaahsil" Hayden's bourbon, not "Baysil" Hayden's bourbon. People invariably ask me if it is pronounced Basil, or Basil Hayden's. I answer with this story:*

I have a neighbor (this is true) who lives six doors down from me, and not only is he a great guy, but he has one of the coolest names I know: Basil Doerhorfer. (I think he's Irish.) He's in his 70s and is about 6'5" tall with a full head of wavy white hair, and he's a real skinny fellow. Every day he walks his little Chihuahua-mix dog in front of my condos, and it just looks funny with him being a slender 6'5" and with that little dog on a leash. One day I saw him and said, "Hey, Basil, how are you doing?" He replied, "Well, young man, basil is an herb, Baaahsil is the name." To which I replied, "Well, in that case I'll just call you Dick then." We both had a chuckle, but since then I've always called him and the bourbon Baaahsil.

21c Museum Hotel

700 W. Main Street

Louisville, KY 40202

phone: 502.217.6300

www.21chotel.com/hotel

The Bar at Proof on Main (Photo courtesy of the Louisville Convention and Visitors Bureau)

What is a museum hotel? Well, everything in the hotel/restaurant is a museum exhibit! It's something to see, and it's not just me who says that. *Conde Nast Traveller* rated it the #1 hotel in the United States, and the #6 hotel in the *world*! A boutique hotel that's not snooty. It has a great sense of humor, as you'll find by the exhibits and the large red penguins that move around the hotel and restaurant called Proof (the cheese grits are to die for). You'll see some of the master distillers and us bourbon ambassadors at Proof from time to time, and when you come in, you'll know why. Even the bathrooms are intriguing. Luxury accommodations with good ole Kentucky hospitality, and it's the only museum in America dedicated solely to art created in the 21st century (get it? 21c?). Whether you visit Proof or stay at 21c, you will not think you are in Kentucky. London maybe, or New York or San Francisco, but thank God it is Kentucky!

The Galt House Hotel

140 S. Fourth Street

Louisville, KY 40202

phone: 502.589.5200

www.galthouse.com

Jockey Silks at the Galt House (Photo courtesy of the Louisville Convention and Visitors Bureau)

The Galt House is located right on the Ohio River and is a large hotel with two towers. The rooms that have recently been renovated and most of them are huge. A.J.'s Lobby bar overlooks the river and Fourth Street Live, and the Jockey's Silks Bar boasts over 100 bourbons, some that aren't even available anymore! Rivue Restaurant sits at the top of the West Tower and overlooks Louisville and the Ohio River for great views of the Bluegrass. Jeff Ruby's Steakhouse is in the front of the Galt House and is one of the hottest spots to sip a bourbon, listen to great music, and enjoy great steaks and seafood. My good buddy and singing partner Robbie Bartlett and her band play almost every weekend there. She drinks Jim Beam Black Label and ginger ale with about five cherries in it, if you want to send one up to her. Jeff Ruby's also has a signature Maker's Mark dessert complete with dripping red icing.

Z's Fusion

115 S. Fourth Street

Louisville, KY 40202

phone: 502.855.8000

www.zsfusion.com

Z's Fusion (Photo courtesy of the Louisville Convention and Visitors Bureau)

Z's offers a blend of European and Asian ingredients and flavors. Z's is one of the newest additions to the Urban Bourbon Trail, and their bartenders offer an array of fine bourbon classic cocktails and some of their own creations.

Maker's Mark Bourbon House (Photo courtesy of the Louisville Convention and Visitors Bureau)

Maker's Mark Bourbon House and Lounge

446 S. Fourth Street

Louisville, KY 40202

phone: 502.568.9009

www.makerslounge.com

The lounge is located right in the center of Fourth Street Live in the tourist block of Louisville. You'll find the Hard Rock Café there and other fun places to hang out. From its name you can tell it's a bourbon bar, and the food there is often paired with bourbon, of course.

Bourbon's Bistro

2255 Frankfort Ave

Louisville, KY 40206

phone: 502.894.8838

www.bourbonsbistro.com

Voted the best whiskey bar/restaurant in 2006 in the Icons of Whisky Awards in *Whisky Magazine*, this is a wonderful place owned by John and Jason, two bourbon fans and all-

Chef Michael Crouch with owners Jason Brauner and John Morrison (Photo courtesy of the Louisville Convention and Visitors Bureau)

around good guys where you'll see almost every night sipping on some good Kentucky straight bourbon whiskey. Located just two miles from downtown, the restaurant is also easy to get to. On Mondays they often have master distillers and ambassadors like myself host bourbon dinners. Call ahead and see if one is going on; they're always fun and educational with delicious food. My favorite meal in the world is there, and if you see the pork chop on the menu, tell them you want it the way Bernie gets it, complete with the glass of Old Grand Dad.

Baxter Station

1201 Payne Street

Louisville, KY 40204

phone: 502.584.1635

www.baxterstation.com

Baxter Station is one of my favorite additions to the bourbon trail; I'm so glad they're on it. It's a nice cozy little neighborhood bar/restaurant with good food and a great casual atmosphere. It's a 100-year-old tavern, and it's just a mile or so from downtown. You're also at the foot of Baxter Avenue and Bardstown Road, where the locals go to eat and drink at locally owned places. If you want to find local flavor and folks, go on down and enjoy the bourbon and food there. Baxter Station just won a 2010 Icons of Whisky Award from *Whisky Magazine*!

Baxter Station (Photo courtesy of the Louisville Convention and Visitors Bureau)

So there you have it, the Urban Bourbon Trail (that's just fun to say, isn't it?). Just remember that several of the accounts on the Urban Bourbon Trail are busier for happy hour or dinner. Blu Café (Marriott), Proof and Bourbon's Bistro have the better later-in-the-evening scene, especially Thursday at Blu with Hickory and the boys playing bluegrass 'til midnight.

There are also several locally owned bars and restaurants you should check out. I'm always one to support the little guy, and the local guy, too. If you want to go to where the locals drink and hang out to get a real taste of Louisville, I'd suggest taking a two-mile car ride to the highlands to one of these accounts. It's also quite a bit more affordable to hang out and have many of the same bourbons at these places, and they all have excellent bourbon selections.

STILL DOWNTOWN:

732 Social–732 E. Market Street–Louisville, KY 40204–502.583.6882. 732 is not on the Urban Bourbon Trail, but you should consider this place for its fine cocktails. Patterned after the Violet Hour in Chicago, this is a hot newish little place that is known for its mixology. Larry heads up the staff there, and they've always got a story about a cocktail. They have good food here, too, so don't overlook this place for a nice dinner.

OUT OF DOWNTOWN:

The Back Door–1250 Bardstown Road–Louisville, KY 40204 (in the back of Mid City Mall). John Dant owns the place, and it is a favorite hangout for locals. Six pool tables, darts and Golden Tee golf all contribute to make this a great place to hang out with friends. They boast a really nice bourbon selection, and Chris, Steve, Flash, Queenie, Carrie, Mary, Steve and the whole staff will give you suggestions on drinks and bourbons. They have Old Grand Dad and just about everything there, as well as some of the best pub grub in town. Helpful hint: Don't order a double, you're getting one anyway. Prices are low there. They are only closed one night a year: New Years Eve. Can you believe it? I asked John why, and he said it was because he got tired of babysitting amateurs.

Outlook Inn–916 Baxter Avenue–Louisville, KY 40204 (at Christy)–Look for the Falls City Beer sign outside (my dad and grandfather's brewery). There are a couple pool tables in the back, but this is just a great little corner bar. They also have Falls City Beer on tap there, so have an old one (old Grand Dad) and a cold one (Falls City).

Molly Malone's Irish Pub–933 Baxter Avenue–Louisville, KY 40204. This is an authentic Irish bar with authentic Irish folk working there. Donnell owns the place, and they've done so well they've opened a second Louisville location in St. Matthews, and another in Covington, Kentucky. They have a trivia night early in the week and great live music on the weekends.

O'Shea's–956 Baxter Avenue–Louisville, KY 40204. Another great Irish pub. Tommy O'Shea owns this place, as well as Flanagan's down one block and Patrick O'Shea's downtown at Second and Main. If the weather is nice, they have one of the best outside areas in the whole state!

Cahoots–1047 Bardstown Road–Louisville, KY 40204 (Baxter turns into Bardstown Road). This is a dive bar, make no mistake, but with very chill atmosphere. If you like dive bars and heavy metal music, you'll *love* this place. It's owned by Marsha, and they have a great bourbon selection. They even carry Old Grand Dad 114, which I highly recommend. Drinks are cheap with liberal pours there.

Highlands Tap Room–1279 Bardstown Road–Louisville, KY 40204 (across from Mid City Mall and Skyline Chili). Tommy owns the place, and Kevin and Will are my buddies there who bartend. The Tap Room is known for the most fun karaoke in town. They have a decent bourbon selection as well and a great outdoor area for conversation and watching folks on Bardstown Road…good people watching.

Shenanigan's Pub–1611 Norris Place (at Deerwood Ave.). Good food, drink and 16 flat screens to watch all the sports and live music ost weekends. Eddie owns the joint, and Rick keeps it rollin'.

Nachbar–969 Charles Street–Louisville, KY 40204 (at Krieger St.). They have an absolutely brilliant beer selection and a nice bourbon list. Retro is big there, so Old Fitzgerald, Old Forester and Old Grand Dad are popular. Chill hipster scene. One of my favorite places to take visitors just to have a nice beer and a shot, and to hang out with friends. It's where all the cool kids hang out.

Third Street Dive–440 S. Third Street–Louisville, KY 40202 (right down the alley from Fourth Street Live!) It's the hang-out bar for all the staff at Fourth Street Live but with much cheaper prices for drinks. For entertainment, there is a real Diamond pool table and darts. Steve owns the place and is from Bardstown, so it has a good bourbon selection. As an interesting side note, he used to be the paper boy for the legendary distiller Booker Noe.

St. Matthews Area – Lots of locally owned pubs and eateries, only 5 miles from downtown

Joe's Older Than Dirt–8131 New La Grange Road –Louisville, KY 40222. Joe's is owned by Gary and Janet Gish, and it's a neighborhood bar that transforms into a larger neighborhood gathering place later at night. It has good food and a great bourbon selection. Check out the case at the entrance and you'll find some really cool Prohibition bourbons on display. This is also an Indianapolis Colts Bar, so stop by to watch a game if you're around during the season. You see, in Louisville we have no pro teams, so fans of different teams go to bars that are headquarters for their favorite NFL teams. It's a pretty cool dynamic and very Louisville! Join in on the fun.

R Place Pub–9603 Whipps Mill Road–Louisville, KY 40242. Known for its outdoor sand volleyball leagues, this bar is owned by Cres and Scott and is a great neighborhood hang-out. Jim Beam's R&D folk have a volleyball team every year playing on Thursday nights, and the Pittsburgh Steelers fans pack in here for football season.

Diamond Pub & Billiards–3814 Frankfort Avenue –Louisville, KY 40207. This is a great pool hall with a dozen or so Diamond pool tables, including a regulation nine-footer! It has a great bourbon selection and great live music almost every night. This is where I play music with my buddy Robbie Bartlett every once in a while, so stop by. Jared runs the bar there and Griff is the owner. Great friendly staff there, and it's a great place to watch all the football and basketball games, with TVs a plenty. Right smack dab in the middle of all the bars in St. Matthews.

Gerstle's Pub–3801 Frankfort Avenue–Louisville, KY 40207. With great live music and a great bar, this is one of the most recognized neighborhood bars in Louisville. My cousin's band, Dallas Alice, performs there from time to time, as do other great acts. It's the home of the Minnesota Vikings, so if you're a fan of the Vik's, get your ass to Gerstle's to watch the game. You can go down and taunt the Packers fans at Dutch's at half-time. The Pranksters perform there, and they are one of the best bands on the entire planet, no joke. They are easily the best band playing on a Sunday night anywhere in the United States. They play every Wednesday and Sunday, but I really love Sundays. They also have Falls City Beer on tap there. The Pranksters play originals and cool covers. They've been together for like 100 years, so they nail everything they perform. They cover "The Walrus." I mean come on, if the Beatles were all here alive today, they couldn't play "The Walrus."

Patrick's–3202 Frankfort Avenue–Louisville, KY 40206. This is a little neighborhood pub just down the street from Gerstle's. It has pool tables and a nice little patio out back, and has one of the coolest beer coolers I've ever seen. It's an antique in the shape of a beer bottle, but it still keeps the beer nice and frosty cold.

Frankfort Avenue Beer Depot–3204 Frankfort Avenue–Louisville, KY 40206 (directly next door and shares a parking lot with Patrick's). It just serves beer (thus the Beer Depot) and has some of the best BBQ in town. Known for "Beerhalla" miniature golf out back, since the "Valhalla" golf course is here in Louisville, too. Relive your own Ryder Cup at FABD as the locals call it.

Brendan O'Shea's Irish Pub– 3921 Shelbyville Road, Louisville, KY40207. Owned by the same folks who own O'Shea's and Flanagan's, Brendan's is right in the heart of St. Matthews and is always lively no matter what night of the week you're there. It has a nice menu and is just a fun place.

Molly Malone's–3900 Shelbyville Road–Louisville, KY 40207. This is Molly's St. Matthews location. If you follow soccer or rugby, this is going to be your spot. Molly's has a great beer selection and nice bourbons to choose from, too. Brendan runs this place, not from across the street but from across the pond in Ireland, and he's a great guy. The whole staff is terrific, and Molly's is always poppin' with fun people. The food is pretty damn good, too.

Dutch's–3922 Shelbyville Road–Louisville, KY 40207. Dutch's has been in business since 1929! It's the home of the Green Bay Packers, so if you're a fan, grab your cheese head and go watch them play, but get there early 'cause it's where all the Packers fans pack in to watch a game. Don't forget to walk down to Gerstle's at half-time and give the Vikings fans a little hell.

PLACES TO EAT

Here are some suggestions of places to eat breakfast, lunch and dinner. Louisville is home to some of the best locally owned restaurants in the country. Per capita we have more restaurants and eat out more often than most cities in the nation.

Breakfast places:

Lynn's Paradise Café, 984 Barret Ave, Louisville, KY 40204 (lynnsparadisecafe.com). Featured in the *New York Times* and on the "Today" show, Lynn's is really something to see and experience. *Bon Appetit* voted Lynn's one of the top 100 best neighborhood restaurants in the United States. Its kitschy décor is fun and the food is great.

North End Café, 1722 Frankfort Ave, Louisville, KY 40206 (northendcafe.com). Located just a couple miles from downtown is a great neighborhood place with great food all day, but I really enjoy breakfast here. They also have a great bourbon selection. Don't be bashful about ordering a Bloody Mary and substituting bourbon for the vodka. It's one of my favorite cocktails.

Toast on Market, 736 East Market, Louisville, KY 40202 (toastonmarket.com). Toast has great breakfast and is always popular any day of the week. Toast is just what a breakfast place should be. You may have to wait a little bit to get a table, but once you get one, it's not a drawn-out thing. It's where Goldilocks would enjoy breakfast; it's just right.

Wagner's Pharmacy – 3113 South 4th Street, Louisville, KY 40214. (4th Street and Central) Since 1922, Churchill Downs is Wagner's and Wagner's is Churchill Downs, and yes, it's inside a pharmacy. It's the city's most famous breakfast joint, especially Derby Week. Racing History drips from the walls and the ceiling. D. Wayne Lucas, Nick Zito, and other horse trainers and celebrities all pack in to this hole in the wall joint across from the track to sop up gravy with biscuits and have some of the best sausage, eggs, and bacon Southern Style.

LUNCH PLACES:

August Moon 2269 Lexington Road Louisville, KY 40206 (augustmoonbistro.com). A fusion of Chinese and Malaysian cuisine, renowned chef Peng S.Looi has been invited as a guest chef at the James Beard Foundation on numerous occasions. You can get an awesome dinner here, too, as you can imagine, with a very cool atmosphere. They have an *awesome* homemade chili pepper oil that is hot and spicy and just wonderful drizzled on anything.

Ramsis Café on the World 1293 Bardstown Road Louisville, KY 40204 (ramsiscafe.com) Louisville, KY 40204–is on Bardstown Road in the heart of the Highlands, where we locals like to eat/drink. Featuring dishes from all over the world, this is one place you'll love to come back and visit each time you come to Louisville.

Dish on Market–434 W. Market Street–Louisville, KY 40202–502.315.0669 (www.dishonmarket.com). My buddy Anderson opened this place, and it's got a brisk breakfast and lunch business Monday through Friday, and they serve up damn good grub. In addition to breakfast and lunch, they have happy hour until 7:00 pm. The restaurant has a nice little bourbon selection, and Anderson has been to several of the distilleries and has a genuine passion for bourbon.

Kern's Korner–2600 Bardstown Road–Louisville, KY 40205–was founded by Mr. Kern, who used to work with my dad at the Falls City Brewing Company. Kern's has great chili, soups and burgers and is a great place to hang out with the locals and have a casual lunch.

Bambi Bar–2701 Bardstown Road–Louisville, KY 40205–is famous for the Bambi Beer Walk and the Bambi Burger. It has one of the best dang burgers in town. The #1 has fries, the #2 has cheese, and the #3 comes with onion rings. It doesn't get any simpler than that. It's a dive bar, folks, so don't wear a tie or a dress, just put on your jeans and go on in.

Dinner places

Jeff Ruby's–325 W. Main Street–Louisville, KY 40202–502.584.0102 (jeffruby.com). Eat where O.J. can't. Jeff Ruby asked O.J. Simpson to leave his place a couple Derbys ago. He serves up some of the best steak and seafood around. My buddy Robbie Bartlett's band plays there almost every weekend. It's not cheap, but it's worth every penny.

Jack Fry's–1007 Bardstown Road–Louisville, KY 40204–502.452.9244 (jackfrys.com, at Baxter Avenue and Highland Avenue at the foot of the Highlands). Many locals will tell you that Jack Fry's is the best restaurant in Louisville, period. Great live jazz during the week, wonderful food, and the décor takes you back to the 1960s. It doesn't get much better than this.

Lilly's–1147 Bardstown Road–Louisville, KY 40204 – 502.451.0447 (lillyslapeche.com). Lilly's bills itself as a Kentucky bistro, and its menu is shaped by the produce and meats available from community farms and its own organic garden. Lilly's is located right in the heart of the Highlands, just a couple miles from downtown hotels.

Avalon–1314 Bardstown Road–Louisville, KY 40204–502.454-5336 (avalonfresh.com). Also in the Highlands on Bardstown Road, Avalon has a great atmosphere and an especially delightful outdoor dining area to enjoy the Kentucky springs and falls. And when it gets hot and humid, they have misters that take care of that, too.

Asiatique–1767 Bardstown Road–Louisville, KY 40205–502.451.2749 (asiatiquerestaurant.com). On the edge of the Highlands just about three miles from downtown, its food, décor, and multilevel dining rooms are all fascinating. They boast Pacific Rim cuisine in a relaxed elegant atmosphere. They have about 40 bourbons and are applying to be a part of the Urban Bourbon Trail.

Blind Pig–1076 E. Washington Street, Louisville, KY 40206. A mile from downtown, this is a great place for lunch or dinner. The Blind Pig is in Butchertown (where all the meat processing plants and stock yards used to be), and the atmosphere, menu and cocktails are great. All the barstools are made from bourbon barrel staves and built by hand by one of the bartenders there. The Bacon Butty and the Ivory Bacon Sandwich are my favorites. What can I say, I like bacon, plus it's the Blind Pig–hello? Good cocktails are crafted by Jeremy and his bar staff. I also like the fact that when the owners go on vacation, the place closes down. I love that! If they're not going to be there, no one will.

Bistro Le Relais–2817 Taylorsville Road–Louisville, KY 40205–502.451.9020 (lerelaisrestaurant.com). Located in historic Bowman Field, Louisville's original airport, the Bistro is fine dining with exquisite French cuisine. Anthony Dike is the owner. first-class service and an intimate, 1940s art-deco interior reminiscent of the café from the movie "Casablanca

Equus –122 Sears Avenue–Louisville, KY 40207–502.897.9721 (equusrestaurant.com)–has great food and a good bourbon selection. Bartender Joy has her book on cocktails there at

Equus. Go there and buy her book and have her sign if for ya!

Corbett's–5050 Norton's Health Care Blvd–Louisville, KY 40241–502.327.5058 (corbettsrestaurant.com). Owned by Chef Corbett from Equus, this location is about 10 miles east. Corbett's features an inventive menu and cutting-edge technology. Built in the historic Von Allmen mansion, which once housed Kentucky's first working dairy farm, Corbett's boasts a stunning interior design, a menu with the highest quality ingredients, extensive wine list, impressive artisanal cheese selection and an interactive digital chef's table.

We also have great neighborhood bars and pizza places in the Highlands and right downtown.

Downtown

Bistro 311–301 W. Market (Third and Market)–502.584.8337–A great place with good food, Bistro is close to the Marriott and other downtown hotels and right across from the downtown convention center.

Bearno's by the Bridge–131 W. Main Street (at the Second Street Bridge)–502.584.7437. Bearno's serves pizza and Italian food, and sometimes acoustic acts there, too. It's a nice little bar to hang out or watch a ballgame.

Patrick O'Shea's–123 West Main Street–Louisville, KY 40202–502.708.2488 (osheaslouisville.net). At the foot of the Second Street Bridge, this gorgeous building is a great place for lunch or dinner. It's a great place to hang out downtown, as well.

Highlands/St. Matthews

Molly Malone's–933 Baxter Avenue–Louisville, KY 40204–502.473.1222 (mollymalonesirishpub.com). This is an authentic Irish pub with authentic Irish people. They have a pub quiz early in the week, and dining inside and out.

O'Shea's Irish Pub–(www.osheaslouisville.net)–Wherever you find yourself either downtown, the Highlands or St. Matthews, you'll find one of these great fun pubs.

Wick's Pizza–971 Baxter Avenue–502.458.1828 (wickspizza.com)–Home of the "Big Wick," this is a Louisville favorite when it comes to pizza. It has good entertainment on the weekends, too.

Impellizzeri's Pizza–1381 Bardstown Road–502.454.2711 (impellizzeris.com)– Famous in Louisville, and right in the Highlands. Impellizzeris Pizza uses only the finest and freshest ingredients, which is why it's no wonder we've been voted "Best Of Louisville Magazine" a whopping SIX TIMES! They offer this award-winning pizza alongside a full menu of Italian-style dishes from appetizers to salads to hoagie sandwiches and mouth watering pasta dishes. A new location on Main Street just down from the new Yum Center Arena too.

LEXINGTON, KENTUCKY

Lexington is a smaller city than Louisville, but it's just as much fun. I went to college there at the University of Kentucky. *The Bourbon Review* is published there, and it's the perfect place to stay when you visit the distilleries on the Eastern Shelf: Buffalo Trace, Woodford Reserve, Wild Turkey and Four Roses.

I'd suggest visiting Wild Turkey and Four Roses one day, and then Woodford Reserve and Buffalo Trace the next. Lexington doesn't have the equivalent of the Urban Bourbon Trail (yet), but there are a few places, including hotels, that carry a nice selection of bourbon.

Downtown Lexington Hotels

Lexington Hilton Hotel–369 W. Vine Street–Lexington, KY 40507–859.231.9000. This hotel is right in the heart of Lexington and within walking distance to many fine restaurants and watering holes. It has the Bigg Blue Martini Bar off the lobby–a great name for being in the home of the Big Blue Kentucky Wildcats. The bar also has a nice bourbon selection and live music often on the weekends.

Hyatt Regency–401 W. High Street–Lexington, KY 40507–859.253.1234. The Hyatt is right across the street from the Hilton and ideally located near downtown watering holes. The Hyatt is actually connected to Rupp Arena where the University of Kentucky plays basketball, so if you want to see Wildcat basketball madness up close, go for it! They've got a very nice lobby bar in the atrium with a nice bourbon selection, so it's a great place to start or end your evening on your Lexington visit.

Crowne Plaza–1375 S. Broadway–Lexington, KY 40504–859.255.4281 Just a mile or so down the road from the Hyatt, the Crowne Plaza Campbell House was renovated in 2005. Bogart's is the bar there, and it has a variety of bourbons.

Marriott – Griffin Gate. Located a few miles out of town and right off I-64, this hotel boasts a great golf course that was host to a couple Senior PGA Tour events. Large hotel, nice bar, too. The Marriott here is located right off I-64.

WHERE TO GO FOR A COCKTAIL/AFTER DINNER DRINKS:

Horse and Barrel–101 N. Broadway–2008 Global Icons of Whisky Award winning account by *Whisky Magazine*. This is a gorgeous bar and well appointed with bourbon and other whiskies from around the world. This bar is attached to deSha's and has a nice bar menu. You have to walk out of deSha's and enter the Horse and Barrel from its own entrance. Home of the "Bluegrass Bourbon Club" where members learn more about bourbon by tasting all 53 bourbons they carry there. Their "Kentucky Margarita" is very popular.

Redmond's–269 W. Main Street, Lexington, KY 40507. This is Larry Redmond's live music bar. Larry is a great singer/performer and has some of the best talent in the area appearing there all the time. If live music is up your alley, come on by and have a good time with Larry and everyone else who's there enjoying the same.

Bluegrass Tavern–115 Cheapside Street–Lexington, KY 40507. Also owned by Larry Redmond, this bar offers more bourbon and American whiskey than any other bar, period. That would be 187; Larry's counted them. Led by head mixologist, Chris, all the bartenders have on a white shirt, black trousers and black tie, and they are eager to help you select a bourbon and/or a cocktail if you need such a suggestion. I've helped train the staff there, too, since I've done a couple bourbon tastings there. It's located right on the pavilion downtown on Cheapside, so in nice weather it's a huge outdoor patio party on the whole block.

Al's Bar–601 N. Limestone, Lexington, KY 40508. Josh is one of the owners and he prides himself on specializing in local "everything," from ingredients in food to over 30 bourbons, and he hosts a great variety of local music talent nearly every night of the week. Their house specialty cocktail is called the "Kentucky Cocktail," which is your favorite bourbon mixed with a local ginger ale called Ale 8. Can I suggest an Old Grand Dad with that, anyone?

Cheapside Tavern–131 Cheapside Street–Lexington, KY 40507–859.254.0046 (cheapsidebarandgrill.com). Good food and live music, too. It's located on the opposite end of the block from Redmond's. My Louisville buddy and singing partner, Robbie Bartlett, performs there from time to time. Cheapside Street has been turned into a pavilion and is one rockin' outside area when the weather permits, which is often!

Austin City–2350 Woodhill Drive–Lexington, KY 40509 (austincitysaloon.com) Just a couple miles from downtown Lexington, this is a shit-kicking country bar with great bands. My buddy Puddin' Howell plays there regularly. This is where Troy Gentry of Montgomery Gentry won a contest sponsored by Jim Beam, and to this day, Jim Beam and Montgomery Gentry have a mutual partnership spreading good music and good bourbon wherever they travel.

The Grapevine–4101 Tates Creek Centre Drive–Lexington, KY 40517. The Grapevine is a comfortable neighborhood bar with good pub grub. They also have TVs to watch all the Wildcats games. They have a stage with live music, where the owner of the joint gets up and plays, too. FUN!

Jakes Cigar Bar–263 East Brannon Road–Nicholasville, KY 40356 (www.jakescigarbar.com). Located just 10 minutes south of downtown Lexington on Nicholasville Road (US 27) in the Brannon Crossing Shopping Centre. Jack Glancy owns the joint and it's only been open since April 2010, but it's the only place you can go in Lexington (or Louisville, for that matter) to enjoy fine cigar brands from all over the world, along with a choice of 50 bourbons. They don't have food, so it's a perfect after-dinner stop. Take the short drive out to Brannon Crossing and have a great smoke, great bourbon and stellar conversation.

Breakfast

Tally Ho's–395 S. Limestone–Lexington, KY 40508. The only place for authentic college grub! This is a little greasy spoon, where extra grease is no extra charge. It takes me back to my college days every time. It's one of the few places in the world where I order a chocolate milkshake with breakfast! Yummie!

Breakfast/Lunch

Ramsey's–496 E. High Street–Lexington, KY 40507–859.259.2708. There are three other Ramsey's in town, so check out their website for them (ramseysdiners.com). Ramsey's offers great breakfast and just good food all the way around. Sunday mornings are particularly fun with their brunch menu. Plan on waiting awhile though, but even waiting for breakfast there is kind of cool.

Dinner

deSha's–101 N. Broadway–Lexington, KY 40507–859.259.3771 (tavernrestaurantgroup.com). In business since

1985, it's right in the heart of downtown on Main and Broadway and across from the Hyatt and Hilton. The chef is very creative cooking with bourbon there, and it was voted by *Whisky Magazine* as a 2008 Icons of Whisky Bar of the Year globally.

Dudley's–259 W. Short Street–Lexington, KY 40502–859.252.1010 (dudleysrestaurant.com). Dudley's Restaurant has been a mainstay on the Lexington gathering and dining scene for the last 28 years. Great food and atmosphere. I like it!

Baker's 360–201 East Main Street–Lexington, KY 40507–859.523.7797 (bakers360.us). Great steakhouse and seafood. A buddy of mine from San Diego recently went there and said it was the best sushi he's ever had, and he's from California! After dinner it turns into a nightclub and bar. Really cool new spot in Lexington.

Portofino–249 E. Main Street–Lexington, KY 40507–859.253.9300. Portofino is in a nicely renovated building downtown and serves northern Italian food. If you're looking for some good wine on your visit to bourbon country, know that Portofino earned the *Wine Spectator* Award eight years in a row, from 2003 through 2010, for their varied selection.

Malone's/Harry's–3347 Tates Creek Drive–Lexington, KY 40502–859.335.6500 (malonesrestaurant.com, in the Landsdowne Shopping Center). Always makes the top 10 great steak houses in the United States by all the inflight magazines I see when I'm traveling around country. Awesome seafood, too. Malone's is the more formal (although dress is casual), and Harry's is the hangout bar area with a great menu as well. Malone's ownership is proud to claim that they carry prime beef that's considered to be the top 1.5-2% of the beef served in the whole world! Now that's a statement. They have the Big Lex cocktail, which is Maker's Mark bourbon with Kentucky Proud blackberries and strawberries which have been infused into a simple syrup with a splash of 7UP and a squeeze of lemon and lime.

Sal's/Oscar's–3373 Tates Creek Road–Lexington, KY 40502 (bluegrasshospitality.com). Actually in the same shopping center as Malone's and Drake's. That's how good these places are: They compete directly with themselves! It's just a great experience, and once you go, it won't be for the last time. The outdoor patio at Sal's is always hopping from Keeneland's spring meet through the summer, of course, and until the fall meet ends before it gets too cold. Trust me, this is where all the pretty people are.

Merrick Inn–1074 Merrick Drive–Lexington, KY 40502–859.269.5417. Merrick Inn is without a doubt the oldest and most traditional dining experience in Lexington. The bar area and patio are an experience all on their own.

Bellini's—115 W. Main Street, Lexington, KY 40507 (bellinislexington.com). Italian cuisine with use of locally grown seasonal ingredients. Bellini's has a great atmosphere, a classy bar, great food and a nice bourbon selection, too.

Eddie Montgomery's Steakhouse–180 Lucky Man Way–Harrodsburg, KY 40330–859-734-3400 (eddiemontgomery-steakhouse.com). Eddie is the Montgomery of dynamic county music duo, Montgomery Gentry. They are Jim Beam guys through and through and are personal friends of Fred and the Beam family. This is quite a showplace in Harrodsburg, which is a little bit of a drive from Lexington (or Louisville), but it's sure a treat and worth the drive.

7
How to Host a Bourbon Tasting at Your Home

"They say that some of my stars drink whiskey. I have found that the ones that drink milk shakes don't win many ballgames."
– Casey Stengel

Now that you know about the history and heritage of our native spirit, and you know how to read a label and find your favorite bourbons, you're going to want to show off your knowledge and host a bourbon tasting for your friends and family. The first thing you'll want to do is figure out a fun tasting of four or five bourbons/whiskies. That might sound like a lot of alcohol, but if you only pour a quarter-ounce of bourbon in each tasting cup, it's equivalent to just one drink. You'll want to start with the lowest-proof bourbon and go up to the highest proof. If you start with the higher-proof bourbons and go lower, their more intense flavors will overpower those of the lower-proof bourbons. Always drink smart and be aware of your guests; if they need a lift home, of course provide one.

Not all of your guests will be bourbon drinkers, so you'll want to have drinks for them as well. You might want to have a featured cocktail for them to try. A delicious cocktail would be Ms. Annis' Bourbon Sour since you can batch them and pour them out as your guests arrive. It's a very refreshing cocktail that even vodka and gin drinkers will enjoy.

Appetizers are a must since you will be sampling spirits. Various sliced meats, cheeses and crackers are always good, and then whatever your favorite apps are for any party.

Map out the bourbons you'd like to sample. It's best to start with a younger bourbon, either 80 or 86 proof, and then move up in age and/or proof. Remember that some bourbons are high rye bourbons (Old Grand Dad, Basil Hayden's, Four Roses), and some use wheat instead of rye (Maker's Mark, W.L. Weller, Van Winkle). And then you have the single-barrel and small-batch bourbons (Blanton's, Knob Creek, Evan Williams Vintage, etc.).

Here are some tastings I've done in the past just as an example for you:

Sample One

Jim Beam Black 8-year-old, 86 proof

Maker's Mark 90 proof

Elijah Craig 12-year-old, 94 proof

Four Roses single barrel 100 proof

Baker's 7-year-old, 107 proof

Sample Two

Basil Hayden's 8-year-old, 80 proof

Woodford Reserve 90.4 proof

Knob Creek 9-year-old, 100 proof

Pappy Van Winkle 15-year-old, 107 proof

Booker's 6-8-year-old, 121-130 proof

Sample Three

Jack Daniel's 80 proof

Jim Beam White Label or Black Label 80/86 proof

Old Fitzgerald 80/86 proof, proof

Wild Turkey 101 proof

Old Grand Dad 114 proof.

You might want to taste different styles of bourbon:

Sample Four

Basil Hayden's 8-year-old, 80 proof (high rye bourbon)

Bulleit 90 proof (high rye bourbon)

Elijah Craig 18-year-old, 90 proof (traditional bourbon recipe, single barrel)

Knob Creek 9-year-old, 100 proof (traditional bourbon recipe, small batch)

Old Weller 7-year-old, 107 proof (wheat bourbon)

Whatever you choose, it will be fun putting bourbons and whiskies together to taste. Pick one or two that you've never tasted before, so you can experience it along with your friends during the tasting.

Now look at your guest list and see how many people are coming and multiply that number by five or six or however many bourbons/whiskies you will be tasting. If you have five whiskies to taste and you have two or three people over, you'll need five glasses for each plus yourself; so you'll need 20 glasses/cups. If you have 15 or 20 people coming, you will need 100 glasses/cups for the tasting. Not many people have 100 shot glasses or wine glasses, so in that case I'd go to the liquor/party store and buy hard plastic or two-ounce or two-and-a-half-ounce shot glasses. They usually come in packages of 50 and cost three or four dollars each.

Next you will need to craft a "tasting mat" for the glasses/cups to sit on. You can make one yourself by using a blank sheet of paper and, with a Sharpie pen, tracing around one of the plastic glasses to make a circle (see my sample on the next page). If there are five bourbons in your tasting, trace five glass-sized circles on the mat with a Sharpie, and then put the name of the bourbon down in the order left to right, using one or two columns. You can print the name of each bourbon/whiskey under the circle. You also might want to note the age and proof and whether it's a bourbon, scotch, rye, Irish, etc.

JOHN'S BOURBON TASTING

WOODFORD RESERVE
NO AGE STATEMENT
90.4°

POPPY VAN WINKLE
15 YEARS OLD
107°

BASIL HAYDEN'S
8 YEARS OLD
80°

KNOB CREEK
9 YEARS OLD
100°

BOOKER'S
6-8 YEARS OLD
121-130°

Put a cup on each circle and pour out the bourbon for your guests right before you all sit down. You don't want to pour more than 30 minutes before you sit down, as that little amount of whiskey in the glass will be exposed to the air and can turn it cloudy. You're only pouring a quarter-ounce or so in each glass. You can use a jigger to pour them out accurately if you prefer, or just use a speed pourer. You will also want to have small bottles of water for your guests so they can add water to the bourbon if they like or just sip between tastes. Crackers on the table would be good, too, so guests can cleanse between tastes if they wish.

Then lead your guests in a tasting. Here's how I'd lead them for each brand, with a little bit about what flavors they will be discovering in each expression.

Start out by telling them that bourbon and rye whiskey are truly American creations. Canadian Whiskey has different grains distilled separately and then blended together. Scotch and Irish whiskies use only barley. Bourbon uses predominantly corn, rye and barley, all ground and cooked, fermented, and distilled *together*. Rye uses those same grains cooked, fermented, and distilled together, but the predominant grain in the recipe is rye.

Corn is the native crop of North America, and because of that and its rich history and heritage in helping to form this country, Congress declared bourbon the native spirit of the United States. President Lyndon Baines Johnson signed it into law in 1964. So not only is it delicious to drink bourbon, it's your patriotic damn duty to drink bourbon! Also share with them some of your stories of bourbon: the proof story, George Washington and Jacob Beam, how the barrel first became charred, and how bourbon got its name.

There are certain flavors you get from the grains. You get the sweetness and the full body from the corn. Rye brings a really nice spice flavor. Think of eating some corn bread, and then some rye bread. This will help you imagine the different flavors of corn and rye. We use just a little bit of barley, and we use it mostly for the starches to help convert the sugars into alcohol by the yeast, so we are getting little or no flavor from the barley. If the distiller uses wheat instead of rye, more of the sweetness of the corn will come through, so wheated bourbons are typically softer and sweeter than rye bourbons.

Aging the bourbon in the charred barrels is responsible for 75% of the flavor of the finished product. All of the red/amber color of bourbon and rye comes from the barrel. The liquor goes in the barrel clear like vodka, and years later the natural sugars in the wood impart the color and flavors to the whiskey. Wood notes you want to look for in these whiskies are vanilla, maple, caramel, ginger, various toasted nuts and oak. Some people with astute noses and taste buds will taste different flavors like leather, tobacco, peppermint, and on and on, but they all come from the interaction of the grains with the barrel. The length of time it spends in the barrel will dictate how many wood notes are in the whiskey. It takes six years to start getting big vanilla notes in a bourbon. So if you taste really pronounced vanilla notes, then that bourbon is probably six or more years old. If you taste more citrus notes in a bourbon, that bourbon is more than likely four or five years old in the barrel.

So let's taste these and see what notes we get. Booker Noe used to tell folks to use these four steps in tasting bourbons.

Step One: Look at the color and compare it to the others on the mat. The darker the color, the longer the bourbon has been aged and the higher proof it will be compared to the lighter ones on the mat.

Step Two: Nose the bourbon/whiskey. Put your nose into the glass, but part your lips so you are not taking all that high-proof alcohol up your nose. This isn't wine, its high-proof alcohol with many layers of aromas and flavors, so don't take it all in your nose at once.

Step Three: Place your tongue on the side of the glass and put enough whiskey in your mouth to get to the middle of your tongue and then "chew" it. This will achieve the same result as "swishing," but since it is high proof, the chewing will distribute the spirit to your entire palate. Fred Noe, Booker's son, calls this the "Kentucky Chew," and it's something his dad taught him. It works really well in tasting bourbon.

Step Four: Assess the finish. Is it short? Medium? Long? Is it empty, does it fade away cleanly or linger? Short finishes usually dictate lighter proof and/or younger aging. For some people a short finish is preferred to a long finish. You just don't want an empty finish or one that is metallic or unpleasant.

Finish off the tasting with the "Bourbon Pledge." This is something I wrote a couple years ago, and it really helps to emphasize to people that bourbon is the native spirit of the United States. It also ends the tasting on a really nice note.

You can copy the pledge from the book here, put four on a page, and print it at Kinko's, too.

THE BOURBON PLEDGE

I pledge to open my heart and my taste buds
to the native spirit of the United States: bourbon!

I acknowledge the history
and heritage of this unique spirit.

I understand that all bourbon is whiskey,
but not all whiskey is bourbon.

I pledge to always have
bourbon whiskey available:

For those who arrive as strangers
yet leave as friends,

And for those who arrive as friends
and leave as family.

This I pledge from this taste forward.

So raise your favorite bourbon to salute our
country's native spirit...BOURBON...Cheer's, ya'll!

8

My Favorite Bourbon Recipes

"My grandmother is over 80 and still doesn't need glasses. She drinks right out of the bottle." –Henny Youngman

There are several classic bourbon cocktails: julep, sour, old fashioned, Manhattan and highball. Each has a great history behind them. The oldest bourbon cocktail is probably the Julep.

Derby Day, 1966–I made my first mint julep

My real first experience with bourbon was tied to the Derby, as it is for many Kentuckians. Since the brewery where my dad worked owned box seats at Churchill Downs for executives and customers, my parents had to go to the Kentucky Derby every year. Darn! They'd leave early that first Saturday of May, and they wouldn't get back home 'til seven or later that night. Four of my dad's sisters would come over and watch us and enjoy the festivities of Derby Day. Aunts Regina, Bernadine, Michelle and Margaret–or as we called them, Jean, Bern, Mike and Maggie–were more like our grandparents than aunts. So it made Derby even more special in our house when they visited.

Now, in Louisville on Derby Day, the local TV stations broadcast the entire day of races and festivities before the featured race, the Kentucky Derby, the most exciting two minutes in all of sport. So it's like the Macy's parade, only all day long. When I was seven years old, my aunt Bern decided to start a new Derby tradition and put *me* in charge of making the family mint juleps. The result is that I make a *killer* mint julep. Aunt Bern had the best recipe; it's *so* easy and works in any-sized container.

To start, you take a silver mint julep cup–or a gallon pitcher, it doesn't really matter–and pour a quarter-inch of sugar on the bottom. Then you pile in about an inch (loosely stacked) of mint leaves fresh off the stalks. Muddle those loose leaves into the sugar with a wooden spoon. Pack crushed ice on top of it and then put the container in the fridge all day (or overnight).

When you're ready to serve, add the bourbon and more crushed ice along with several sprigs of mint sticking out of the top so you can bury your nose in it as you sip and savor and enjoy! The melted ice and sugar make the simple syrup for the julep. Just so you don't think too poorly of my Aunt Bern, she's the one who always added the bourbon when I was seven. I wasn't in charge of alcohol until I was at least nine.

Right before the big race, when "My Old Kentucky Home" played, we would all sing along and pass the silver mint julep cup around to everyone in the family, young and old. And then when the bell rang and the gates opened up and the track announcer said, "And they're off..." we would again pass around this tasty refreshing piece of history as we watched the race unfold on TV. I swear it was one of the most thrilling times to be alive! I get goose bumps and a little misty just writing about it here. (Let me go grab a drink–ahhhh OK.) So who won the Derby that year in 1966 when I made my first mint julep? Kauai King with Don Brumfield up.

In my comedy act, I explain the Derby to folks who have never been there. I say that the Kentucky Derby is like Mardi Gras, except everyone's facing the same way.

When you see me at different events, more than likely I will have one of those cups from my family's sterling silver mint julep sets. Since my parents and my aunts are all drinking with the angels now, it's a way to pay tribute to the important place bourbon has had in my history.

As a side note, the mint julep is based on an Arabic drink called a "julab" made with water and rose petals. Hmmmm ... a drink made from water and leaves. Is it just me, or does that remind anyone else of tea? It morphed into the mint julep here in the United States with either rum or bourbon and mint leaves. The bourbon version has been the most popular, as it has been the official drink of Churchill Downs and the Kentucky Derby since 1938. Who won the Kentucky Derby that year? Lawrin with Eddie Arcaro aboard.

Aunt Bernadine's Mint Julep

Ingredients:

Sugar

Basil Hayden's eight-year-old 80-proof bourbon–you want a lighter bourbon that doesn't overpower the mint, so pick your bourbon accordingly.

Fresh mint

Ice/water

In the bottom of any container (works with a glass, a pitcher, or an infusion jar) put about a quarter-inch of sugar. Add a small amount of water, pull 10 or more mint leaves off the stems, and then muddle them in the bottom of the container with the sugar. Fill the container with ice and place in the fridge for several hours. Pull from fridge and fill the container with Basil Hayden bourbon. Top it off with water, if needed. If larger than a glass, put in 1.5 ounces per every 12 ounces of the container. For example, if it's a 24-ounce container, put in three ounces of bourbon. If it's a 36-ounce container, put in 4½ ounces, and so on.

Sour

The whiskey sour is a classic and was written about in the very first cocktail book in 1862 by Jerry Thomas. Jerry is the father of American mixology. His creativity and showmanship established the image of the bartender as a creative professional. His book in 1862 was titled, *The Bar-Tender's Guide* (alternately titled *How to Mix Drinks* or *The Bon-Vivant's Companion*).

The sour recipe I will share with you is my absolute favorite and a favorite at every bourbon festival. I first had it at the Bourbon Gala about six years ago. It's the Noe family's recipe, and it's so simple and so delicious!

Stocking your bar with bourbon

So now you know what bourbon is, how it's made, even how to read a label. Now it's time to go out and stock your bar with some great bourbons so you can share with your friends and family. You can't really go wrong with any bourbons, so don't be afraid. When asked my advice on what bourbons to stock at home, I always say go for the classic old-school bourbons with the iconic names and history. Follow the history, and you'll find yourself with some great stuff. If you've been paying attention in this book, you should have a pretty good idea of what bourbons I'm talking about. Then go out and have some small-batch and single-barrel bourbons at a bar or restaurant and find the ones you like and add them. Like when you build a house you need a good foundation before you can add the amenities, it's the same deal here. Get a nice foundation of all types of bourbons and ryes, and then you can add to them with the small-batch and single-barrel bourbons. So if you're asking me, here's what I'd put on my bar for my foundation:

Old Grand Dad–*86, 100 bonded and 114. Get one or all three, you can't go wrong.*

Heaven Hill–*bottled in bond 100 proof–a good bonded bourbon you just gotta have*

Evan Williams–*86 proof–It doesn't get much more classic than that.*

Old Crow Reserve–*86 proof – old school and a great four-year-old bourbon for the price*

Old Forester–*86 proof, 100 proof–the flagship for Brown-Foreman and just a great bourbon*

Wild Turkey–*101 proof–the Kickin' Chicken*

Old Overholt Straight Rye–*80 proof–classic Monongahela-style rye*

Rittenhouse Rye–*bottled in bond 100 proof–classic Monongahela-style bottled in bond rye*

Jim Beam–*four-year-old 80 proof, and Black Label eight-year-old 86 proof–It is the #1 selling bourbon in the world, for goodness sakes, find out why for yourself.*

Old Charter–*eight-year-old and 10–year-old–high corn recipe and good value for the years aged*

Ancient Ancient Age–*10-year-old 86 proof–10-year-old bourbon, nuff said!*

Old Fitzgerald–*86 proof–This is what Pappy Van Winkle made famous, and it's a wheat bourbon, so it's a nice way to top your bar off.*

Right here you're not even at $200.00. Isn't that crazy?

From here you can then start adding your Knob Creek, Basil Hayden's, Maker's Mark, Elijah Craig, Blanton's, etc. Find out if you like a high rye bourbon or a wheated bourbon and then play around with all of those that share similarities in recipes, ages and proof. Find out your common denominators.

Ms. Annis' Bourbon Sour

Fred Noe's mom (Booker's widow) made this recipe. It's a refreshing twist on a classic.

Ingredients:

Take equal parts of:

Jim Beam Black

Orange juice

Frozen concentrated lemonade

Ice cubes

You can pre-batch them for a party. Just take the equal parts of Beam Black, frozen lemonade and orange juice, mix, and then pour over the ice in a glass. You can just use the lemonade container as your measuring cup. If you want to make them frozen in the summertime like Fred Noe does, put the mixture in a blender. We serve these every year at the

Bourbon Festival in Bardstown, and they are a hit with everyone. People don't believe us, but Fred and his wife, Sandy, son Freddie, and friends all work together and pre-batch them for the Bourbon Gala. We save a jug for our table because they're just that delicious!

Old Fashioned

The old fashioned is the first drink we know of that used bourbon as the base spirit. The drink was invented by a bartender at the prestigious Louisville gentleman's club, the Pendennis Club, around 1870. A member and distiller, Colonel James E. Pepper, asked him to make a bourbon drink in the "old-fashioned way." The bartender took that to mean as a "smash" with muddled fruit. Colonel Pepper liked it so much he ordered it wherever he traveled and brought it to the Waldorf Astoria in New York City, where it became a standard.

The drink was so popular that the lowball glass it was served in began to be known as the old-fashioned glass.

Ingredients:

Slice of orange cut in a half moon

Cherry

2-3 dashes of bitters

Sugar - small lump or a cube

Soda water

Knob Creek bourbon

In a lowball glass, add a cherry, half-moon orange slice, a sugar cube and a splash of water. Muddle the contents and then add a shot of Knob Creek bourbon and ice, and top off with soda water.

Old Tub Bottled in Bond Toast

Fred Noe is the seventh generation of Beams to run the Jim Beam distillery...which just happens to make them one of the most illustrious distilling families in the world. Yet Fred takes the time to text or call me and wish me a happy birthday. He takes the time to talk to anyone who is interested in bourbon. He is more than a mentor, he is a friend.

The Bourbon Fest 2007 previewed the first bottles of Jim Beam with Fred Noe's image added to the family pictures on the label. They had a big media event for that special day, of course. There was an empty rocking chair to represent each of the six previous generations, and Fred's dad, Booker's, chair had his fishin' hat and can on his. Fred and Booker used to travel around doing the Great Whiskey Debate. The Great Whiskey Debate was something that was created by their PR partner and friend, Jim Kokoris, at which Booker or Fred would debate that bourbon was the better whiskey of the world, and Richard Patterson of The Dalmore Scotch would debate that scotch was the better whiskey of the world. It is a great event to witness. One of the "props" they used was a full bottle of Old Tub Bottled in Bond Bourbon (a brand that was first made by third-generation David Beam and continued until the 1970s). Jim and Fred always said they'd open that bottle some day. So later that week when we were all at the Bourbon Q BBQ celebration, Jim brought that bottle of Old Tub to the party to give it to Fred.

Fred took that bottle of Old Tub Bottled in Bond Bourbon, and everyone took turns getting pictures with it. Now you can't get Old Tub anymore, but Fred insisted we not just open the bottle but finish it off. I mean, how many times do you get your picture on the side of one of the biggest icons of American history? But still, a lot of people I know would have saved that bottle and never opened it. Not Fred. We all took a taste and toasted Fred's milestone on the porch of Colonel Jim Beam's house with all that history around us...It's a moment I'm sure I could never describe as vividly as it happened, but I know I will never forget it as long as I live.

The Manhattan

The Manhattan was created in 1870 for Winston Churchill's mom, Lady Randolph Churchill (Jennie Jerome), at the Manhattan Club in New York City during a fundraiser she hosted for presidential candidate Samuel Tilden. The success of that party made that drink fashionable, and people started ordering it by referring to the name of the club where it had originated. It was made with American whiskey, sweet vermouth and Angostura Bitters. It can be made with rye whiskey, a bourbon, or even a Canadian whiskey, but the classic Manhattan is now made with bourbon or rye whiskey.

Ingredients:

Knob Creek bourbon

Sweet vermouth

Bitters

Mix three parts Knob Creek, one part sweet vermouth and add bitters to your taste. Put ingredients in a Boston shaker glass first without ice, then add ice ¾ to the top of the glass. Using a bartender spoon, stir the Manhattan, do not shake. Stirring adds just enough water to the Manhattan, shaking would add too much. When the cocktail comes up to the same level as the ice, you've stirred it enough. Strain the drink into a martini glass, garnish with a cherry (classic) or a lemon peel, and serve.

Highballs

A highball is simply a shot of bourbon (or any spirit) topped off with a carbonated mixer (ginger ale, 7UP, cola, soda, etc.). Back in the day, trains were the fashionable way to travel. On the train there were two lights in each compartment, one on top of the other. When the train left the station and got up to speed, the train's engineer lit the light on the top position, and it came to be called the "highball." When the highball was lit, people knew it was OK to walk to the club car. They knew it was time to go get a cocktail.

Whiskey Professor–a.k.a BBG (originally called a *Horses Neck*)

Ingredients:

Old Grand Dad 86 or the Bonded (or if you're up for it, the 114)

Ginger ale

Aromatic bitters

Lemon peel

Sprig of mint

Ice

In a highball glass, pour a shot of bourbon, then two to three dashes of aromatic bitters, and top off with ginger ale. Garnish with a spiral of lemon. (The spiral of lemon is reminiscent of a horse coming out of the stall, and for us in Kentucky, that's something we know about.) I've changed the name of this drink to the whiskey professor, because I can, and because it's my favorite bourbon cocktail and I'm spreading it all over the world, so there! We also call it the BBG for my buddy and master mixologist Bobby "G" Gleason, who first turned me on to these. (BBG–get it?) BBG also stands for the ingredients: bourbon, bitters and ginger ale. The first time you tell a bartender what BBG stands for, you'll never have to tell him again, he'll know. So order a whiskey professor and enjoy!

Presbyterian – a.k.a. Press

Ingredients:

Old Grand Dad 86

Ginger ale

Soda water

Peel of lemon

Fill a highball glass with ice and add one shot of Old Grand Dad 86-proof bourbon. Fill the rest of the glass with equal measures of ginger ale and soda water. Take a slice of lemon peel and zest it on top of the drink.

It's said that when people had parties at their homes back in the '50s and '60s, bourbon and ginger ale looked pretty dark, and folks knew they were drinking a cocktail. But if you added soda water, it looked like your Presbyterian neighbor was just drinking ginger ale, since the soda lightened it up. Truth or fiction? I don't know, but it's a damn good story.

Here follows some bourbon twists on other classics

BLT (IT'S A BLOODY MARY WITH BOURBON AND A COUPLE OTHER UNIQUE TOUCHES)

Ingredients:

Jim Beam Black eight-year-old bourbon or the equivalent

Bloody Mary mix (preferably homemade, but your favorite mix will do)

Hickory bacon salt

Two slices of thick-sliced crisp bacon

Celery (the "L" of the BLT here)

Rim a tall glass with hickory bacon salt. Make a Bloody Mary as you usually would in your favorite way, but use Jim Beam Black Bourbon instead of vodka. Take two slices of thick-sliced flavorful gorgeous crisp bacon and make an "X" over the glass. Take a bite of the bacon and sip and you have a BLT. Let,s face it, vodka adds no flavor whatsoever to the Bloody Mary, but the eight-year-old bourbon adds those great

SPEAKING OF BACON...

Every Tuesday night at Harris Grill in Pittsburgh is "Bacon Night," With free bacon at the bar from happy hour, and just a dollar at the tables "'til the pigs go home." My friend Lori Martin turned me on to the Harris Grill, its owner Rodney and Bacon Night. How can you not love a place that has Bacon Night? Next time you're in Pittsburgh, head on over Tuesday night and enjoy some bourbon and bacon. (5747 Ellsworth Avenue {in the Shadyside neighborhood}– 412.362.5273-www. harrisgrill.com.)

barrel notes after aging, that compliment the Bloody Mary. The bacon, well, if I have to explain that, you shouldn't be drinking it!

I attend the annual New Orleans convention celebrating the art of the cocktail–Tales of the Cocktail. Whatever you do, *go* next year. Go to the website and find seminars to attend and make plans to attend the different dinners and events. I've found that New Orleans as a city makes the best Bloody Marys by far. My guess is they are more familiar with hungover people than most cities. Right behind the host hotel, the Monteleone, is a little corner bar called the Chart Room. I call it the "Back Door of the French Quarter," so you know I love it. During Tales of the Cocktail, you can find master distillers, ambassadors and the top mixologists in the world there at any given time. I walked by one morning and saw my buddy Phil who owns the famous whiskey bar in New York, Daddy O's, my buddy and teammate, Matt, and a few others sitting at the bar at the crack of 11:00.

When you see a collection of professionals like this, you know it's going to be a long day and night, so you definitely need your vitamins. I then introduced them and the bartender Julie to the BLT. They didn't have bacon, but Julie made up the best damn Bloody Mary with Old Grand Dad *bonded* in it...and let me tell you, it was delish. I will not rest until Old Grand Dad is the Pabst Blue Ribbon of bourbon, and I won't rest until all the Bloody Marys made around Bourbon Street are made with bourbon in them. Help me spread the word.

Bourbon Mimosa

Ingredients:

Knob Creek bourbon, or your favorite that works with this

Chilled sparkling apple cider

Cinnamon

In a champagne flute add a shot of Knob Creek bourbon and then top off with chilled sparkling apple cider. Sprinkle some cinnamon on the top. If you want to get real fancy, garnish with a thin slice of apple and slide it on the rim.

This drink is an absolute hit when I attend Kentucky Derby morning parties before we go to the race track. For any occasion you would be drinking a regular mimosa, think of this as an alternative. It's a great way to enjoy bourbon, especially for vodka and rum drinkers.

Cook Like a Whiskey Professor

I don't cook much, but when I do, I like to cook with bourbon. (Surprise!) Here are a few of my favorites for you.

Bernie's Spicy Bourbon Chicken

Boneless skinless chicken breasts

Your various favorite spices

½ cup brown rice

Broccoli, or any combination medley of your favorite vegetables

Chicken broth

Old Grand Dad Bonded 100-proof bourbon whiskey

Preheat oven to 450 degrees. Slice chicken breasts in half. On a piece of aluminum foil, place each boneless chicken breast in its own piece of aluminum foil on the shiny side. Make sure the foil is long enough to be able to hold chicken inside and fold at both ends.

Sprinkle your favorite seasonings and spices on the chicken. I like ground cayenne, cumin, freshly ground black pepper, poultry seasoning and a little ground paprika for really nice color. Don't be bashful with any of these spices. After seasoning both sides, you may add broccoli or any other veggies, too. Then join the long end of the foil at the top and fold shut. That leaves the two ends of the foil. Fold one end shut and then add up to a tablespoon of chicken broth and the same amount of bourbon. Seal the final end. You'll figure out which amount of broth and Old Grand Dad you like after you make this recipe a couple times.

Place the chicken in the foil on a baking sheet on the center rack for 20 minutes. Prepare a half-cup of brown rice while the chicken cooks.

The chicken will be perfectly done after 20 minutes. Be careful opening the end of the foil (the steam escaping is very hot since you just pressure-cooked it in the sealed foil). Pour the bourbon/broth "gravy" in a bowl, and then the chicken. Slice the chicken in the broth with the veggies, and add rice.

The best thing about this is you can make several of these aluminum packs of chicken and put them in the fridge. It just takes the time to preheat and 20 minutes of cooking. Perfect for dinner for one or two, but it can also be perfect for a dinner party. It looks like you've slaved and prepped all day. They'll never know how easy it is.

Bernie's Bourbon Cream

Wine glass

Mint chocolate chip ice cream

Baker's seven-year-old, 107-proof bourbon

This is the easiest dessert to serve at home or take to someone's house. It's *always* a hit. All you do is take a wine glass and add a couple scoops of mint chocolate chip ice cream into them. Then pour over it a shot of Baker's seven-year old, 107 proof bourbon. Garnish with some fresh mint and, if you want to get really fancy, add some fruit, but that's it. When your guests spoon out the ice cream and the bourbon, it's just like a mint julep dessert! So simple, and you'll be the star every single time, especially with the after-dinner drinks you make with the leftover bourbon!

9

Bourbon: Our Native Spirit

As a nation, "... we have improved man's lot and enriched his civilization with rye, bourbon, and the martini cocktail. In all history has any other nation done so much? Not by two-thirds."
–Bernard DeVoto, *THE HOUR: A Cocktail Manifesto*

In 1964, Congress declared bourbon the native spirit of the United States. Why would the U.S. government take the time to bother with bourbon? It's because bourbon whiskey developed in tandem with United States history. Let's face it, folks, if there was no bourbon, there'd be no NASCAR! And what would America be without that?

President Lyndon B. Johnson signed it into law. Then the United States Senate in 2007 unanimously passed the resolution declaring September as National Bourbon Heritage Month. Like I said, it had to be a unanimous decision by the Senate. Bourbon is the one and only alcohol that is designated as our native spirit. So it is not only delicious to drink bourbon, it's also your patriotic duty!

Just think about all the rich history and heritage surrounding bourbon: how the United States has used bourbon and whiskey as money and paid our troops with bourbon whiskey; the way bourbon has become its own style of whiskey, unique from Irish, scotch, Canadian, and Tennessee whiskey; the corn that gave it sweetness and the charred barrels that gave it magic, color and characteristics. Just think about all of the family names that are still in the bourbon business: Elijah Craig, Evan Williams, Dr. James Crow, Edmund Taylor, the Medleys, the Ripys, Albert Blanton, George Washington, Colonel Oscar Pepper, the Beams, Pappy Van Winkle, the Samuels, the Browns, the Wathens, the Willets, and on and

Bottling Bourbon

Bourbon was first bottled and labeled in 1870 by a pharmaceutical salesman named George Garvin Brown. One of his friends was a doctor who was a Civil War hero with a sterling reputation, and the doctor would often complain that the bulk whiskey he prescribed (barrel whiskey) wasn't consistent. He would say he just couldn't rely on it. Being an enterprising man, George Brown bought several barrels of bourbon, used a hydrometer to measure the proof, bottled it, and sold it as superior medicinal bourbon. For credibility, he put the name of that noted physician and Civil War hero, Dr. William Forrester, on the label, and Old Forrester was born. After Dr. Forrester passed away, the distillery dropped one "r" and the Old Forester brand is still around today. As a matter of fact, it is the only bourbon that was available before, during and after Prohibition. I quite like the Signature 100 proof.

Other distilleries adopted this practice of bottling and labeling their bourbons, but mostly after 1897 with the Bottled in Bond Act. George Garvin Brown and his brother J.T.S. Brown went on to found Brown-Forman in Louisville, Kentucky. J.T.S. Brown was the preferred bourbon of Fast Eddie Felson, played by Paul Newman, in the movie The Hustler. *J.T.S. Brown bourbon is still around today, too. What does the J.T.S. stand for? John Thompson Street Brown–I* love *that name.*

on. It's great to see people embracing bourbon in the manner they have in the past 10 years. I believe that with the increased interest people have in visiting the Bourbon Trail and all the distilleries on it here in Kentucky, the industry might easily double and triple in size. But don't worry about the quality. Remember, we *can't* cut corners.

I think that what Ben Parley Moore witnessed in Kentucky in 1857 is still true today. When you meet my fellow whiskey professors, distillers, ambassadors and me, you will surely be greeted by gentlemen with our hearts in our right hand, and our right hand in yours, and surely in our left a bottle of unequalled old bourbon.

Appendix:
Frequently Asked Questions

You can imagine that as a whiskey professor, I get asked a lot of questions about our native spirit when I tour the country. A lot of them get repeated, so I figured that putting down some of the most frequently asked questions here might help. Also, after reading this book, you just might know the answers yourself. Cover up the answer and see how well you do:

When distilling the distillers beer or mash into white dog, are different cuts of the distillate used to make different labels of bourbon (e.g. more middle run for higher quality labels vs. more first cut or tails for lesser quality)?

When you use a column still, you don't make "cuts" as you do with a pot still for single-malt scotch. With pot stills you trim off the heads and tails on each batch. Column stills are very efficient. You only have to trim off heads when you start the still up, and then it brings the spirit off the still at a constant proof 24 hours a day, as long as you run the still, which is usually five or six days. Then you only trim off the tails on the last day. We do that with all our bourbons, not just small batch. There's no such thing as "good cuts," "bad cuts," or "best cuts. They are all the best cuts. What separates the bourbons therefore is age and proof. A greater age on a bourbon and higher proof can make the bourbon more expensive. But they are all made with the same exacting, high standards by the laws that define bourbon from other whiskies. (i.e. 51% corn, distilled to no more than 160 proof, aged in a brand new charred- oak barrel at no more than 125 proof, bottled at no less than 80 proof, with nothing added to the bourbon other than water to get it to barreling or bottling strength).

Even when using pot stills and separating heads and tails on each batch, they would never use the heads and tails, only the heart. There would be too many fusel oils and congeners in the heads and tails.

Are there any bourbons distilled outside Kentucky? If so, what are they?

Ninety-seven percent of the bourbon in the world is distilled in Kentucky. But there are more and more bourbons made outside Kentucky as the popularity of bourbon continues to climb. The biggest brand made outside Kentucky is *Virginia Gentleman*. Hudson Baby Bourbon is being produced up in New York. There are bourbons being distilled in Austin, Texas, Colorado and Florida, too. But these are tiny little craft distillers and probably will be available only in their local markets, kind of like a local brew pub. So bourbon can be distilled anywhere in the United States, but since the overwhelming majority is distilled in Kentucky, a lot of people think that it has to be made in Kentucky. That is one of the myths of bourbon.

What type of glass is best for drinking bourbon neat?

I like to use a snifter or a nice rocks glass, sans the "rocks." I like a glass that I can get my nose into a bit. But that's a personal preference. There are some who like a tulip-shaped glass, and those are nice, but I can't get my schnoz into them, so I like a snifter. Try some out and see what works best for you; there are no rules. When you visit, you'll find out that we bourbon drinkers are not as pretentious as the scotch drinkers.

I have put together a whiskey cellar with roughly twelve different bourbons right now. Most of these are sealed with a cork. How should store them? On their sides? Upright? How long will they keep before they go "off"?

Keep your bourbons standing straight up, and if the corks are a good seal, they should never go "off". Unlike wines, bourbons are distilled at a higher proof, so they won't get "corked" or go bad. Bourbon will not age in the bottle, either. Just keep them out of direct sunlight, and you'll enjoy them for years. But don't wait years to enjoy them; we've got lots of barrels resting in our rack houses for you, so enjoy all you want … you keep drinking it, and we'll keep making it.

When my uncle introduced me to good bourbon, he had a bottle of "branch water" on his bar. I tried to find "branch" on the Internet but it does not seem to exist anymore. Does anyone sell it or has bottled water replaced it?

"Branch water" is a term that refers to the water from the head of a stream before it "branches" off. Not many of us are lucky enough anymore to live on acreage that has such magical properties, so I'd suggest we use a good nonmineral bottled water, or water from a purifier.

WHEN DID DISTILLERS START STORING WHISKEY BARRELS IN RACK HOUSES, RATHER THAN STACKING ON THE FLOOR OF OTHER BUILDINGS? I'M WONDERING IF IT WAS BETWEEN THE 1860S (STILL ON FLOORS) AND ABOUT 1880.

I've been doing research on this one for a while now, and it's been pretty fun. I'm glad you've asked the question. I know that one of my heroes in bourbon history, Colonel Edmund Taylor, was very influential in bourbon-making and aging. In 1869 Colonel Taylor purchased a small distillery on the banks of the Kentucky River at Leestown, Kentucky. Colonel Taylor was the first person to employ the "rick" system in warehouses on a consistent basis. The ricks lifted the barrels off the floor and into the ricks we still use to this day. They are stacked three barrels high per floor in the "one high," the "two high," and the "three high," and rolled down the ricks which are two 4x4's designed to hold 11+ barrels deep in a rack house.

Colone Taylor was also a supporter who helped pass the Bottled in Bond Act of 1897, the first consumer protection legislation in the United States. The B.I.B. Act states that a bourbon must be at least four years old, exactly 100 proof, from one distillery (with the actual maker listed on the bottle) and barreled in one season. So raise a glass of Bottled in Bond Old Grand Dad to Colonel Taylor! We employ today a lot of what he pioneered long ago.

I'm used to drinking Jack & Coke, but a friend turned me on to the Knob Creek bourbon. Since I like to mix my drink is it OK to mix the Knob Creek with Coke or something else, or do you prefer not to?

I'm glad your friend turned you on to bourbon and especially one of my favorites. The only rule I have about it is one I picked up from my buddy and master mixologist, Bobby "G." Drink what you like, like what you're drinking, but know what you're drinking. If you like it mixed with Coke, by all means mix it with Coke.

Jack Daniels tends to be younger, meaning it hasn't been aged as long as Knob Creek (nine years in the barrel) or Elijah Craig (12 years in the barrel), for example. Even the white label Jim Beam (four years old) drinkers tend to like Coke, 7UP, or ginger ale mixed in with their bourbon. The longer the bourbon has rested in those barrels, the more of those vanilla, maple, caramel, and ginger flavors are there, and the less you might want to add to it so you can taste them. This is why a lot of folks just use a cube or 2 of ice, or just a splash of water or ginger ale.

If you like it with cola, by all means drink it that way, but know that cola tends to mask the flavors that we have been aging for. It also contains a lot of sugars and flavors on top of that to boot. Ginger ale actually brings out some natural vanillas and other flavors from the barrel. So try it with ginger ale sometime, or half ginger ale, and half soda. This is also called a Presbyterian. It's a classic drink and very refreshing.

But if you like bourbon with Coke, you drink it with Coke. Booker Noe was asked by a woman one time if it was a sin to mix Booker's Bourbon and Coke. She really liked the taste of it. Booker looked at her and said, "Ma'am, if you take the best bourbon in the world and mix it with Coke, you'll have the best damned bourbon and Coke in the world."

How do you measure alcohol content? How do you regulate it during production? How much variability is there from batch to batch?

That's a great question. And we have to thank technology for helping us make it a little easier and a lot more consistent now. In the 1980s, computers were being used more in the actual cooking and distilling. Before that, people had to turn valves and control temperatures, etc. Now it's all done by computers, so it's controlled a lot more tightly. Once the computer has the steam under the still, it can keep the bourbon pouring off the still at a desired proof. But we still use the old-fashioned way and use a hydrometer to check the proof level every hour, just like Dr. James Crow did back in the 1800s. So there is hardly any variability on a run (batch). Keep in mind that a "batch" is five or six days long. That's the advantage of using column stills instead of pot stills. The proof stays constant. Two people in the control room overseeing the computer system can do the job of 15 people turning valves and adjusting dials by hand. The operators can override the computer system and open valves, but still by using the computer system. If that totally fails, they can go down into the distillery and turn the valves by hand. With as much technology as we have today, we still have to have guys like Fred Noe, Craig Beam, Tommy Crume and other distillers who know how to go in and do it by hand if needed.

Can a whiskey still be considered a bourbon if it contains more than 80% corn, or does that automatically make it "corn whiskey"?

This is a question that is debated over and over, and I don't know why. The laws are really clear here. The law on bourbon whiskey states that it must contain at least 51% corn. It mentions no upper limit for percentage of corn or other grains specifically, so yes, as long as it follows all the laws of bourbon, the whiskey can be 80% or more corn and still be considered bourbon. Period. Corn whiskey is defined as "whiskey produced at not exceeding 160 proof from a fermented mash of not less than 80% corn grain, and if stored in oak containers stored at not more than 125 proof in used or uncharred new oak containers."

If you're more inspired now than ever about the native spirit of the United States and want to attend some of the events and meet folks like myself, Fred Noe and all the whiskey men and women who are ambassadors, please come and enjoy. Some whiskey events across the country include: Bourbon Festival in Bardstown, KY, Whiskey Guild/Whisky Life and Spirits Cruises, WhiskeyFest, Whisky Live, Tales of the Cocktail, Aspen Food and Wine, Epcot Food and Wine, Beer Bourbon and Bar-B-Q, and the Philadelphia and Pittsburgh Whiskey Festivals. Just Google these and they'll pop right up.

You can also follow me on Facebook and Twitter.

You can see a video of me on YouTube singing a song I wrote and performed with Hickory and the boys titled, "The Bourbon Trail." I mention 18 bourbons in the song:

THE BOURBON TRAIL, BY BERNIE LUBBERS, 2009

G C
My ***Old Grand Dad***... he passed away
G A D
But he lived 94 years to the day
G C
He's laid to rest, right up on ***Heaven Hill***
G D G
With a spray of ***Four Roses*** on his grave

He'd drink a quart - each and every day
Of some good store bought ***Jim Beam***
Doctor ***Forester*** said "Hey ***Pappy***" you better cut it down
But then the good doc passed away, so who's to say!
Chorus:
C G
So raise a **Red Eye** to ***Old Grand Dad***
G A D
He lived to be an ***Ancient Age***
G C
That ***Old Crow*** sure left his ***Makers Mark***
G D G
And now he's **drinking with the angels** far away

A Final Note

As I finish this book, I'm on holiday in Munich, Prague and Berlin. Most people hate airports. I love them. True, they can be a pain, but what the hell, you're going somewhere! I also love train travel. Since I took the train between cities in Europe, I knew it would be the perfect opportunity to finish this incredible project. I'd like to thank my employer, Jim Beam, for the opportunity to serve as whiskey professor on behalf of their great brands. Also, I can't thank Fred Noe enough for his never-ending passion and the knowledge and experience he shares so graciously with us all. When I asked him if he would write the foreword for this book, he didn't hesitate and added that it would be his *honor to do it. What a class act! Fred makes you feel like you're a part of the Beam family, and when you meet him, you'll feel like you've known him all your life. This is also true of all the other master distillers: Jimmy and Eddie Russell (Wild Turkey), Greg Davis (Maker's Mark), Harlen Wheatley and Elmer T. Lee (Buffalo Trace), Parker and Craig Beam (Heaven Hill), Fred Noe and Kevin Smith (Jim Beam), Jimmy Rutledge (Four Roses) and Chris Morris (Woodford Reserve). I've learned a lot from all of them, and they're all inspiring to be around.*

I also want to thank my buddy Tom Mabe (comic, musician, jingle writer, TV show host) for introducing me to my publisher. I heard stories of getting rejection letter after rejection letter with publishers, and I must tell you, I'm one for one. I approached one publisher and he said, "I want to do it." Thanks, Tom Doherty and everyone at Blue River Press!

I encourage you to sign up and become members on the websites of your favorite brands: jimbeam.com, knobcreek.com, makersmark.com. When you sign up, you'll be invited to cool tastings and gatherings. Most brands have websites, so Google your favorite brands and sign up for all the ones you enjoy.

, tag the ending with

ırow ***Old Fitz*** if he didn't get that **Sour Mash**, and now he's
with ***Booker*** far away!

ngels' share is surely higher now today

:2

en the weekend rolled around, oh the stories they would flow,

ke branch water pourin' down ***Knob Creek***.

van Williams start to sing - ***Brother Elijah's*** voice would ring

And **Jimmy** passed the jug to **Fred** and ***Elmer T***.

CHORUS

Verse 3

Wild Turkeys they all were, and like ***Eagles*** they were ***Rare***

They **bottled & bonded** all the day.

And on into the night, at ***Basil Hayden's*** shear delight,

They'd tell stories 'bout the whiskey men they were!

18 bourbons referenced:

Old Grand Dad – Heaven Hill – Four Roses – Jim Beam – Pappy Van Winkle – Old Forester – Ancient Age – Old Crow – Maker's Mark – Knob Creek – Evan Williams – Elijah Craig – Booker's – Wild Turkey – Eagle Rare – Basil Hayden's – Elmer T. Lee – Old Fitzgerald

Other bourbon referenced:

Red Eye–Bottled in Bond – Angel's Share – Branch Water – Sour Mash

Whiskey men referenced:

Jim Beam – Doctor William Forrester – Pappy Van Winkle – Evan Williams – Elijah Craig – Jimmy Russell – Fred Noe – Elmer T. Lee – Basil Hayden – Booker Noe

10668833

GATE

The Gate Theatre presents

THE FLU SEASON

by **Will Eno**

First performed at the Gate Theatre on 7 April 2003

THE FLU SEASON

by **Will Eno**

Cast in order of appearance

Prologue	**Martin Parr**
Epilogue	**Alan Cox**
Doctor	**Damien Thomas**
Man	**Matthew Delamere**
Nurse	**Pamela Miles**
Woman	**Raquel Cassidy**

Director	**Erica Whyman**
Designer	**Soutra Gilmour**
Lighting Designer	**Anthony Simpson**
Sound Design	**Michael Oliva**

Assistant Director	**Hanna Berrigan**
Stage Manager	**Fiona Green**
Set Builder	**Simon Plumridge**

The design of the Flu Season has generously been supported by Jenny Hall.

The Company

Hanna Berrigan Assistant Director
Hanna graduated from RADA and King's College with an MA in Text and Performance.
Credits as a director include: The Wheel (Rosemary Branch) The Birthday Party (Edinburgh Festival) The Secret Rapture (Moser Theatre).
As an assistant director: The Price (Tricycle Theatre) Kuehltransport (Mainz Staatstheater).
Hanna is currently on both the Trainee Directors scheme at the Gate and the Directors Programme at the National Theatre Studio.

Raquel Cassidy Woman
Theatre credits include: Possible Worlds (Tron Theatre) Tree Houses (Northcott Theatre, Exeter) Blessings (Old Red Lion) The Promise (Everyman, Liverpool) Dogs Barking (The Bush) Threesome (LPB Prods/Old Red Lion) Othello (Bury St. Edmunds) The Bone Room (Young Vic Studio) Twelfth Night (National Theatre) The Censor (Royal Court Downstairs) Couch Grass and Ribbon (Watermill, Newbury) Stealing Souls (The Red Room) Walking with Mr. Brownstone (Southwark Playhouse) The Song from the Sea (West Yorkshire Playhouse) St. James and the Tattoo Man (London New Play Festival).
Film credits include: Do I love You?, Before You Go, Perdie.
TV credits include: Trevor's World of Sport, Trust, Red Cap, Teachers, Table Twelve, Thin Ice, Hearts and Bones, Nature Boy, Killer Net.
Radio credits include: Baby First, The Love of a Life Can Show Below.

Alan Cox Epilogue
Alan trained at LAMDA.
Theatre credits include: The Lady's not for Burning, Hock and Soda Water, On the Razzle (Chichester) Passions (Tristan Bates Theatre) The Duchess of Malfi (Salisbury Playhouse) The Daughter-in-Law, The Dark River (Orange Tree) Strangers on a Train (Colchester) Barefoot in the Park (Jermyn Street Theatre) The Importance Of Being Earnest (Chichester/ West End) Three Sisters (Birmingham Rep) The Seagull, Wild Oats, Absolute Hell, An Enemy of the People (National Theatre) The Dumb Waiter, Desire Caught By The Tail (The Landor) Beggar's Opera, The Winter's Tale, Anthony and Cleopatra (RSC) The Drummer (The Watermill) Strange Interlude (Duke of York's) The Warp (Three Mills Island).
As a director: A&R (Latchmere Theatre).
Film credits include: The Auteur Theory, Mrs Dalloway, An Awfully Big Adventure, Death of a Schoolboy, Young Sherlock Holmes.
TV credits include: The Dinosaur Hunters, The Odyssey, The Thin Blue Line, Young Indy, Adam Bede, A Voyage Round My Father.

Matthew Delamere Man
Mattew trained at Central School of Speech and Drama.
Theatre credits include: Les Enfants du Paradis (RSC) Mansfield Park (Chichester) Of Mice and Men (Nottingham) What the Butler Saw (Sheffield Crucible) Laundry Room at the Hotel Madrid (Gate Theatre).
Film credits include: Shadowlands, Under the Skin, Eight and a half Women, The Trouble with Men and Women, Hellraiser – The Deaders, Dumping Elaine.
TV credits include: Fields of Gold, Holby City, Merseybeat, Spooks.

Soutra Gilmour Designer
Theatre includes: Antigone (Citizens' Theatre Glasgow) Peter Pan (The Tramway Glasgow)The Birthday Party (Sheffield Crucible) Fool for Love (English Touring Theatre) Macbeth (English Shakespeare Co) Hand in Hand (Hampstead Theatre) Modern Dance for Beginners (Soho Theatre) Tear From A Glass Eye, Les Justes, Ion, Box of Bananas (Gate Theatre) Witness (Gate Theatre & BAC) The Woman Who Swallowed A Pin, The Winter's Tale, Through The Leaves (Southwark Playhouse) The Shadow of a Boy (National Theatre).
Opera credits include: Eight Songs For A Mad King (World Tour) El Cimmaron (Queen Elizabeth Hall Southbank) Twice Through the Heart (Cheltenham Festival) Bathtime (ENO Studio) A Better Place (ENO, Colesium).

Pamela Miles Nurse
Pamela has worked extensively in repertory work at Lincoln and tours with the Welsh Theatre Company. Other theatre credits include: King Lear (Bristol Old Vic), The Norman Conquests (Windsor Theatre Royal), Bedroom Farce and Habeas Corpus (Nottingham), Circe and Bravo (Coventry) Soapbox (Manchester Library Theatre) Equus (Sailsbury Playhouse) The Orchestra (Kings Head) Over Garden's Out (Royal Court Theatre Upstairs) Animal Farm,The Garden of England (National Theatre) Hamlet (New Shakespeare Company, Regent's Park) Sherlock Holmes (RSC, Broadway) Julius Caesar (Compass Theatre Company) Miss Bronte and I (Colorado).
Film credits include: A Fish Called Wanda, Under Milk Wood.
TV credits include: The Voysey Inheritance, 84 Charing Cross Road, Going Out, The Family, Cold Enough For Snow; Rumpole of the Bailey, Inspector Morse, The Good Guys, Midsomer Murders, The Doctors.
Recent radio credits include: Darkness Into Light, The Head of Medusa, With Great Pleasure.

Michael Oliva Sound Design and Score
Michael trained as a biochemist and now teaches composition with electronics at the Royal College of Music.
Scores and sound design for theatre include: Fool For Love, Love's Labours Lost (English Touring Theatre, RNT Studio) The Glass Slipper, The Winter's Tale, The Old Curiosity Shop (Southwark Playhouse) Tear From A Glass Eye, Les Justes, Box of Bananas, Ion (Gate Theatre) Witness (Gate Theatre & BAC) Knots (in the Dark) (BAC) The Birthday Party (Sheffield Crucible).
As well as live computer improvisations with Hannah Marshall (Coccyx), concert works include More Bless'd Than Living Lips, an opera Ocean, Chase and Hannah's Dream, a collaboration with the painter Susan Haire, The Speed Of Metals, Ultramarine, Cyclone and Torso.
Michael is currently working on his opera Black And Blue.

Martin Parr Prologue
Theatre credits include: Vanity Fair (Northcott Theatre) The Rivals (Swan Theatre) Rutherford and Son (Salisbury Playhouse) When We Are Married, The Importance of Being Earnest, White Devil (Leicester Haymarket) Perfect Days (Derby Playhouse) The Belgrade Trilogy (Tristan Bates Theatre) The Country Wife (Bridewell Theatre) Tenant of Wildfell Hall (New Victoria Theatre, Birmingham Rep) Maddie (Lyric, Shaftesbury Avenue) Rough Side of the Boards, Candida (Bolton Octagon) The Entertainer (West Yorkshire Playhouse) Wind in the Willows, Pygmalion (Birmingham Rep) Macbeth, Fantastical Banquet (Stratford).
Film credits include: This Rough Magic, Lionel's Birthday.
Radio credits include: The Red Story, The Strange Affair of Adelaide Harris.

Anthony Simpson Lighting Designer
Antony studied Drama & Music at Middlesex Polytechnic. Recent design credits include: Early Morning (The Oval House) Habitats (Gate Theatre) The Weir, Waiting For Godot (Royal Theatre, Northampton) Someone Who`ll Watch Over Me (Southwark Playhouse) Arcadia (Royal Theatre Northampton / Salisbury Playhouse) Under the Doctor (The Comedy Theatre, London) Berkoff`s Women (The Ambassadors Theatre, London) Cooking with Elvis (The Whitehall Theatre, London) Falstaff & Hansel and Gretel for Palace Opera (QEH, London) La Traviata (Duchy Opera) The Cherry Orchard (The Duke of Cambridge) Burdalane (BAC).
Recent Associate Design credits include: RNT`s Life x 3 (the Savoy Theatre, London & UK tours) An Inspector Calls (the Playhouse Theatre, London & UK tours). Re-lit The Weir for The Royal Court Theatre (UK, Sicily & Australia) Les Liaisons Dangereuses (Mobil Touring Theatre) Amadeus (Los Angeles & New York, UK tour & The Old Vic, London) re-lit Therese Raquin for The Royal Opera House.

Damien Thomas Doctor
Damien trained at RADA.
Of 36 major repertory productions, including three seasons at Regents Park Open Air Theatre, most recent credits include: Possible Worlds (Tron Theatre, Glasgow) Eyes of the Kappa (Gate Theatre).
Films credits include: The Message, Tiffany Jones (Peter Walker) Pirates (Roman Polanski) Sinbad and The Eye of The Tiger (Sam Wanamaker) The Merchant of Venice (Orson Welles) Twins of Evil (John Hough, Hammer).
Roles in over 40 major TV productions include: Shogun, Noble House, Beau Geste, Jane Eyre, Tenko, The Talisman, Blake's 7, Anno Domini, House of Cards.

Erica Whyman Director
Erica trained at Bristol Old Vic on the Director's Attachment, and with Phillipe Gaulier in Paris. Erica was awarded the John S Cohen Bursary for Directors at the National Theatre Studio and English Touring Theatre. Directing credits include: Silence and Landscape (NT Studio) The Gambler, Oblomov (Pleasance, Edinburgh and London) her own adaptation of To The Lighthouse (Bloomsbury Theatre) Blue Remembered Hills (Bristol Old Vic) The Little Violin by Adrian Mitchell (Tricycle Theatre) Fool For Love (English Touring Theatre) Three Wishes (Pleasance, Edinburgh) The Birthday Party (Sheffield Crucible) A Shadow of a Boy (National Theatre).
As artistic director at Southwark Playhouse she directed The Glass Slipper, The Winter's Tale, The Old Curiosity Shop. For the Gate she has directed Tear From A Glass Eye, Les Justes, the devised piece Box of Bananas, Ion and Witness (also at BAC).

For the Gate Theatre

Artistic Director	Erica Whyman
Producer	Kester Thompson
General Manager	Daisy Heath
Production Manager	Chris French
Technical Manager	James Glanville
Assistant Technician	SJ Anthony
Box Office	Paul Long
Trainee Directors	Hanna Berrigan Jennie Fellows
Head Reader	Sophie Craig

Thanks to our volunteers: David Linton, Jennifer Tebo, Marisa Lapiana, Julia Deutsch, Lucy McMahon, Jess-Luisa Flynn, Katie Jeffery and to all our volunteer crew, who often work long and unsociable hours in order that this theatre may survive.

Gate Theatre
11 Pembridge Road
London
W11 3HQ

Box Office:	020 7229 0706
Administration:	020 7229 5387
Fax:	020 7221 6055
E-mail:	gate@gatetheatre.freeserve.co.uk

The Gate's work is supported by:
The Jerwood Foundation, The Arts Council of England, Charles Glanville, Jenny Hall, The Paul Hamlyn Foundation, Oberon Books and The Gatsby Charitable Foundation.

Gatekeepers:
Sir Ronald and Lady Cohen, Jenny Hall, Hart Brothers, Oberon Books, Georgia Oetker, The Really Useful Group Ltd, The Really Useful Foundation, and Mr and Mrs Tack.

Special thanks to the following for all their help and support on this production: Paul and all the staff at The Prince Albert Pub, Vicky Jones, Mark Goddard, Paul Murphy, Kate Wild, Herta Quierazza, Neil Sutcliffe, Crumble, Georgia Oetker, Tamzin Griffin, Lizzie Dudley, Roger at Ken McReddie, Paul Miller and Jennie Fellows.

The author would like to thank: The Dramatists Guild Fund, The Foundation for Contemporary Performance Arts, Erica Whyman, Kester Thompson

Damien Thomas and the Gate would especially like to thank Stephanie Jenke.

Very special thanks go to Jenny Hall, and The Gatsby Charitable Foundation, without whom the Gate would be a very different place.

THE FLU SEASON INTERMISSION

First published in this collection in 2003 by Oberon Books Ltd.
(incorporating Absolute Classics)
521 Caledonian Road, London N7 9RH
Tel: 020 7607 3637 / Fax: 020 7607 3629
e-mail: oberon.books@btinternet.com
www.oberonbooks.com

Copyright © Will Eno 2003

Intermission © copyright 2002 by the Antioch Review, Inc.

Intermission first appeared in the *Antioch Review*, Vol. 60, no. 4.
Reprinted by permission of the Editors.

Will Eno is hereby identified as author of these works in accordance with section 77 of the Copyright, Designs and Patents Act 1988. The author has asserted his moral rights.

All rights whatsoever in these plays are strictly reserved and application for performance etc. should be made before commencement of rehearsal to Will Eno, c/o Oberon Books at the above address. No performance may be given unless a licence has been obtained, and no alterations may be made in the title or the text of the play without the author's prior written consent.

This book is sold subject to the condition that it shall not by way of trade or otherwise be circulated without the publisher's consent in any form of binding or cover or circulated electronically other than that in which it is published and without a similar condition including this condition being imposed on any subsequent purchaser.

A catalogue record for this book is available from the British Library.

ISBN: 1 84002 370 8

Printed in Great Britain by Antony Rowe Ltd, Chippenham.

Content

THE FLU SEASON, 15

INTERMISSION, 67

THE FLU SEASON

'We step in the puddle, you know, and we do not. We live, these bright cold days on earth, and we don't. We tell our little story, staring out. We devise the beginning knowing the end, and this is trouble. We trudge on, losing ground, looking back, trying, telling a tale of summer, a sinking feeling amid the leaving geese and slush. It's coming, little one. Truth. Now, where's my shoes?'

–from the film *By Dint of the Bridge's Collapse*

Dramatis Personae

PROLOGUE
A Narrator. He should differ physically from Epilogue. Perhaps he is large, and Epilogue is skinny. Where Prologue is warm and tender, Epilogue would be cold, might even have a flair for a seductive kind of cruelty. Both narrators remain discretely on stage, except where noted. Though Prologue is not aware of Epilogue, the latter is aware of the former.

EPILOGUE
A Narrator. As above

MAN
late-twenties

WOMAN
late-twenties

DOCTOR
late-fifties

NURSE
fifties

Setting
The play takes place in a mental health institution of a not very specific type. The play also takes place, certainly, in a theatre, as each narrator makes clear.

Acts and Scenes
There are two acts. The first is made up of nine scenes. The second, twelve scenes.

A Note

Special attention should be paid to the casting of the roles of the two narrators. Ideally, it is through them that the feelings of the play pass, on their way to the audience. Through its relation to the narrators and the narration, the audience is meant to feel those feelings – attraction and ambivalence, desire and self-rebuke – that are felt by characters in the play. In this way, the audience is meant to participate in its own love story, and not just watch someone else's. In this way, the audience may feel tenderness, loss, and disappointment, in a new and improved way. Also, there is action that occurs off-stage whose only expression is in the narrators' emotional (or unemotional) relation to it. This is not to say that there is anything terrifically complicated going on here. These are all only means to a feeling.

PROLOGUE: (*Enters, in darkness. Footsteps. Pause.*) Darkness. Footsteps. A little pause. (*Pause.*) It's quiet and dark. But you knew that. (*Pause.*) I could leave it all alone. I could let us shudder by ourselves. Leave us uncomforted by the shaky fiction of anything shared, of any common story. I could let us wreck ourselves in the dark, shiver closer to death, slowly, unnoticeably, instead of making such a big production out of it. But I won't. So, savor it, the dark. Like everything, it's ending. Yes, as for the darkness, at least: The End.

Lights up.

Hello. My name is Prologue. What else would it be. Welcome to a play whose title is 'The Snow Romance'. It is a chronicle of love and no love, of interiors and exteriors, of weather, change, entry-level psychology, and time; but, oh, lo – what chronicle isn't. Composed one spring, it follows the lives of four or five people living in the season just previous. I'll be brief. We are in a sort of hospital. The time is almost winter. The lights fall.

The lights don't fall.

EPILOGUE: Right. About the title, the play is now called 'The Flu Season'. A lot of down-time has gone by since the first draft was written, or, quote, composed. The new title stands for the fatigue, for all the sick-days wasted in coming up with a title at all. 'The Flu Season.' I don't know. Could use some work, another year of scribbling, erasing. There's always a different word, some other title, something better the language might cough up. My character, we'll call him Epilogue. Could have also been called Regrets. Or, Mr Sorry-So-Sorry. Could have been called, I don't know, Steve Stevenson, the names don't matter. Can you hear me, all right? Can you see me?

(*Motioning to PROLOGUE.*) He can't. Strange. Theatre. This. Certain things we have to live with. Anyway, I come later, after, more coldly, and with a little less optimism. I'll revise a line, add an afterthought, subtract a feeling. I'll try to speak plainly. But I liked that last part. It describes life. I quote: 'I'll be brief. We are in a sort of hospital. The time is almost winter. The lights fall.'

Lights lower on PROLOGUE and EPILOGUE.

ACT ONE

Scene 1

DOCTOR enters upstage, near a door. MAN is sitting downstage, in darkness.

DOCTOR: All alone in the all-dark, are we? Sitting in the twilight of the Exit light, licking our wounds with our wounded tongue, dreaming of some great difference, some healing hand, some heavenly or electrical light? Or just sitting there? Which? There is a difference. Tell us. The shuffling coughing world awaits. Give us a little of your disquiet.

MAN: I'm not doing anything.

DOCTOR: Well, not anything or not, we still need the light.

He turns on a light switch. Lights up.

It adds a sort of decorum to our proceedings, brightens up the otherwise muted décor of our shadowy procession. And it helps us to see, finally. But how was it, without it?

MAN: Darker.

DOCTOR: I see. Less light. But what about you? How are you?

MAN: No.

DOCTOR: (*Pause.*) I'm sorry? I said, 'How are you?'

MAN: I'm sorry, I thought you said, 'Who are you?'

DOCTOR: (*Brief pause.*) Even if I had, wouldn't 'No' still have been the wrong answer?

MAN: The mind doesn't work this way.

DOCTOR: What way?

MAN: Quickly. Talkatively. I don't know. Quickly.

DOCTOR: I'm sorry?

MAN: Nothing. Can I go lie down?

DOCTOR: First, I have to quickly ask you a question or two.

MAN: (*He inhales and begins holding his breath. He speaks with great difficulty.*) Yur tha dogdor. You know bess. I yield doo tha medigal prefezhional.

DOCTOR: The first question is, (*He reads.*) 'In your personal dealings with people, with the certain persons who people your immediate surroundings, have you ever personally felt it humanly necessary to present, solely for the sole and lone purpose of individuality itself, a persona, such that…'

MAN is turning blue.

This is not that important. Would you like to go lie down?

MAN: (*He exhales.*) I really would.

DOCTOR: We can talk later. I do need you to sign something. Nothing very serious or breathtaking, just more paper for the future to shred. A form. Strictly a formality.

DOCTOR begins to fill out a form.

MAN: (*Watching DOCTOR from across the desk.*) How do you do that?

DOCTOR: Do what?

MAN: Write upside-down like that?

DOCTOR: (*Flips the paper around, showing that he was writing right-side up.*) Voila!

MAN: Oh, right. I get so used to seeing things from my own perspective.

DOCTOR: I see. From *my* own, I guess, yes? Please sign.

MAN: (*He signs.*) Voila. (*Looking at his signature.*) Look at that. It really is strictly a formality. This is me – strictly, formally me – but it's not the only me. There's a hundred ways I could do it, all different, all mine. Looking at my little slanted mess of a signature, I have to wonder where my life will take me.

DOCTOR: I'll show you your room.

MAN: (*Looking back down at signature.*) I should have seen that somehow.

DOCTOR and MAN exit. NURSE and WOMAN are on the other side of the stage. NURSE at desk, WOMAN seated before it. Lights up.

NURSE: I think that would be fine.

WOMAN: (*Pause.*) What would? No one said anything. You're just going to start talking to me, totally out of the blue?

NURSE: Yes, dear. I am. I think people will understand. Maybe you've seen a baby born, or a grown-up die. Amazing. Totally out of the blue. And, as someone once said to someone, everything has to start somewhere.

WOMAN: Well, so, then, start.

NURSE: In fact, dear, we're almost finished. So, lastly, any allergy or injury or personal personal history that you would like to make public. Any distinguishing marks, inside or out? A birthmark in the shape of anything? Some internalized agony wholly without form? Any even sketchy sense of your character to help us empathize with you, to help us live more empathically, more heroically, within the life-size form of our own familiar pain?

WOMAN: No.

NURSE: Splendid. I will duly note that. (*She writes for thirty seconds in her notebook.*)

WOMAN: Are they still spelling 'No' with just two letters, or is it more, now?

NURSE: Oh, this – I'm sorry. I'm just scribbling. You're probably wondering where my little scribbles will take you. Yes? Either way, it all comes to something. A period, at least. A comma, or, dot-dot-dot, in some sad cases. (*Pause.*) Well, I think you'll be a wonderful –

WOMAN: (*Interrupting.*) No, I won't. I won't be a wonderful anything. Whatever noun was about to come out of you. I will be here until I leave here, and I was only here because some family – reportedly mine – brought me here, and left me here.

NURSE: Families are only groups of people. And groups of people mean well, they try. Unless they're angry mobs with broken bottles and golf clubs, and even then, they still – in their way – try. Here we also try to create a familial atmosphere. Or at least we try to act like a group of people. And the grounds are beautiful, this lovely time of year. The temperature dropping. Fall. Us, trying. All the nasty allergens dying off or flying somewhere warmer. The wonderful maple trees.

WOMAN: Yes, wonderful wonderful. Beautiful trees shedding their leaves, as I disintegrate into an animal, snow gently falling onto the uncombed hair of me, a cold cold girl, a sometime bitch in heat.

NURSE: Yes, well, you're tired, I'm sure, and possibly a little more elegiac than the situation seems to call for. I'll show you where your room is.

They exit.

PROLOGUE: In the world of our world, it is now late afternoon, a few days later. Our new admissions are settling in. The setting autumn sun is streaming through the thinning trees on the hospital property's edge. We are in the Crossroads Psychiatric Retreat Center. We are at a pay phone in the hall.

EPILOGUE: Very nice, fine. No argument here. A few days later, a pay phone in the hall.

Scene 2

MAN is standing near a pay phone, WOMAN enters.

WOMAN: I need to call somebody.

MAN: I'm waiting for someone to call.

WOMAN: I'll only be a second.

MAN: What if you suddenly find something else to talk about?

WOMAN: What if your phone call never comes?

MAN: What if the place you call is filled with people you haven't talked to in years? A line of loved ones and distant cousins, lined up through the house, waiting for their chance to get on the phone and twirl their hair and talk to you?

WOMAN: What if the person you're saying is going to call wrote the number down wrong and then lost the tiny piece of paper and was lying in the first place when he said he'd call at all?

MAN: It's a she. And she'll call. Go make your second-long call somewhere else. This is for normal human use. Phone calls lasting into the minutes and hours, years of long-distance and polite chatter, trailing off into raging and expensive silences. Humanity, on the horn. Conversation.

WOMAN: So make some conversation.

MAN: I will. (*Pause.*) Nice weather I'm having. Yes, I would have to agree with myself, there. That's a nice haircut I have. Yes, thank you, it is but a sign of human civilization. Like standing up straight and not eating worms, it's not something I can really take credit for.

WOMAN begins to walk away.

And I see you wander through life in a social architecture called the family, the rubbley remains of which we build our new relations on. Yes, we do, and we use the same name and share the same features and we all move apart so as to later hold reunions.

WOMAN is gone.

Ice cream, you scream. This is how the mind works. Poorly. Around. On the ruin of the last thought. I'm glad we had this little chat. Et cetera. 'Social architecture.' I'm an idiot. She has nice hair. My last ruined thought.

PROLOGUE: He is certainly outgoing and verbal, certainly expectant and full of hope, standing by a phone that doesn't take incoming calls. She is walking back and forth somewhere, ingoing, unverbal, biting her nails, rethinking the last scene. But cut to the offices of the doctor and the nurse! It is morning, days later.

EPILOGUE: In a little while, we begin to depart from reality, from the little mess of real life we built our play on. Hardly even noticeable. The lying and pretending, the trying and revising into ruin. A signature move. It's only natural. If we could control life, it wouldn't be life. If we could control our likeness of it, it wouldn't be a likeness.

Scene 3

NURSE in chair, with WOMAN on couch. On the other side of the stage, in very separate light, DOCTOR is in his chair, with MAN on couch.

WOMAN: He stayed waiting, I left. That's the story. I don't know. (*Pause.*) Can I leave?

NURSE: In a little. Once – I am reminded – I didn't know, either. On a train, in a dress, in the winter. Me, and the snow coming down, as if in some famous short story, into the ocean off the shore of some rocky land. I saw a horse, from the train. I was on my youthful way south to see if someone might marry me, a man I had already given my hand and the rest of my body to, because that's what you did when you did that in those days. Only a pony really. Are you cold? He said no, go home – essentially, go to hell. That horse looked cold, standing in the middle of such a snowy and fictional-seeming winter. Or, pony. All the frozen marsh water around her. I never understood. The tall dead grasses. I assume it was a female. I was pretty. Not as pretty as you. Pretty enough, I thought, but, maybe not. What changed, I wanted to ask him. Cute, I guess you would say. No. Pretty, I was pretty when I was young. The way you are. The way you, I mean this as a compliment, will have been.

WOMAN: Thank you. I'm sorry, can I go?

NURSE: No, dear. What I learned from all this is that I didn't learn that much. Live and learn – but not that much. (*Pause.*) We still have some time.

DOCTOR: How goes life here, too fast, too slow? Happily, lamentably, timelessly, around, not at all – how goes it?

MAN: I saw someone, the other day. I tried to make conversation.

DOCTOR: Yes, I saw someone, once. Once, I, standing ankles-deep in a brook watching geese flying by. I was thinking of the shape of a horse and trying to picture the cloud that might best represent it. Who comes along but – life is too remarkable – a woman. She was so pretty-looking, her collarbones, or, you know, clavicle, her clavicles, and so on, down the bones of her body. I climbed out of my water, crying hello, crying hi. I proposed all sorts of things to her. She slowly declined, over the coming months. I invited her to the ocean. She said no and no and never and then, one coming month, yes. We were together for a time. She threw me a surprise party. I had a mild stroke. Everyone came. She gave me an antique train set and I was rushed to the hospital. Some people knock looking backwards as a way to live. I do not. Never did.

NURSE: I've felt a lot. As many people have. Where I distinguish myself is, I stand outside at night. I try to make new constellations out of the old stars, if there are old stars out. Sometimes it rains. Or there's sleet, or nothing. I remember I was so hurt. I stand there. Or I don't. I'm a professional. This may all seem as if it's… I don't know. But it isn't. Unless it is. And if so, then, there you go. But all you need to know is that I, like the rest, sit here with a serious history, with little and real fears and dreams, a heart and two eyes, looking out, from a body of bones, watching you and the rest of the world for some sign. We have a little more time.

DOCTOR: I loved her and felt ugly. I grew to hate the way I walked, my stupid posture. I saw my dull reflection glaring at me from windows and mirrors, saying to me, 'What are you looking at?' I asked myself, 'Am I beautiful, inside?' No response, inside, except gurgling. None, without, except a different gurgling. People died. Winter and Summer Olympics passed. I slowly declined. I used to love the Butterfly, in swimming. The Downhill, in skiing. You probably don't see me as a man who loved so much. I, like everyone, was and was so for very long. Summer or winter, I cheered for everyone. I learned the stories of our nation's young athletes, their role models, subjects they failed in school, how hard they worked, and in such awful weather. I loved a lot. Instead of her. I don't know why.

NURSE: My one true love: a meaningless fling. I looked for the horse on the ride home.

DOCTOR: It wouldn't have killed me if things had been different.

MAN: My life is going to be different.

WOMAN: My life story unfurls itself before me in gleaming ripples and hopeful waves of never-ending and over-written difference.

NURSE: I'm surprised, as I get older and people look me less and less in the eye, how nothing is ever different. It seems that the way things seem is the way they're going to stay seeming. There's that old saying: Buck teeth are buck teeth. And that other old saying: Horses always smell like horses.

WOMAN: Are those really old sayings?

NURSE: They will be, someday, if people start saying them now. (*She looks at her watch.*) Speaking of someday, we don't have any more time, for today.

MAN: You know what's probably pretty interesting, is that I have never really –

DOCTOR: (*Interrupting. He is making notes. His pen appears to have run out of ink. He shakes it, vigorously.*) Hang on a sec. (*He finds another pen, has to draw scribbles with it for a moment, in order for the ink to begin running.*) There. I think we made some real progress.

PROLOGUE: It's evening. The cold air, dark sky, and historical stars. Faraway traffic goes unhonkingly by, with daylight savings over, the beaches uncrowded. It is past twilight. Geese are flying noisily overhead, mated for life, as the duck-hunting season opens. Houses and corporate headquarters are festively decorated, empty except for the light. 'Tis the season hardest to suffer, and better to hibernate through. So now we, to the TV room, for some television.

EPILOGUE: Winter isn't sad. You've had happy times in winter. And sad ones in summer. Life goes by year-round. People get married in sleet storms. People get cancer on soft summer evenings, sitting by the radio, looking up words in a dictionary. You know this from experience, if you've ever had any. And there's nothing necessarily sad about anything. Or happy. I just wanted to make that clear. Am I making myself clear? It doesn't matter. You don't care. You're thinking about yourself. Our scene moves to the TV room.

Scene 4

WOMAN turns on the television. The television faces upstage.

TELEVISION: – cars with their lights on coming down Main Street, through this once darkened little town, now alight with grief. All, in a state of shock at the loss – the drowning – of the popular Williams family. The area always has a tragedy to grieve, but rarely one as grievous as this. A family, in whole, pulled drowned from the local pond, after an evening of skating, a winter's outing undertaken too early in the season. We are all on thin ice, but, for some of us, it is even thinner. Young and old, they still wore their skates, tightly tied on to make up for their weak ankles. Whatever they wore, all those generations now are now gone; and, though this reporter understands that this would have happened eventually, this reporter also understands it is tragic it happened now. One bright spot, they leave no family behind. They are survived by only their neighborhood and house. No legal battles will ensue. It's all settled. They're dead. Live, I am in Carlisle. Stay tuned for some holiday gift ideas and tips on ways to keep your car battery from freezing. Reporting for channel –

WOMAN turns off television. Pause. MAN enters.

MAN: Hi.

WOMAN: Well, if it isn't you.

MAN: Yup. Or, nope? Hi.

WOMAN: Did your phone call come?

MAN: That thing doesn't take incoming phone calls, it turns out. Did you find somewhere to make yours from?

WOMAN: I decided not to call.

MAN: I feel bad.

WOMAN: It isn't your fault. It was better I didn't call. I'm glad.

MAN: Oh good. I'm glad. I still feel bad. (*Pause.*) Not because of anything to do with you.

WOMAN: I'm sorry.

MAN: It isn't your fault. As I think I just, you know, pretty clearly, said. Do you have change for the laundry room?

WOMAN: I might. (*She begins to look for change.*) Did you watch the sun go down tonight?

MAN: (*Pause.*) Don't you see what's happening here?

WOMAN: No.

MAN: Me neither.

WOMAN: Me neither. Did you see the sunset?

MAN: Oh, right – the sun, going down. No. I didn't. I think I can honestly say, I did not.

WOMAN: You should have. It was pretty. It was cold-looking. A person could come up with all kinds of words, if he sat down and tried.

MAN: I'm sure. (*Pause.*) Bye. (*Begins to leave.*)

WOMAN: Do you have anyone come, for visiting hours?

MAN: I'm separated.

WOMAN: Is your wife near here?

MAN: Oh I'm not married. I just kind of meant –

WOMAN: Me neither.

MAN: I thought I would be divorced by now. Sometimes I see a rickety little house with broken shutters and a tiny swimming pool and I think, 'I'd like to get married, and then get divorced, and then live there.' But I never met the right person. See you around.

WOMAN: Didn't you need quarters?

MAN: No. No, thanks. That was just a need I had. Something to act on. And so I did. And here we are. Bye, again.

He exits. WOMAN exits.

PROLOGUE: Do things seem aimless? Maybe that's how things are. Do you think anyone has a future? An aim? The man and woman? The Nurse and Doctor? Are you an optimist? Do you see a love scene on the sunless horizon? Are you good at making things up? And can you properly repress? My questions won't get us anywhere. Nor, probably, would my answers. But, so, to the Group Therapy Room, for group therapy, in the morning.

EPILOGUE: Is the main action of the play a man with a pencil in his hand, sitting at a desk in the morning, trying to come up with a word for sunset? Is the through-story (so-called) thrown away? As he tries to revise the play and create ornate metaphors for simple things? As the old fears creep in. The old story. Is repetition a failure in daring, or a step toward deliverance? Could be both. Don't know, never knew. So, to the Group Therapy Room, for group therapy, in the morning. I quote. Or, repeat. Because, why wouldn't I? That's what we do.

Scene 5

DOCTOR, NURSE, MAN, WOMAN, are seated together.

DOCTOR: It was always one of the most beautiful places and times in the world for me.

NURSE: (*Pause.*) What was?

DOCTOR: Didn't I say? I'm sorry. The Netherlands, when I went when I was young. The days were girls. Blue skies, yellow flowers, the world's largest diamond. Decent drugs, Anne Frank's attic, tall blonde Dutch women on vintage bicycles, and me. I saw the King at a tennis game.

NURSE: (*Pause.*) How does traveling make people feel?

WOMAN: I've never been anywhere. No, yes I have.

MAN: Sad.

NURSE: I'm sorry?

MAN: Traveling makes me feel sad.

NURSE: Why, do you think?

MAN: Why do I *think*? I guess because –

NURSE: (*Interrupting.*) Why do you think it makes you feel sad?

MAN: I don't *think* it makes me feel sad. Traveling makes me feel sad. F, E, E, L. S, A, D.

NURSE: Oh, a speller.

DOCTOR: Maybe – M, A, Y, B, E – it has something to do with all the things going past in the window. The sadness, I mean. Life life life, mile after mile. You're a smiling baby, a reckless teen, a tax-paying adult, a corpse. Bang bang bang. You're just getting the hang of the toilet and, suddenly, time to pick out a coffin. I'm kidding. Or, exaggerating. Slightly. (*Brief pause.*) Amsterdam.

Everyone looks at DOCTOR. Pause.

WOMAN: Once I lived a whole summer with a friend's family. I did everything they did. I got stung by bees and tried drinking and simple kinds of kissing. It was hard being away and then hard being home. Is that something like what you were looking for someone to say?

NURSE: Just like, dear. Thank you. I guess we're all away from somewhere. Away from some house on some street, or from some position in relation to the body of the mother. By dint of our being here. Did anyone know that 'dintless' was a word?

MAN: Did anyone ever see a movie called 'By Dint of the Bridge's Collapse'?

WOMAN: Is that where the shoe-shine boy is always staring at the girl who sells flowers? But there's no reason to buy flowers and no one has good shoes because the whole town is poor and totally sad. He's a poet. Or he's thinking about it. The girl only eats vitamins.

DOCTOR: And she was played by Susette de Baronelle, who I was a little in love with. Still a little am.

NURSE: Movies are wonderful. I didn't see that particular one.

MAN: And his brother keeps bringing different animals home and naming them all the same thing. And, right, the main boy stares at the main girl. You never know if they ever meet, or ever fall in love. The town is in a sort of quarantine.

DOCTOR: (*Looking at his watch and his notepad.*) I know this has only been a few pages, but we have to stop. (*He takes out an appointment book.*) Sorry. Funny, life. We don't even have time to misrepresent ourselves. We hardly have time to make a tragic error of our lives. Oh, well, ah, well. Now, before everyone leaves, I need to change next week. (*He begins writing in appointment book. Pauses.*) I'm starting to think it was Belgium I went to, and that I only read about Amsterdam.

PROLOGUE: The weeks change anyway. Another little pause in the world. (*Pause.*) Then, right on cue, here comes more time, giving us life, rushing past, taking it away. Time. Do you feel it? Ladies and gentlemen, do you? It's there. I wouldn't know how it feels. In words.

That's all right. It's late on an early winter's evening, and we, to the rec. room, rush!

EPILOGUE: In other words: tick-tock, tick-tock. But, again, well-enough said. 'The weeks change anyway.' Time is important here, to us. The general sweep of it, not its particularities. 'Sweep' is the wrong word, but, you'll live with it. Gentle, deadly. Slow and violent, it just goes by. I wouldn't look for some life-changing event. Except life, or illness, or death. This is all supposed to be at least plausible, after all, our play. Real contemporary realism. But, so, what changed your life? Forever. Whatever it was, it's probably still doing it. Tick, tock. Or to put it another way, at what moment did your life suddenly stay the same forever. It's night in the rec. room. We claim. You're sitting there in the dark. Strangers on either side.

Scene 6

MAN is assembling a balsa-wood toy airplane. WOMAN walks by in the background, upstage. She stops to look and listen, unseen.

MAN: All quiet, as I assemble a balsa-wood toy airplane. I'll use a rubber band to drive the propeller. Once finished, once this project of mine is done, when the little toy can finally fly, it won't help anything, but it will fly beautifully and sputteringly high above this dirt-bound life, without changing anything, and then crash, without end, until it's over.

WOMAN exits.

PROLOGUE: Night's over. And it's morning. And we return to rooms we thought we left. We return to the rec. room. It makes you wonder. Have life and the whole world already been written – been foreseen, foretold, long been forborne? Is the ending of the story already in your bones? The fevered climax already long in your cold blood?

EPILOGUE: Maybe. Probably. You know what's what. But you hope that along the way there will still be, sometimes, a surprise. We're back in the rec. room, yes. The woman enters, yelling:

Scene 7

WOMAN: Surprise! (*She enters holding a lit candle. The balsa-wood airplane is completed. She sings.*) Happy Birthday to You. (*She speaks.*) You know the middle part. (*She sings the final line.*) Happy Birthday to You. (*She speaks.*) I guess you know the ending, too. The fevered climax is probably already long in your cold blood. But it seemed unkind somehow, or anti-art, not to sing it.

MAN: My birthday isn't until spring.

WOMAN: How would I know that? We've hardly talked. That's what makes this so gracious an act. So mysterious.

MAN: It is pretty gracious an act. Pretty mysterious. Thanks. (*He holds up the candle.*) Was there a cake that came with this?

WOMAN: My uncle died on his birthday last year.

MAN: I'm sorry. He's in a better place, I guess.

WOMAN: We don't know. He lived on a nice street. He died.

MAN: I'm sorry.

WOMAN: It's not your fault. Is it? It isn't. His gravestone read, 'Here lies the late myself, dead as far as the eye can see.'

MAN: Cake? (*He feeds her an imaginary piece of cake.*)

WOMAN: Mmmm. Not bad. Here, you. (*She feeds him a piece. Pause.*) You put your hand in my mouth, just then.

MAN: Ditto you yours in mine.

WOMAN: What a cold and intriguing sentence. I remember, once, I don't know why I remember – oh, I know why: it was cold. And intriguing. To me. But, so, up north, once, I threw all this outdoor furniture off the roof of a museum. Chairs and tables and glass ashtrays. That was the start of my adulthood. I was trying to become a lifeguard. I was supposed to be rescuing things. Around that point, people stopped returning my calls, generally. I started acting really psychological. When I bled – you know, girl stuff – I bled too much.

MAN: Oh. A lot of that kind of went over my –. So, did you ever become a lifeguard? (*Pause.*) Wasn't the water cold up there? I got really emotional next to a screen door, once. So there was that. (*Pause.*) Have you seen outside? It looks like rain. Or snow.

WOMAN: What does?

MAN: It does, what else, the – I don't know – sky, the firmament. The, um, welkin. (*Pause.*) We pretended to eat cake. I find that sort of interesting.

WOMAN: I would have to sort of agree. I'm looking forward to seeing you again.

MAN: Are you leaving?

WOMAN: No. It was for children, I should add.

MAN: What was? The museum was?

WOMAN: I should go.

MAN: Did I say something?

WOMAN: Did it sound to you as if you said something? I didn't hurt anyone, throwing the stuff off. Even though I broke everything. And could have killed someone. I feel as if I should go. And that usually means I should go. Bye. (*Exits.*)

MAN: Bye. (*To himself.*) I feel as if I should go. (*Pause. Exits.*)

PROLOGUE: Despite winter coming at these two from every angle and direction, one can sense a little spring in their speech. Them two, warming toward each other. Our scene moves ahead one week. And it has snowed. And it is night. On the grounds, somebody built six snowmen, facing different ways, standing too close together. And our love story has progressed without us. Will we catch up to it, overtake it? Either way, to the sunroom, in the moonlight.

EPILOGUE: The birthday scene was a happy scene. But let's not be precious. If not these two talking, then two others. Or one of them and someone else, some third person. The history of plays and the history of the world is a set of the same conversations being had by different people. We've all been through them. 'You are the only one, forever,' we swear, having sworn it twice, or more. People are liars, but, liars are people. Take me. Forgive and forget. Then die and be forgotten. Or, I don't know – maybe there's more to it. But in the meantime these two are becoming sort of lovely together. I admit. A handsome couple. Either way, we are in the sun room. A week later, a night, the Winter Solstice.

Scene 8

NURSE and DOCTOR are seated, wearing winter jackets. They have skates. There is a bowl of plastic fruit on the table before them.

NURSE: They're probably having one of their very particular conversations, in which they both take such solace. I remember those conversations, those whispered times – so original, such pure meaning and total motivation. You go ahead. I'll wait.

DOCTOR: No, no. I'll wait with you. It'll make the time go by faster. (*Pause. The time doesn't go by faster.*) I haven't skated in a while.

NURSE: How about that heartbreaking story of that family skating. And the ice broke and they all fell through? Williams, was it? The name?

DOCTOR: I think, yes. Imagine, a dead family. When they dragged the bodies out, the whole town could hardly keep staring. I thought I might speak about it, might try to bang it up into words, at the conference on the National Grief in the spring. To the which, by the way, I would, I must say, of course – it goes without saying – love you to come.

NURSE: Please, Doctor. Must you be so forward?

DOCTOR: I'm sorry, you're right. I use a lot of dashes and commas when I get nervous. But it would be wonderful and helpful. Give it some thought. Period. Speeches about grief during the day, a whirlpool, a shower, and then cocktails at seven. It's in one of those little sea towns. We could take the train down.

NURSE: I haven't been to the ocean since I was a girl. I was a girl at one time, Doctor, as you are probably aware.

DOCTOR: We could play golf. Doctors are pretty good at golf. I never played. Don't tell anyone, I could lose my license. And I was aware.

NURSE: I would love to see the sun set over somewhere that wasn't here.

DOCTOR: So it's decided. Is it decided? Well, you think, and then decide.

NURSE: I will.

DOCTOR: (*Looking at the bowl of fruit.*) These are fake, I just noticed.

MAN and WOMAN enter.

NURSE: And here they are! Come on, you two. Everyone is waiting.

WOMAN: You go ahead. I'm cold. I want to put on more clothes.

DOCTOR: Okay, but quickly now. Time's a-wasting. There's only so much cocoa. That's my philosophy.

NURSE: You can't go wrong with a philosophy like that. Also, 'Don't get sick in Portugal,' someone once told me. (*To MAN.*) You need a hat. And hurry. We're going to light some sparklers.

NURSE and DOCTOR exit.

WOMAN: Let's stay. I've seen a sparkler before.

MAN: Okay. Are you thinking what I'm thinking?

WOMAN: Are you thinking about when I burned my hand one year on New Year's Eve?

MAN: No.

WOMAN: Then no.

MAN: You look pretty.

WOMAN: Maybe I am pretty.

MAN: That would explain it. (*Pause.*) Where were you hiding yourself today?

WOMAN: In the basement, behind the hot-water heater, in fear.

MAN: You missed exercise this morning.

WOMAN: I said I was under the weather. And behind the hot-water heater. I always liked exercise.

MAN: I bet you throw like a girl.

WOMAN: I am a girl.

MAN: Oh, hello. Are your mother and father still together?

WOMAN: My father is. But don't change subjects so fast. Because, just don't, please. Swimming is an interest I have. Let's talk about that. 'What Swimming Is Like.' Begin. Discuss. Enlarge. You have an average lifetime.

MAN: Swimming is different. From walking.

WOMAN: I see.

MAN: It's fun.

WOMAN: I see. Go on.

MAN: I'll never be how you think.

WOMAN: Oh.

MAN: Whales swim.

WOMAN: They do. Every day of the week.

MAN: There's enough room in the ocean for everyone in the world to have room to drown in. Do you see? (*He looks at the ceiling.*) But don't leave me, don't leave me,

She moves to his side.

please don't leave me –

WOMAN: (*She interrupts. Puts her hand on his shoulder.*) Here I am, I'm right here, it's all right, I'm right –

MAN: (*He interrupts. Unkindly. He shrugs her hand off.*) Listen, can't you see I'm in the middle of something?

NURSE: (*Enters.*) I forgot my scarf. Come on, you two. Don't just sit around here and miss everything. Okay, Miss Everything? (*She playfully flicks WOMAN with her scarf.*) And Mister Everything Else. The world is racing by and Doctor is skating around backward. He also just proposed to me that we all build an igloo. Is my lipstick all right? Is my mouth on right? Do I look crazy? Do I look, would you say, crazed, at all? Anyway, hurry. (*Exits.*)

MAN: I'm sorry I yelled.

WOMAN: You didn't yell. (*Pause.*) I don't want to miss everything. I really don't. I like everything.

MAN: Me neither. (*Pause.*) I meant to yell.

WOMAN: (*Pause.*) Name a season.

MAN: Winter.

WOMAN: Name another.

MAN: Spring.

WOMAN: We were made for each other.

MAN: Name an animal.

WOMAN: The otter.

MAN: Name another.

WOMAN: No thanks.

MAN: We were.

WOMAN: Can we go be alone somewhere?

MAN: I know just the place.

WOMAN: Where?

MAN: I don't know.

WOMAN: How about your room?

MAN: If you don't mind the state it's in.

WOMAN: No.

MAN: And you don't mind that it's mine.

WOMAN: No.

MAN: Or that everything in it is mine. If you don't mind that loss shall be yours. And then even that will be taken away. And it might be messy. Are you allergic to dust?

WOMAN: No.

MAN: I want you to have the last word.

WOMAN: (*Pause.*) Sympathy?

They exit, him carrying her.

PROLOGUE: What more could anyone want? What would anyone add? And why? And how would he phrase it? (*Pause.*) I'll say this. Their skin is young. And they know nothing. Unlike ourselves, whose skin is old and who know nothing. But onward. There is no need to show what we all can so easily imagine, what we all so often and easily imagine. For instance, her taking his hand in hers and running it over her mouth, wetting it, running it over each breast, to down between her legs. All in a single fluid movement. And then him responding in kind, whispering into her eye, gently pulling her hair.

They both say, 'God.' They both come to an understanding. And it's over. They lie all over each other. (*Pause.*) Now it's late. The skaters have all come in. What cocoa is left over is frozen. The doctor fell and sprained his ankle, having fun and showing off. Nobody drowned. Winter has officially begun. Somebody lost a mitten. It's quiet and nothing more need be said.

EPILOGUE: Probably not. Probably not. (*Pause.*) But, feelings between the man and woman, yes. The two characters seem right, beside the other, like the character of the bird and the rock in ancient Chinese writing, beside the other. One bird, one stone. What is between the man and the woman is starting to seem inevitable, as with the rock and the bird. Will they be beside themselves forever? Do you follow my drift? From away from where I was? Is it noticeable yet? For I have one, a drift. All will painfully make itself painfully clear. Oh, but for now, such splendor, the liquid movements, the responding in kind, the hair, the hands, my God. Almost makes you… I don't know. (*He stares off, wistfully. Returns abruptly.*) The room of the man.

Scene 9

MAN: Do you see children anywhere on your horizon? A little baby screaming out of you? A new father standing frozen in horror behind his rented video equipment, trying to smile and focus? And a new voice in the world, crying? A new cry. Is that so crazy-sounding?

WOMAN: No.

MAN: Okay. Then, plus, when I was younger with my arms unbroken and my dreams undreamt, a sister in a snowsuit, leaving you soon, seeing red, and do the Netherlands still have a king? I don't know and my mouth on you and parting the ocean and your legs and baying at the moon and earth, crying, 'Mother Mother,' and 'Not Mother, Not Mother.' Crying, 'Writing.' Crying, nothing. Wanting only to be alone in the quiet and dark, so as to be lonely and home, so as to be drenched on the inside with blood, waiting, a man in house, *Wo est der zoo*, et cetera, and let slip the dogs of love while I go change into something more tennis-oriented. (*Pause.*) Is that so crazy-sounding?

WOMAN: A little. But I could see a child. We could take family trips to the beach. You could look for a place for our towel. I could pull my suit down from where it had ridden up. Us, on the world, sunburned, hungry– a little family. Taking showers under those little weak showers that they have in front of the giant ocean. And something to eat, after. Also, lowering your fly while we're driving home. A wet road map. The baby, asleep. Showering at home. You have pretty bones in your face. I would always lose my keys. You could type upstairs. Is this too scattered-sounding?

MAN: No.

PROLOGUE: Ah, love.

WOMAN: You should have the last word.

NURSE and DOCTOR enter at other side of stage, but remain in a separate playing area from MAN and WOMAN.

MAN: Sympathy is such a good one. But let's see. Ocean, no; Medication, no; Redemption, no; Cocoa, no; Myself, no; Salvation, no; It isn't Summer, Trust, or Honesty, no. It's from Latin I have a feeling. I don't know. Dire? Is dire Latin? Is Latin Latin?

MAN and WOMAN exit.

NURSE: I think it's beautiful.

DOCTOR: It's a little unheard of, isn't it? I never heard of anything like this. I fear for them.

NURSE: I'm sure they fear for themselves just fine.

DOCTOR: How far have things progressed? If I may use so clinical a term. See, there's the problem. A growing clinicality. The old heart-breaking songs don't break my heart anymore. I haven't cried for the last five Olympics. But, how far?

NURSE: Far, I imagine, from the distant look they give each other. Those old songs will break your heart again, or the new ones will, when they're old. (*Pause.*) I saw people ice-fishing driving in this morning. There was a little bird flying over all the holes. How is your ankle healing?

DOCTOR: Correctly, I think, I thank you. I'm glad it's not broken. You'd have to carry me all over that conference.

NURSE: Which I would do with a smile. A grimace, I guess. A sort of pained, burdened, hyperventilating but not unhappy grimace. A smile.

PROLOGUE: Outside the window, a kite in a tree is covered in ice. People's bodies looked changed in the distance of the parking lot – hunched, closed, as seen in ultrasound – as they struggle with their frozen car door locks. Something to behold. And how long can they be beheld? How long can an image be kept in mind? I wouldn't hold your breath. Go stretch. I need to relieve myself. We'll take a little break, an intermission. Please come back, and, if you do, maybe you'll find that the cushion of your seat is cold and has given up the shape that you gave it, that there is no trace of you but your absence and a few gum wrappers. No trace. Imagine that. Hard to conceive. Almost impossible for us to conceive. See you soon.

EPILOGUE: (*He seems to be considering many things, preparing to make a long speech.*) Fifteen minutes.

Lights down.

ACT TWO

Scene 1

Lights up on MAN and WOMAN, seated. They exit.

PROLOGUE: You've come back. Some time passed, in the last few minutes. Christmas did. Life continued. Christmas ended. Those decorations that made it through the wind and cold unbroken now are all down and put away. Whatever was frozen, froze harder. On the south lawn are snow forts and snow angels losing their child-made form. Very very north of here, a polar bear is eating a seal cub. And far over that, a dead satellite launched from Florida, America, during an earlier presidency, is floating out of control in freezing outer space. Back on Earth, we are in the reading room, in the Common Era.

EPILOGUE: What if you were writing a play and your feelings changed? You didn't even know how you felt anymore, or what you thought. You couldn't keep going. The image disintegrated. Your mind wasn't up to it, or your heart. Would your claim to realism be lost if you didn't somehow incorporate the change, the not-knowing, the cold feeling? Would you just abort the whole thing? Wash your hands of the whole bloody mess? What would you do, back on Earth? We move our scene to the reading room, sure, why not, in the Common Era.

Scene 2

Lights up on MAN and WOMAN. He is reading.

WOMAN: Where were you yesterday?

MAN: I had to take some tests.

WOMAN: What kind of tests, blood tests? History tests?

MAN: I took a Spielberger Rage and Anger Index, a Van Beck Depression Composite, a Taylor Manifest Anxiety Scale, and, just out of curiosity, a Minnesota Multiphasic Personality Inventory.

WOMAN: (*Pause.*) How did they go?

MAN: I think I did really well.

WOMAN: (*Pause.*) What are you reading?

MAN: The dictionary.

WOMAN: How is it?

MAN: You know the joke. It's a little wordy. The verbs are good, at the beginning. You get sick of them.

WOMAN: I'll wait for the movie. (*Pause.*) You don't think that's funny?

MAN: Listen to this, (*He reads.*) 'Hilaktia: Disorder named for Greek ruler whose vivid nightmares of winter caused him to die and his body to manifest all signs of having frozen, despite the season being summer, the weather being warm. He wrote several plays, which survive in fragments or not at all. The disorder is characterized by a flight of ideas, a fear of the mind, and disregard for language; also paleness and change, hatred. Treatable, with bright light, photographs, medicative therapies.'

WOMAN: (*Pause.*) What am I supposed to think about that?

MAN: You got me. Something, though. You'd think you'd think something. (*Pause.*) Don't you ever change clothes? I'm sorry I said that. But don't you? Forget I said that. Forget I said I'm sick of you and your body and sick of our story. One side of me seems to say – I don't know. Forget it. Listen to me, my sucky vocabulary. Blah!

Blahhh! I wonder if I have that General's disease. Or, whatever, 'ruler'.

WOMAN: Maybe you just need –

MAN: (*Interrupting.*) Thanks, I'll try that.

PROLOGUE: Do you remember somebody mentioning an otter? When verb followed noun, when the man and woman spoke lovingly and plainly in simple yups and good old household nopes? The beautiful woman said – it was such a beautiful line – 'Yes.' I forget what the beautiful man had asked her. I forget the exact feeling. But I can say the word beautiful. I could say a lot of words, if I sat down and tried. And I do know where this is going. So, to someplace! Lights, action!

EPILOGUE: Darkness, inaction. As an aside, have you ever been stung by a bee that had nothing against you? Or bitten by a dog who otherwise seemed to like you? Or gotten stuck in freezing rain? Or fell, due to a gravity not your own? Or hurt someone you loved, or used to love, or never did? Ever suffer loss? Ever slowly lose control of something? Ever slowly lose control of everything? Fail? Ever fucking really badly fail?

Scene 3

WOMAN: Interesting people have interesting names. This is sort of a juncture. For us. Would getting one of those books of children's names be a good idea?

MAN: Theoretically.

WOMAN: You have to have some feelings. Name some names.

MAN: Lawyer Malloy. Bodhisattva. Steve Stevenson, I don't know. I think Alexander Graham Bell has a certain ring to it.

WOMAN: A first name will be fine. And what if she's a girl?

MAN: Then you can name her You, after you. Or, I don't know. Simone? Isn't there a human name, Simone?

WOMAN: Please, darling, try.

MAN: All right, darling, I will.

WOMAN: Now, think.

MAN: I'm thinking. (*Pause.*) I've thought. (*Pause.*) I should speak. This might hurt. (*Pause.*) What if there is someone else?

WOMAN: There's everyone else.

MAN: No, no there isn't. What if I don't care about this, because I'm in love with someone else. That would be quite a turn. The famous, 'another woman'. She studied trumpet and she's teaching me the harmonica. We play in the snow. I gave her the children's book you gave me that I said I had lost.

WOMAN: I'm sorry? I'm preoccupied with the baby, yours, inside of me. You said something about a trumpet?

MAN: I said something about my lying and cheating and going back on my word. Listen to this, the following words: my feelings changed. From away from ones of love.

WOMAN: Stop it.

MAN: I already did. It'll be as if I never started. I would have told you sooner, but, I don't know.

WOMAN: You're serious.

MAN: Not really. I don't know. Probably.

WOMAN: What is her name?

MAN: Again, with names. You wouldn't believe me if I told you.

WOMAN: Why not?

MAN: Because I'd be lying.

EPILOGUE: Ah, love.

WOMAN: (*Pause.*) How could you do this?

MAN: This? Is that how you would denote my million million feelings: 'this'? Or do I mean 'connote'?

WOMAN: Just the other day we were talking –

MAN: (*Interrupting.*) I know I keep interrupting, but, 'The Other Day and The Other Day and The Other Day. Life is but a bucket boy drumming for loose change, a person playing pots and pans on the street as a way to get some food. Or, not really, not at all. That isn't at all what life was, The Other Day, The Other Day, The Other Day.' It ends a little weakly, kind of tails off, but how's that for a soliloquy?

WOMAN: Please listen. Just to this one little thing. I want you to listen. When I was little, before school or anything –. You gave her the book I brought back from Ireland? I walked forever. I went through miles of stupid Irish rain to buy that stupid book. I loved that stupid book. *Sleepy Time Rhymes.* We colored it together. And you gave it away to some bitch to remain unnamed?

MAN: Don't swear. I hate swearing. When you hear swearing you know the person has lost the feeling. But, that book, I believe you mentioned that book, *Sleepy Time Rhymes.* It made her happy. She loved it, too. She cried over it. We read it to each other and went through it with White-Out and uncolored it. It was our best night.

WOMAN: What did I do?

MAN: Nothing. Somewhere, though, someone did something. It would seem. Once, there was a pretty pretty girl. Maybe she's the one who did something. Time will take of her. We'll see what pretty bones her face is made up of. Her, I loved. Unlike you and the woman I'm now leaving you for. Her name is Margaret, too.

WOMAN: My name's not Margaret.

MAN: No, I know. I just meant that she's another person with that name.

PROLOGUE: Welcome to a play whose –. Parlez-vous anglais? Sprechen Sie Englisch? Niwappi inglappa? Schones totes Kind, estos zapatos son cuellos? Esti palid. Mimi niliyeona nasema hivi. Wo est der Zoo? I speak English. Or, I used to. We now rejoin –. This doesn't cohere. I can't make this make sense. (*He exits.*)

EPILOGUE: He just said, (*Reading.*) 'Welcome. Do you speak English? Do you speak English? Do you speak English? Beautiful dead child, whose shoes are those? You are pale. I who saw say thus. Where is the zoo? I speak English. Or, I used to. We now rejoin –. This doesn't cohere. I can't make this make sense.' I quote. For what it's worth. Which is probably very little. But maybe not. I'm not big on assigning values. (*He looks to where PROLOGUE has just exited.*) We now rejoin the man and the woman. It doesn't matter where.

Scene 4

WOMAN: You can stop loving me overnight?

MAN: I started loving you overnight.

WOMAN: We took walks. We undressed each other. You said such beautiful true-sounding things.

MAN: Go to hell.

Pause. DOCTOR enters.

Say, what do you think we should name the baby?

DOCTOR: Did you both forget? Everyone's going out on the hill for a big photograph. We're losing daylight, so rush. We need everyone. I would come back if I could. I heard you fighting.

MAN: Just she was fighting.

DOCTOR: One person can't fight.

WOMAN: Yes one can. I was, just. Me, alone, fighting.

DOCTOR: I'm wrong, then. Malpractice, my old friend. But let's go outside. We never get good weather, so let's not let it blow over. Winter is going to kill everything and we want to have a photograph to look at to keep us warm while we suffer through it. I know this is a bad time, but it's for the Crossroads brochure.

WOMAN, MAN, and DOCTOR exit.

PROLOGUE: (*He enters. His hair is messed up, his clothes are disheveled. He has a glass of water.*) I apologize for the awful languages that I was using before. It's just that…oh, I don't know. Sometimes I wish… (*He regains some composure. Pause.*) Anyway. They all go. They stare at the camera. Like life, it's over, like that. Long complicated life histories, over, click. Documented. Flat. Where did all the talk about the ocean go? Down some drain, out to sea? And you? How are you? Think of yourself when you were younger. Did you ever love anybody? I bet you did. You looked so proud. Your nice shoes and clothes are still somewhere. You may be thinking of that. As you live on, as you lose some more of the rest of your life quietly, wrecking yourself in the dark. (*Pause.*) Everybody leaves. The photographer gets in his car. Day is over again.

EPILOGUE: Right. Right. One more thing. There's more snow in the forecast, moving in like a hungry animal from somewhere out over the ocean. If you'll forgive me the simile. Which you probably don't. So I take it back. It's black, out. The freezing shitty night settles. I've lost the feeling. This is useless. I don't care about the time or where anyone is.

Scene 5

WOMAN, MAN and DOCTOR enter. A pause, almost a minute long. They stand, not knowing exactly where they should be, as neither narrator has set the scene.

NURSE: (*Enters.*) Good morning, everyone. (*Pause.*) I see our scene has moved to the group therapy room, for group therapy. (*They all move across stage and seat themselves.*) Did someone get sick in the hallway?

WOMAN: Is this an experience experienced by anyone? Where it's just you and someone, and you lay and lie and lie in a room. This someone is lying next to you in the breathing dark but he doesn't know who he is, and that makes you start to slip. And you make the statement: I am not in control of my body or my mind. And you state the question: So then what is the 'I' that is the subject of the assertion. And then you tender the inquisition: Who is the liar, the breather, the nobody, lying next to me? And who is the one lying inside me, kicking? You won't recall this time in your life with any warmth. And you feel sick. And as you suffer all that and grow great with mistakes, you can't even count on anyone to be – not even faithful – but just humane? Just at least recognizable? Anyone? Any goddamn body? I never swear.

DOCTOR: Why doesn't everybody take a few deep breaths and –

WOMAN: (*Interrupting.*) Why doesn't everybody not do that. I've breathed deeply enough, thank you. I think I'll go be sick again. That would be the most expressive thing I could do. Word. (*She gets up, seeming light-headed.*) Excuse me. I'm sorry. I'll be all right. Or I'm wrong. I'm sorry and I won't be all right. And I'm not sorry. (*She walks downstage, stares at the audience for a moment, then exits.*)

DOCTOR: Why don't I go see if I can say anything. (*He exits.*)

NURSE: (*Long pause. Not unkindly.*) Well. You seem to be living with yourself. I don't know exactly what to say. (*Pause.*) It's supposed to be a beautiful sunset, tomorrow night. Or the night after that. Or that's what they said. Why don't we... I should...

NURSE exits. MAN exits.

PROLOGUE: Traffic lights are changing alone across the suburbs, the tundras, the empty urban intersections. Not that it has anything to do with anything.

EPILOGUE: Click, click. Tick, tock. This last night is now weeks ago. A new routine has set in. We are in evening. The action moves to a waiting room. Enjoy.

Scene 6

Lights up. WOMAN is sitting, staring into the audience. Pause. Lights down.

EPILOGUE: And to a laundry room.

Scene 7

Lights up. MAN is sitting, staring into the audience. Pause. Lights down.

EPILOGUE: And to an office.

Scene 8

DOCTOR: She says she'll take care of the child. She keeps saying, 'Me and the world will carry on.' Then she looks at a lamp or a pile of books and says, 'Won't we, world?' It makes you want to cry to hear.

NURSE: He says he never did well when people tested his personality. Then he says, 'This is just a stage.' Then he doesn't say anything. Except, then he says, 'Everything will end, happily.' The comma makes me worry. I listen and nod and say something I've said before.

DOCTOR: And then there's me. I stand here, idly. An empty white coat, a dry pen in my pocket. My oath is to first do no harm. But I don't do anything, ever. Except this. I stand outside and tilt my head and listen to the traffic and wonder if it's people coming or people going and revel at how it all sounds the same. Is that a promising entrance or heartbreaking exit? Then, like everyone, I go make notes, enter a journal entry on a scrap of paper to be left behind or recycled. Maybe I doodle a little design, heave a heavy – I don't know – sigh. I'm glad you're here. I've told you my hobby. What do you like to do?

NURSE: I'm glad you're here. Everything will quiet down eventually. I'm too busy for hobbies. Except reading and skiing and landscape painting, quilting, a little modern dance, tennis, calligraphy, comparative philology, and astronomy. I'm kidding. I thought a little levity might…

I think I'd like listening to the traffic. (*Pause.*) Spring will be pretty, the birds and the bees, and your speaking engagement. Then of course you'll have to decide how you're going to injure and embarrass yourself in the inter-hospital running race.

They share a little laugh.

PROLOGUE: Ah, finally, kindness. Love is deep and real and everywhere. All is well and all will be even better. We can see this all around us, clearly.

EPILOGUE: What a pain. I'm sick of the story. I'm sick of you. Next scene. It's got flowers in it.

Scene 9

WOMAN is asleep in bed. NURSE enters, carrying a neatly folded sweater.

NURSE: Here are some flowers, dear.

WOMAN: (*She is waking.*) Who? Did I light myself on fire and they put me in an insane asylum? Who broke into me? My father said I shined. I was in a boat or something. Everyone was there.

NURSE: Hello, darling. Easy, slowly. It was just a dream. I know it's hard. It gets harder and more awful, but it never ceases being beautiful. Or this is made up, and I'm lying. Either way, here are some flowers.

WOMAN: Could I brush my hair?

NURSE: I remember wanting to do the exact same thing after my empty-handed train ride. And after I underwent this same procedure, an abortion. Not to put too fine a point on it. I was to remain an unwed non-mother.

MAN appears at the door.

And who is that young man, so boyishly entering. I'll leave you two alone. Yell, if it gets too lonely. (*She exits.*)

MAN: They said you were sick.

WOMAN: How kind of them to phrase it that way.

MAN: Is there anything I can get? (*Pause.*) Is it contagious?

WOMAN: No. I had them evacuate the fetal material attached to my uterine wall. Can you think up a better name for that? Gilly, Sam, Jessamyn. There are so many pretty names. (*She closes her eyes.*)

DOCTOR and NURSE enter. PROLOGUE leaves his narrator's position to join them. NURSE is holding the sweater. DOCTOR has a tray of food. PROLOGUE has a heart-shaped box of candy. One by one, they set these things down, on a table or at the foot of the bed, and exit. PROLOGUE returns downstage to where he narrates from.

(*She opens her eyes.*) That was nice of everyone. You know, it physically hurt. It still really physically does. You don't know. Once, sweat from you got in my eye. It physically burned and I liked it. Will this be going into your play? And do you wonder whether you'll allow me to recover? What would be your name for this? This procedure, you and I? Our life? I should go. But I don't think I can walk. So, you. Come on, go. Consider yourself forgiven, your almost pretty eyes forgotten. Hand me that candy, please. I will be polite up to the end. I was never a person who swore, even though you had me swearing. Please go. No, wait. (*Pause.*) Now go.

MAN exits.

PROLOGUE: I –. I wish –. Now we –. The –. (*Pause.*) I could misquote the old books. That might be meaningful. What flowers could grow out of this rocky garbage? A gross of broken statues and a pile of overdue books.

Maybe the thunder will say something motherly. Maybe someone will say something kind.

EPILOGUE: (*He steps a step forward, a tiny shrug. He lowers his head, slightly, and steps back.*)

PROLOGUE: (*Pause. He is holding a photograph.*) Here is the picture from the hill that everyone stood on. You can see their breath. Aren't pictures of people beautiful. But, our story! Our scene moves up the coast, to the dazzling, cold, and pacific Atlantic Ocean! Quickly! To a young family, in the sun, happily. With all speed, fly!

EPILOGUE: Oops.

Scene 10

WOMAN: (*The scene is WOMAN in bed, still. She is taking pills, one with each sentence.*) This little piggy went to market. This little piggy is not careful. This little piggy's bladder relaxes, as she wets herself, as she did when she was little. And someone blew my house down. I was trusting, *Mein Schones totes Kind.* I will huff and puff and die. *Uff-hay* and *uff-pay*, in Pig Latin. *Ipso facto*, in regular non-Pig Latin. I am killing my body, in English. I knew everything. Dad? Tell me the story of me. A sleepy time rhyme. Italicize my life. This little. (*She closes her eyes.*)

PROLOGUE: (*He stares at the scene of WOMAN in bed. He turns to the audience, pauses. Begins to open his mouth. Closes it.*)

EPILOGUE: Stop crying. Practice holding and kissing your pillow, for when the day comes you really need to hold and kiss it – this is what I tell myself. There's a philosophy for you. Or, for me. And don't get sick in Portugal. Life is a word game. (*Pause.*) I don't know what else. Everything is worse, including our desire for improvement. Of a life, a life story, a play. All are awful, worse, the same, but, in the end, to be lived with. Life is fine. It's spring. In fatigue and a lack of creativity, we fall back on the device of a telephone.

Scene 11

DOCTOR: (*He is speaking on the telephone.*) I would like you to come down. I need to speak with you about your daughter. (*Pause.*) I would like to speak to you in person. Here. (*Pause.*) Please come. I'm sorry for being difficult. Thank you. (*Pause.*) I really need to speak with you, here. Person to person is best. Yes, a right turn after the big wooden ice cream cone. Thank you. (*He hangs up the telephone.*)

EPILOGUE: (*Pause. Looks over at PROLOGUE, who stares into the audience.*) Nothing to say? Cat got your tongue, and the rest of your body? No more scribbley poetry to throw at the moment? Lost your nerve? Can't do it? I guess I can understand. (*To audience.*) It is weeks later, again. Spring, more flowers. A desk. Sunlight. A patient sits near the desk with his belongings in a bag marked 'Patient's Belongings.'

Scene 12

NURSE: (*She is filling out paperwork. MAN is watching.*) Isn't it amazing how I can write upside-down like this? We're going to miss you. Do you have a forwarding address?

MAN: I do, but I don't know it yet. Is the doctor coming in, today?

NURSE: He said he'd try. Do you have any nice Easter plans?

MAN: I'm so sorry. I thought I loved her. Then I thought I didn't love her. That was the end, I thought. Then everything kept ending. How is her family, her father? I know he was close. How is he taking –

NURSE: (*Interrupting. Their lines overlap.*) He's very sad and –. I'm sorry, dear. You go ahead.

MAN: Should I say that I was… I don't know. What should I say? I never knew.

NURSE: Yes, dear, of course you didn't. I know. (*Pause.*) If you get out to Old Town, say hello for me. Get down to that wonderful bridge they have. I went there once with a beau. We had quite a time of it down in the weeds by the water. It's one of life's wonders how pretty it is. The river going by, people going by us, us saying to each other, 'Quiet. Quiet,' while our lives and those people went quietly by. Oh, the daffodils, and all the other flowers, all so prettily named.

MAN: I'll try to go.

DOCTOR enters walking with a cane. His face in swollen. He has trouble speaking.

NURSE: Well if it isn't you.

DOCTOR: Yub. Or, nobe? Hi.

NURSE: How are we today, Doctor Oh-So-Wonderfully-Handsome?

DOCTOR: Nod bad, thang you.

MAN: Doctor, what happened?

DOCTOR: I wath looging for my trhain thet in the attig and I god thtung by beez. I broak my toe drying to ghet away from thehm. Thirdy-five bee thtings in one segond, they thaid. I cand feel one thide. Bud, ind warth my band thide, ainway.

NURSE: I'm sorry?

DOCTOR: It wath my bad thide. For dayging pithurth.

NURSE: Thank goodness your good side was twice as good-looking to begin with. Maybe we'll take some pictures this afternoon.

DOCTOR: Thang you. You are nod thow bad yourthelve. Do wee haff thum way of reathing him?

NURSE: He'll let us know.

DOCTOR: (*To MAN.*) You ghan alwaith contag uth, here. (*Pause.*) Whad a fath winder. Lod off yhangeh. (*He is saying, 'Lots of changes.'*)

NURSE: I'm sorry, Doctor?

DOCTOR: Lahdz, ough, yhanghes.

NURSE: (*She doesn't understand.*) Yes.

DOCTOR: Ihthh –. (*He has to swallow.*) Ith your vhamly gumming?

NURSE: We called a taxi. (*To MAN.*) Which you should get out front for. And we have some new people arriving. May I walk you to your office?

DOCTOR: Thang you. All hride. Bhee goohd. Wheel mith you.

MAN: Thank you, Doctor. Good-bye. I loved –. I was –. Thank you.

In the following two lines, PROLOGUE and EPILOGUE both begin to speak over one another, then PROLOGUE needs to pause to drink some water.

PROLOGUE: Later, the Doctor is in his office, the Nurse–

EPILOGUE: Not that anyone cares, but this is not really the way –

EPILOGUE stops, steps back, in a moment of kindness and deference, to allow PROLOGUE to speak.

PROLOGUE: (*He clears his throat.*) Later, the Doctor is in his office, the Nurse in hers. The body of the woman, gone, and the tiny empty swaddling clothes on a shelf in a store, unbought. The body of the man is in a taxi, and then on a train. He sees the reflection of his reflection looking out the tinted window and sees the land and trees fly past. Towns fly by. People. 'Whad a fath winder.' There is a long long pause, no sound at all – it is like the quiet I deprived us of at the start of this. If it's my fault, then, forgive me. Pardon me. (*He exits.*)

EPILOGUE: It is neither not winter nor not summer. The body of the man, some man, is in another white room, alive, staring at another white wall. There was never any woman, never any nurse, nor doctor, nor certainly any man. Isn't that sad. There was never any abortion. There was no toy airplane. It was a pile of words. Isn't that sad.

PROLOGUE: (*Enters with flowers.*) How does the earth manage? But, us? Finally, we come to rest. The sun is setting, the great sad past in the air, all of your life is in the air this evening. Another sunset in another unseasonable season. The doctor and the nurse soldier on. The beauty of the suffering, suffering.

EPILOGUE: Life. Writing. Try again some other year. This was a mess. The wrong words at the wrong time. This is awful. So cold.

NURSE: Isn't it a pretty light? Aren't we lucky.

DOCTOR: Yes. It's a very pretty light. We are lucky.

NURSE: Doesn't it look quiet.

PROLOGUE: Thank you for coming. The End. Good night.

EPILOGUE: Thank you for coming. There is no end. Good night.

DOCTOR: It does look quiet.

PROLOGUE has his bouquet of flowers, and he turns, lifting them, not knowing to whom he should give them. Lights fade.

End of play.

INTERMISSION

Dramatis Personae

MRS SMITH /
RECORDED FEMALE VOICE TWO
sixties

MR SMITH /
RECORDED MALE VOICE ONE
sixties

JILL /
RECORDED FEMALE VOICE ONE
twenties

JACK /
RECORDED MALE VOICE TWO
twenties

Setting

The play is set in the audience of a play called *The Mayor*. The time is the intermission between acts of *The Mayor*. At the beginning of the play, recorded voices come from the back of the theatre, directed at the audience on stage, as if they were the voices of actors coming from a stage.

The play begins in almost dark. We see the actors seated on stage, as if in an audience, barely lit.

We hear the beeping of a heart-monitor machine.

RECORDED MALE VOICE ONE: Nothing is happening yet. This is not the moment. It will very gently come. Very natural and gentle, the moment – when it's time. You can hold his hand. I will tell you when. Gently, he will just go. We just turn off the machines. There's no plug; that's just an expression. I'm saying gentle so much. It will be dignified, dignity, reality, life, gentle. I need you to sign here.

RECORDED FEMALE VOICE ONE: Words fail me, in the face of this. Living life didn't prepare me for this. Studying English didn't prepare me for words failing me, vis-à-vis this. And I didn't imagine signing anything.

RECORDED MALE VOICE TWO: He looks so unpeaceful. So uncalm. As if it's all a crazy wiry machine of anxiety. There were so many things he never got to do, so many sarcastic things he never got to say.

RECORDED FEMALE VOICE ONE: He is a good man, your father. I wonder how life will be for us tomorrow. I wonder how it will be for us the day before that.

RECORDED MALE VOICE TWO: Meaning today.

RECORDED FEMALE VOICE ONE: Yes.

Lights fade up on four or more people applauding, seated as if an audience, facing the real audience. Recorded applause also plays. One or two people hold programs for a play called 'The Mayor'. The lighting on-stage gives the impression of house lights.

RECORDED FEMALE VOICE TWO: There will now be a brief intermission.

MR SMITH: (*A long pause.*) Well.

MRS SMITH: 'Well.'

JACK: Do you want to stay?

JILL: I guess. I wonder what happens next.

MR SMITH: (*Pause.*) I think I'll get a drink, or go to the bathroom.

JILL: (*To JACK.*) Do you need to get a drink, or go to the bathroom?

JACK: Not right now. Sometimes.

JILL: What do you think so far?

JACK: I don't know if the writing is, quite, I don't know. It's sort of boring. Somebody gets old, somebody dies.

MR SMITH: (*He stretches. A little irked by the above remark. Looking at his watch.*) Yes, sir. I believe I'll go to the bathroom, or get a drink. Liquids, one way or the other.

JACK: (*Pause. Looking at his program.*) I think it's a little over-written. Or underwritten. And I don't necessarily feel for anyone. And he looked so lively and now he's dying? And people don't talk the way they talk.

MR SMITH: No, true. Interesting point – people don't talk the way they talk. People don't seem how people seem. I am not the way I am. There's a subtlety to someone like me, or someone like anyone, that this play doesn't really capture. And who ever died that didn't once look lively?

MRS SMITH: Dear, please. Maybe there will be some gun play and swearing coming up, something to engage your great intelligence.

(*To JACK and JILL.*) My husband is unthinkably intelligent.

JACK: (*Looking again at his program.*) I guess the next part is supposed to take place in the future.

MR SMITH: Is it.

JILL: It's had its moments. Wasn't that a beautiful scene when the Mayor stepped down.

MR SMITH: Little towns like that in New England don't have mayors, they have a Board of Selectmen.

MRS SMITH: Did the sound of my husband's anger eating him alive from the inside-out bother either of you two during the first act?

JACK: A little.

JILL: No, of course not.

MR SMITH: No? Oh, good. I think – if I might reiterate – I'll go try to exercise my rights. Can I get anyone anything, while I'm up? A ginger ale, some toilet paper, nothing?

MRS SMITH: Thank you, dear, no. Wasn't that wonderful when the dying mayor's wife came out and made that wonderful speech: 'I'm afraid that the social economists have it wrong. It is the head of state, and not The State, that will gradually wither away.'

JILL: You could see in his eyes he wanted to live. Do you think he dies?

MR SMITH: In my limited experience, yes, I think he does – given time.

JACK: What was the meaning of her crying and eating the tissue paper?

MR SMITH: The meaning? The meaning. What would be the meaning of her not crying and not eating the tissue paper?

JILL: That part reminded me of someone. Or some time, I think, a holiday.

Pause.

I liked it, though. And that line: 'Whither our Mayor? Oh, gradually, wither, our Mayor away.' I thought I was going to cry.

MR SMITH: But you didn't?

JILL: No. But I thought I was going to.

MR SMITH: But you didn't.

MRS SMITH: I haven't seen you cry since that baseball game. When that older pitcher pitched that historical perfect game.

MR SMITH: That would have been the last time you'd seen me, yes. Something suddenly huge and saddening about the idea of perfection. Someone making history, in the daytime, the humidity, in the middle of an average July. A human being being perfect. In wait for nothing. You only see or read about that a few times in your life, if ever. An obscure joy, this of mine, but what joy isn't? Little life, in its blazing imperfection. Its terrible countability and incompletion. How many more intermissions? The number would scare you to death.

Pause.

And since when did crying become the standard to measure everything by? When I was little, and I was little, I cried if it was cold out, or if the dog lost a tennis ball under the couch. These were not moments of some wild disheveled intensity, or some soul-forming encounter with the Unknown. I cried to cry. I was little. Little children cry. Grown ups don't, or do, less. Listen, all of civilization was built on the basis of people having learned how not to cry.

MRS SMITH: I love when anyone starts a sentence by saying, 'Listen.' What if that were all the person said: 'Listen.'

Pause.

And all across the non-crying world is nothing but the sound of chairs creaking, people listening, the breath. I almost cried during that part about 'whither the Mayor,' too.

MR SMITH: Yes, I almost felt something, too.

Pause.

Here was a cry. Someone at the animal hospital called to say our dog, our actual dog, had torn a ligament in her actual leg and – being too old to risk an operation, and her other legs being too weak for her to stand on if they amputated the bad one – would probably best be put to sleep. I cried. I cried, completely, I cried recklessly, not stopping once to think of myself as a person who was crying, nor to see myself in the act of crying, which I will always do when I am crying at the death or funeral of a person. Always. Her eyes. This wasn't that.

MRS SMITH: Dear?

MR SMITH: The feelings I felt hearing a neighbor say, 'She fell.' They're not to be shared or represented – unless they just were. But you won't see a play about that. Little dog Emily, filled, filled, nothing-but-filled with nothing-but-love. In all my years in our animal kingdom – a boy and his puppy, an old man and his animal, destroyed. When do you get that? You see that, when? So have your recreational cry at the sadness of the pretend Mayor's pretend illness, his even-more-pretend assisted-suicide. But, really, what are you crying for? For what faraway little dog in what faraway little heart? Is there something closer by?

MRS SMITH: Darling, that was beautiful. Wasn't it? I never knew you had it in you.

MR SMITH: Had what in me?

MRS SMITH: Anything, really. But certainly nothing like that. Which was beautiful.

JILL: Maybe some people need help.

MR SMITH: Certainly, some do.

JILL: I mean, crying.

MR SMITH: I know.

Pause.

Yes, I think you're right.

JACK: What happened to the dog?

MRS SMITH: She died.

MR SMITH: She didn't die. I had them put a splint on it. She whimpered herself to sleep. Her leg got caught in doors and she gently fell down stairs. When they were doing it, finally, the dog up on a stainless steel table, the person there asked for the dog's name and I said, 'Emily,' and the dog, who could hardly hear, could hardly walk, her ears went up, because she thought I was calling her to go for a walk somewhere, down some non-stainless-steel path, through some weedy un-hygienic field. We were in an animal hospital. I drove her down there. She was happy. Her ears. They injected the beautiful thing with something. She was happy for the attention of everyone and thought it was exciting to be on a table. I've seen complicated things in life, but, this, no. To watch her old eyes, watching me, change, and then see her ears go down and her lowered head lower down the last half inch. Then, my dog is gone. Or, from her perspective, I am. No better, gentler thing ever lived. I'm sorry, darling – but none did. We buried her bowl with her. It said DOG in nice old-style letters on it.

JILL: She's in a better place.

MR SMITH: Yes, our backyard. Underneath a piece of plasterboard and a few feet of – . Yes, a better place.

MRS SMITH: She was a good dog. She was like a member of the family.

MR SMITH: No, in fact, she was not like a member of the family. My father was like a member of the family. I'm like a member of the family. She was The Dog. Always there, never moody, or never for long, barking into the night, humble through the days, asleep in the sun or eating butterflies, living better and truer through life than any of us, by at least a factor of seven. She gave us many beautiful people years.

He is possibly beginning to cry.

MRS SMITH: Are you –

MR SMITH: Yes. Whatever you're asking: Yes, I am. Would anyone like anything from concessions?

MRS SMITH: (*Pause.*) Thank you, no.

Pause.

The people are very experienced. The cast. They're good.

JILL: I guess you really loved that dog. Emily.

MRS SMITH: (*Pause.*) Well, yes, I guess, he did. He never told me how much. I knew you liked to walk with her, but I thought you just liked walking.

JACK: (*Pause. Looking at his program.*) One of the actors thanks her dog. (*Reading from program.*) 'Everything important happens before and after everything else has happened. We live and are alive only in the moments in between the moments. Waiting for the heart to stop, the light to change, as the vital signs grow trivial, and the Mayor's eyes close. And after. In the still parts, when nothing else is happening except people by themselves, being themselves, by themselves.'

Pause.

'Be sure to join us next summer for another incredible season.'

MR SMITH: It isn't real.

MRS SMITH: I suppose it is just a play.

JILL: No, it isn't just a play.

MRS SMITH: No?

JILL: No.

MRS SMITH: I almost couldn't stand it when he collapsed in front of everyone. Someone with nothing.

MR SMITH: Are there bathrooms or refreshments somewhere?

JILL: Or when he was saying, 'Loosen my tie. Do I have a tie? Could somebody loosen something?' What do you think will happen?

JACK: (*Nodding toward MR SMITH.*) His kidneys explode and he dies of thirst.

JILL: That's awful.

(*To MR SMITH.*) I'm sorry.

MR SMITH: Not at all. It's the truth. Kidneys fail. People die of thirst. But, son, do you have a mother? Do you have anything? You are comparing this to what?

JACK: I didn't mean anything.

MR SMITH: (*To JACK.*) If you do, look at her next time you see her. Look at her hair. Note your mother's elbows, son. See what the long march of these un-monumental moments the program refers to can do to a person, after enough time. To anything living. In real life. Things begin to fail you never even knew were working. Just you wait. You 'didn't mean anything'.

(*To MRS SMITH.*) Do you want a drink or a snack?

He begins to leave.

MRS SMITH: (*Pause.*) Very old-fashioned – all of us sitting here, in rows, having our various responses, responding to each other, all lit up. It's nice.

(*To MR SMITH.*) No, thank you, dear.

MR SMITH wanders back toward his seat.

JILL: (*To MRS SMITH.*) Did you get another dog?

MRS SMITH: No.

JILL: (*To MR SMITH.*) Do you have children?

MR SMITH: (*A long pause. No response.*) At least it never gets confusing, with too many little sub-plots. It stays very focused on the Mayor, the play.

JILL: True. Although I'd like to know more about everybody.

MRS SMITH: Maybe it's intentional that we don't know that much. And that the family is all these ghostly people. They are only things that make shadows, people we don't really see.

JACK: Is everyone really so moved by this? This isn't that serious. Is it? They're all caricatures. These are police sketches of people.

MRS SMITH: As I sit here and think of them, now that they're not here –

MR SMITH: (*Leaning across MRS SMITH. To JACK.*) Someday you may see something. Something on someone's dresser or hanging over a doorknob. A person's head in a certain position, or an animal's. Some little movement, a wife gardening in the distance, a little thing. In line at the bank or in the middle of a play or traffic, you'll be waiting for something and something else will come, something close enough. There it is, before you: it, this vision, your happiness. You'll regale people with the tale of it, your memory of the tale of it, with misty eyes, with tell-tale quivering voice. You'll assume it has the same force, meaning, and sadness to the others listening. They listen, their eyes dry, their voices even, and they nod. 'You old sentimental old nothing,' they think. 'Fool.' But you will not be a fool, should this ever happen to you, which it probably never will, making you a fool after all.

MRS SMITH: (*To JACK.*) And I don't want to gang up on you here, sweetheart. But maybe all people are police sketches of people. We're smudgy drawings, outlines, rough guides, height and weight, eye color. I am. For instance,

She stands, a statuesque pose.

what is my reality? I am what?

JACK: Wait, give me a minute. Okay, you are an older –

MRS SMITH: (*Interrupting. She sits.*) I was being sort of rhetorical. Do you get to the theater often?

JILL: Sometimes. More and more.

MRS SMITH: (*Pause. She stands. She straightens her dress.*) My reality is I'm not what I used to be anymore. My reality is trips to doctors, dentists, ophthalmologists, pharmacists and skin cancer specialists, to keep myself from falling apart in reality, which, as I mentioned before, consists of nothing but trips to doctors and the hospital, to keep me from – . My reality is I am dry everywhere. Who I am is the little old lady you will see in the background of things, outliving husbands, walking with serious and grave intent down meaningless streets to save a penny on nothing, with a flower embroidered into one of the three sweaters I wear to fight off the cold of a warm and sunny day.

She sits next to JILL.

I'm sorry. You were going to say something.

MR SMITH: Darling.

MRS SMITH: (*Amiably.*) Darling, nothing – darling. You've always had a wonderful knack for reality. No need for any darling theatricality, now. Life is very simple, the next little bit of future. We sit, we watch, we think, we cheer for the actors who played the family, for the actor who played the doctor. We stand, we stretch, check under our seats and go. Underneath all this, something else. And then gratefully, gracefully, waitingly, humanly, into the night we go. As with all good and bad things. I've been thinking of the little dog, and how he wrapped her in a raincoat before he buried her. I've been thinking of the poor little family the dog is survived by. People whose only progress is getting slightly better at not knowing what to do.

(*To JACK.*) Do you feel for me, necessarily? People talk the way they talk.

JACK: I'm kind of speechless.

Pause.

I didn't think –

MR SMITH: Just stay kind of speechless, son. We understand.

MRS SMITH: (*To JILL.*) Do you get to the theater very often?

JILL: I've been coming a lot recently.

MRS SMITH: Do you enjoy yourself?

JILL: I do. A lot. Afterwards, I never know what to say.

Lights lower three times, signaling that the intermission over.

JACK: (*Pause. Reading from his program.*) 'Time: later. Place: a graveyard.'

The lights fade to their initial low setting.

MRS SMITH: It's a beautiful experience.

MR SMITH: Isn't it.

All lights fade.

The End